Studia Fennica
Historica 10

The Finnish Literature Society (SKS) was founded in 1831 and has, from the very beginning, engaged in publishing operations. It nowadays publishes literature in the fields of ethnology and folkloristics, linguistics, literary research and cultural history.

The first volume of the Studia Fennica series appeared in 1933. Since 1992, the series has been divided into three thematic subseries: Ethnologica, Folkloristica and Linguistica. Two additional subseries were formed in 2002, Historica and Litteraria. The subseries Anthropologica was formed in 2007.

In addition to its publishing activities, the Finnish Literature Society maintains research activities and infrastructures, an archive containing folklore and literary collections, a research library and promotes Finnish literature abroad.

Editorial board
Anna-Leena Siikala
Markku Haakana
Pauli Kettunen
Leena Kirstinä
Teppo Korhonen
Johanna Ilmakunnas

oa.finlit.fi

Editorial Office
SKS
P.O. Box 259
FI-00171 Helsinki
www.finlit.fi

Moving in the USSR
Western anomalies and Northern wilderness

Edited by Pekka Hakamies

Finnish Literature Society • Helsinki

Studia Fennica Historica 10

The publication has undergone a peer review.

© 2005 Pekka Hakamies and SKS
License CC-BY-NC-ND 4.0 International

A digital edition of a printed book first published in 2005 by the Finnish Literature Society.

Cover Design: Timo Numminen
EPUB: eLibris Media Oy

ISBN 978-951-746-695-0 (Print)
ISBN 978-951-858-023-5 (PDF)
ISBN 978-951-858-022-8 (EPUB)

ISSN 0085-6835 (Studia Fennica)
ISSN 1458-526X (Studia Fennica Historica)

DOI: http://dx.doi.org/10.21435/sfh.10

This work is licensed under a Creative Commons CC-BY-NC-ND 4.0 International License.
To view a copy of the license, please visit http://creativecommons.org/licenses/by-nc-nd/4.0/

A free open access version of the book is available at http://dx.doi.org/10.21435/sfh.10 or by scanning this QR code with your mobile device.

Contents

ACKNOWLEDGEMENTS 7

Pekka Hakamies
INTRODUCTION
Migration and local identity in former territories of the USSR 9

Antti Laine
MODERNISATION IN THE 1940s AND 1950s IN THE PART
OF KARELIA THAT WAS ANNEXED FROM FINLAND ON
13 MARCH 1940 19

Marina Hakkarainen
"WE WERE UNAWARE OF THE HISTORY.
 JUST TOOK... OUR RISK
"The past, cultural landscape and identity in migrant communities
in Ladoga Karelia and the Karelian Isthmus 42

Ekaterina Melnikova
RECOLLECTIONS OF "NATIVE LAND" IN ORAL TRADITION
OF RUSSIAN SETTLERS TO KARELIA 66

Oksana Filicheva
"ONE IS DRAWN TO ONE'S BIRTHPLACE" OR "THE PLACE
WHERE ONE FEELS AT HOME IS ONE'S MOTHERLAND"
Concepts of homeland by migrants from Ladoga Karelia 79

Pekka Hakamies
NEW CULTURE ON NEW TERRITORIES
The Karelian Isthmus and Ladoga Karelia in post-war years 91

Irina Razumova
ON THE PROBLEMS OF LOCAL IDENTITY AND CONTEMPORARY
RUSSIAN "MIGRATORY TEXTS" (WITH REFERENCE TO THE
NORTHWESTERN REGION OF RUSSIA) 110

Alla Sokolova
CONTEMPORARY IMAGES OF THE SHTETL AMONGST THE
UKRAINIAN POPULATION OF URBAN-TYPE SETTLEMENTS
AND VILLAGES OF PODOLIA 130

CONTRIBUTORS 161

Acknowledgements

Several persons and organizations have offered their support for this project during various phases, from the very beginning to the ultimate editing of this current publication. We owe a special expression of gratitude to Yurii Petrovich Svinarev in Melnikovo, and Nina Tunina and, posthumously, Leopold Neiken in Lahdenpohja for their local knowledge and assistance in helping us to find people for interviews. Ilia Utekhin and Sergei Shtyrkov at the European University in St. Petersburg particularly assisted the project in organization of our field-work. Greg Watson edited the English language, and Maarit Viljakainen helped with the technical editing. The Finnish organizations of the former inhabitants of Räisälä and Kurkijoki supplied some material and, particularly, photographs of the ceded territory. Some of the illustration materials were obtained from the archive of the National Board of Antiquities. Finally, funding from the Academy of Finland made the extensive field-work and completion of this edited volume possible, and the Finnish Literature Society kindly agreed to publish the results of our research.

Joensuu 4.2.2005
Pekka Hakamies

PEKKA HAKAMIES

Introduction

Migration and local identity in former territories of the USSR

The book at hand is a result of a project which had been financed by the Finnish Academy during the years 2000–2003. The aim of the research project "Conditions for Constructing a New Russia: Interactions of Tradition and Europeanness in the Development of 20th Century Russia" was to examine developmental processes in contemporary Russia and conditions delimiting its choices in the light of the central turning points of twentieth-century Russian history. The central question deals with the westward interaction between Russia and Europe from a Russian perspective. In other words, how has the tradition of Russia's culture and history set the conditions for its developmental and political choices.

The project concentrated, in particular, on the changes in Russia's relationship with Europe during the 20th century. The issue of the clash between Europeanness (the Zapadniks) and traditional Russianness (the Slavophiles) concretely highlights the two central factors that have affected Russia's development. The question of Europeanness and its ideals linked to the Enlightenment, often interpreted as universal, has divided Russian society for centuries. Ultimately, the question deals with the problem of whether Russian development leads towards modernization, in the European sense of the term, or whether Russia will continue on its own developmental path, unifying, once again, European influences with Russian specificity. Is there only one way to achieve the modernity which the western European countries have shown to the rest of the world, or are there alternatives (cf. Kumar 1988:5–10)? This problem also involves the question that deals with the aims of western politics towards Russia and how realistic these aims are. Thus, what are the conditions that stem from, and which are determined by, the reality of Russia, its history and culture that fundamentally affect its future development and political choices?

Common threads and particular traits of this collected edition

From this viewpoint, it is natural that the topics of the articles within this publication focus on the western borders of the former Soviet Union. This area has been a contact zone between Russia and Europe, but also a battlefield. The World War Two changed borders in several regions in eastern Europe, and these changes offered a channel for new influences to penetrate into Russia and the minds of Russians. During the initial stage of the second world war, the Soviet Union had already annexed the eastern part of pre-war Poland, according to the Molotov-Ribbentrop treaty, and a little later the Baltic states as well as the Northern Bukovina from Romania had also been annexed. The secret part of this treaty that dealt with the "spheres of interest" of Nazi Germany and Soviet Union allocated Finland to the Soviet sphere of influence. The Soviet-Finnish border was one to be moved, but as the political leaders of Finland were unwilling to consent to the demands of the Soviet Union the latter tried to reach this goal by force. The Winter War period of 1939–1940 and its historical consequences are presented in detail in the article of Antti Laine.

One result of the border change drawn up in the Moscow peace treaty of March 1940 was the evacuation from the ceded territory to the remaining Finland of 400,000 Finnish citizens, more than 10% of the entire population of Finland. During the "Continuation War" of 1941–1944 in which Finland fought as a co-belligerent of Germany against the Soviet Union, many of the Karelian emigrants were able to return to their old homes, but the conditions of the armistice in the autumn of 1944 sealed the fate of the territory, in that it became a part of Soviet Union, so the Finns, once again, had to leave the region.

The process of settlement and incorporation of new territories by the Soviet Union is the topic of many articles of this book. New settlers brought their economic and social structure, culture and toponyms with them to areas that were left practically totally empty by Finnish inhabitants. Analogies to the processes of culture and place formation can be found in the former East Prussia, which suffered a similar fate as the ceded Finnish Karelia. Both areas were incorporated into the Soviet society and received new, Russian-speaking inhabitants as a result of decisions at a high level of Soviet administration and an active recruitment campaign.

The main differences between the former Finnish Karelia and the former German East Prussia seem to be in the war-time history of the territories: East Prussia was heavily devastated in the battles in the final stage of the war, whereas a large part of the territory of Karelia, ceded by Finland to Soviet Union, mainly regions on the West coast of Lake Ladoga, were almost intact except for some bombing by the Soviet air force and some battles in the summer of 1941. Another significant difference was the total evacuation of Finnish inhabitants from the ceded territory. In East Prussia, approximately 130,000 Germans stayed in 1945 but they were deported to Germany until the beginning of the 1950s. So, the new settlers did have an opportunity to familiarize themselves with Germans and their way of living and the Germans did engage with the Soviet society. (Vostochnaya Prussiia, 185, 224.) Another difference was the repetition of the evacuation of the Finnish inhabitants in 1944, and in the meantime, in 1941, the evacuation of the newly arrived Soviet settlers. So, the former Finnish Karelia has created several layers of evacuation recollections and refugee stories.

Western Poland also had, in some aspects, an analogical fate: there the Germans who formed the majority of inhabitants were expelled after the Second World War and place names were changed into Polish ones that were found in old, sometimes medieval, archive sources (discussion at the Finnish-Polish symposium in the University of Tampere, April 2003).

The new western territories the Soviet Union gained in the Second World War are not the only regions in which migration was an important factor of settlement formation. The history of Russia is partially a history of migrations, as Irina Razumova states in her article in this book, and this has been particularly important in North Russia, where the population has been scarce until Soviet times. Nevertheless, these regions had rich natural resources which had to be exploited when the development of industry became the main goal and means of the Soviet modernization. Workers were needed and actively recruited into the new towns and villages in the process of building a new society, especially after the Second World War. This process created a stratum of population that forms the majority in the towns but which has a certain migrational identity and world view. Irina Razumova has collected and studied the oral traditions of families in the Republic of Karelia and elsewhere in the North-West Russia during several years and her current article is based on her own field work in the Murmansk region.

Many towns in the North-West polar region of Russia are of recent origin. As Irina Razumova's article reveals, their inhabitants or the parents of the inhabitants have moved from elsewhere and, in general, they do not know very much about the past of their new place nor its former inhabitants. However, the inhabitants have constructed their own places there and a certain local identity. As the ties to the region are not very tight and there are no deep roots among the inhabitants, migration and reasons for it are an important part of the family history of these people. For them, the possibility of migration is a fact and the younger generations, especially, are inclined to think about this alternative, that is, to live and work elsewhere for a period of time.

Formation of migrational identity occurred not only as a result of mass resettlement of a population from one region to another, but also as a result of the accelerated transformation of countrymen into townspeople, undertaken by the Soviet authority in order to provide a base for the industrialization of the country. Alla Sokolova has examined the process of the mental adaptation of settlements in former market townships, in Podolia, Ukraine, which was accomplished by Ukrainian migrants from suburbs and neighbouring villages. Jews formed, in the mentioned region, the majority of the population of these settlements until the Second World War. They lived within the limits of the old town market centre which can, as a matter of fact, be treated as an ethnic enclave surrounded by Ukrainian suburbs.

The destruction of the Jews during the German occupation of 1941–1944 has led to a profound change in the face of the settlements. The loss of a significant part of a traditionally urban population has aggravated problems caused by the character of the Soviet urbanization, which in connection with the transformation of the historically formed architectural environment of townships can be described as de-urbanization.

Many notions spread among the Ukrainians concerning the arrangement of the urban life of the region both in the distant and in the recent past are connected with Jews. Traces of the Jewish presence preserved in the cultural landscape serve, for the re-settlers, as reference points in the comprehension of the world around. In a transitive-type situation, which can be considered the resettlement from a village to a town, these reference points are especially significant.

In those settlements which were in the Romanian zone of occupation during the war where the total destruction of Jews was not carried out, replacement of the Jewish population by Ukrainians only occurred in the 1990s when mass Jewish immigration to Israel, USA and Germany began. The Ukrainians, natives of the villages, are only now becoming accustomed to the Jewish houses they recently received. Many peculiarities in the structure of the houses, their details, as well as the position of the Jewish settlements in the towns of Podolia have attracted the attention of the Ukrainians and they have explained their experiences of living in the former Jewish homes or close to them.

One of the articles, written by the historian Antti Laine, is based on literature and archive sources opened to research during the 1990s in Russia. Its topic is the same as in some other articles which are based on interview materials, the Soviet occupation and incorporation process in the former Finnish Karelia. Antti Laine's article does not study the grass-root level of personal recollections but the process of the creation of the Soviet regime at the higher levels of administration. The annexation of this territory was important for the Soviet Union, not only for the sake of security for the city of Leningrad but also for economic reasons. Laine presents the general characteristics of this process and also some case studies – of how Soviet society was created in a concrete place.

Four more articles are in common with Antti Laine's topic but use oral narratives, interviews, as their research material. The papers are based on common field work in the former Finnish Karelia, in Melnikovo (Finnish *Räisälä*) on the Karelian Isthmus and Lahdenpohja and Kurkijoki on the West coast of Lake Ladoga in the Republic of Karelia. Marina Hakkarainen has as her theme the understanding of history and the local past among the present inhabitants. Ekaterina Melnikova has studied the image and importance of the place of origin of the inhabitants. Oksana Filicheva has examined the concept of *Rodina* – the place of origin and its many meanings for the inhabitants, and Pekka Hakamies has had as his themes the formation of local toponyms and the way places are constructed, as well as the image of Finns constructed by the new inhabitants on the basis of what they found upon arrival and in the first phase of living.

Fieldwork

All in all, six articles share a common viewpoint and quality of materials. They belong to folklore studies in the broad sense of the concept but similar research has also been carried out in the field of ethnology and oral history. The material that has been collected and used is mainly from interviews – personal narration and oral history, as not much has been documented in archives, particularly not on the perceptions and experiences of ordinary people.

All field work undertaken in this project has a common historical context. The Soviet Union collapsed in the beginning of the 1990s and this fact, together with the preceding perestroika era, has led to a critical review of Soviet ideology and achievements, when many unsolvable problems of the Soviet society became public. The only achievement in the history of the Soviet Union left intact in its previous glory, without criticism, is the victory over "fascist" Germany and its allies during the Second World War.

The past of the Finnish part of the territory of the Soviet Union gained as a result of the Second World War has been revised, although it may not be an exaggeration to state that until the perestroika era this area did not have any Finnish past in the public Soviet history. Since the beginning of the 1990s there has been a flow of Finnish visitors to their former houses – or what is left of them – and this has opened up new contacts and possibilities for the local inhabitants, which, in turn, has increased their interest and created a positive attitude towards the Finnish past of the region. In the border region, some economic cooperation with Finnish enterprises has also emerged. Apparently, the general attitude would have been different in the 1970s, if it would have been possible to record similar material and filter out conscious Soviet propaganda. But at that time, the western coast of Lake Ladoga was a closed border zone to which even external Soviet citizens could enter only with special permission.

The article of A. Sokolova is mainly based on materials from field studies conducted in 2001 but also includes field materials collected in 1998–2000. In 1998–2000, when the main goal of the fieldwork was the examination of the architecture of traditional Jewish houses preserved in the townships of Podolia, the records of interviews had no fixed theme but they determined a thematic field for the present research. In 2001 and 2003, field studies on the theme of the article in this book were carried out in the Khmel'nyts'kyi region and in the Vinnytsia region, in the Ukraine, where 16 informants were interviewed (14 hours of recordings).

In 2001–2002, Irina Razumova collected information for her research from about 100 persons, not only in Apatity, Monchegorsk and Kirov in the Kola Peninsula but also in Petrozavodsk and Saint-Petersburg. Several texts were recorded by handwriting, many informants wrote their own story, and there are approximately 20 hours of audio recordings. The collected records have been archived and preserved by the authors.

The fieldwork group, consisting of Pekka Hakamies, from the University of Joensuu in Finland and Marina Hakkarainen and Ekaterina Melnikova, from the European University in St. Petersburg, Russia has recorded in 2001 interviews of local inhabitants in Melnikovo, the Karelian isthmus, approximately 30 hours from 25 persons, and in the Lahdenpohja and the Kurkijoki region in the West coast of Lake Ladoga, in the Republic of Karelia in 2002 and 2003 altogether approximately 64 hours from 69 persons. Veronika

Makarova participated in the work in 2001 and 2002, and Oksana Filicheva joined the group in 2003 – both are from the European University.

Common concepts and theoretical questions

One of the central issues in the articles of this publication is *experience*. Experience can be seen as a profound dimension of human life, and Renato Rosaldo extends the question to fundamental issues of anthropology: how should ethnographers represent other people's lives (Rosaldo 1986: 133). The contributions of our book are modest in relation to this ultimate question and tend to offer some pragmatic case studies instead of profound theoretical contemplations. Edward M. Bruner has characterized experience, based on the philosopher Wilhelm Dilthey and the anthropologist Victor Turner, as an active, conscious receiving of an event (Bruner 1986: 4–5). An experience is an unavoidably subjective act, and for the research, which tended to be inter-subjective, it is a problem that other people can only tell us about their experiences and in this way we gain our experiences about the representations of others' experiences.

Bruner makes a distinction between life as a lived reality, life as experienced and life as told. (ibid. 5–6). Some of the authors emphasize the disruption of routine behaviour in the experience. Roger D. Abrahams makes a difference between two kinds of an experience: ordinary experiences rise right out of the flow of life, whereas extraordinary ones are those for which we plan and to which we look forward to and which can be called presentations (Abrahams 1986: 63, 70). In our study, experiences are usually ordinary parts of everyday life and not special performances. Nevertheless, these experiences have initially been, to some extent, exceptional, because the whole context in the former Finnish Karelia was alien to the Russian settlers, and, similarly, the settlers in Podolia and the North-West polar region of Russia have experienced something new and unknown in the places they began to inhabit. It has been the differences from the past daily life which have been the essence of first experiences in the new and alien surrounding.

Practically all the articles of this book based on fieldwork materials rely on what people tell us about their experiences at the places and stories of how the places are experienced. So, we have a certain thematic group of narratives that could be labelled "place narratives". This leads us to the other main concept in these articles – the *place*. All authors of the book are inclined to study place as an issue based on lived, subjective experiences of the inhabitants and the narratives representing those experiences, as the place is usually defined or characterized in the research literature (cf. Tuan 2001: 33; Feld & Basso 1996; Rodman 2003: 205–213). Thus, our understanding of the place is based on writings of cultural geography and geographically oriented cultural anthropology. A place is not just a point defined by some coordinates, it is a totality of accumulated experiences and memories making the place significant as a part of the past life of the people living in the place.

Edward S. Casey emphasizes in his article concerning the formation of place from space, relying on phenomenological philosophical frame of reference and, for instance, on the writings of Immanuel Kant, the role of experience as the beginning of knowledge. But as Casey puts it: although the experience is primary, it is always an active event and is constituted by cultural and social structures. For Casey, in the beginning there is not just blank space, which is gradually transformed into places, first at the level of the perception and later culture, primary perception is always a part of concrete action and, simultaneously, constituted by cultural and social structures. (Casey 1996.)

The authors of this book may not commit themselves totally to this theoretical viewpoint, yet, nevertheless, narration about experiences form the basis of their empirical material. Many articles also share the starting point that people studied do not have very deep roots in the places they inhabit and neither do they have close and long-lasting contacts with the previous inhabitants of the places. Their parents or grandparents have moved to the territory and they and their children know only superficially the past of the place, but nevertheless they seemed to feel the place as their own home.

Another uniting trait for the articles is formed by the viewpoint towards our materials. Stories told by people about their pasts and experiences are used in many sciences that study human culture. Historians have also used this kind of material under the label "oral history". Some oral historians have in the recent past argued for the validity of oral materials in comparison with written documents. Paul Thompson has confessed there are defects in oral material but he denies the superiority of written documents and statistics which can be equally imprecise or distorted (Thompson 1978: 94–96). Nowadays, oral documents as a source material are generally valued in a different way. Personal stories and recollections do not compete with archival sources but complement them. They reveal another dimension from the past and reflect subjective experiences and attitudes of people experiencing various phases of history and, thus, give a voice not usually heard in written documents.

Alessandro Portelli has characterized the quality and value of oral sources in his books as follows: "Oral history, then, offers less a grid of standard experiences than a horizon of shared possibilities, real or imagined." (Portelli 1997: 88.) "Oral history tells us less about events than about their meaning... Oral sources tell us not just what people did, but what they wanted to do, what they believed they were doing, and what they now think they did." In this way, oral history is not a direct and objective documentation of the past, and it is not possible to reconstruct the past reality based on oral history – recollections of ordinary people. "The diversity of oral history consists of the fact that "wrong" statements are still psychologically "true", and that this truth may be equally as important as factually reliable accounts."(Portelli 1991: 50–51.)

There is a difference in the viewpoint and goals between history and folklore studies – how important is it to know whether people do remember "correctly" and that the recollection narratives are historically true? Is it crucial to know if there were real visits or raids of Finns to their former houses or other transgressions of the state border? For historians, the relationship of the materials to the past reality is usually significant – the classic ideal is to find out "wie es eigentlich gewesen ist" – 'how it really has been'. Folklorists, in turn, pay less attention to this dimension. In folklore studies, it has for a long time been usual to look at the historical texts from a type of relativist, some could say, postmodernist viewpoint - how the texts relate to each other – and to not give much importance to the relationship with reality. We do not aim to disclose the "false consciousness" of the people living in the former Finnish Karelia or other territories of the past Soviet Union.

Most of the authors of this book come, in practice, close to some kind of weak or modest constructionism but without conscious involvement in it: the past is constructed in the interview dialogues based on the memories of the interviewees. These memories, in turn, are constructed on the experiences of the people and their later interpretations and, ultimately, their experiences are based on real events and the characteristics of the region. In this way, the interviews tell us about the real past indirectly through various filters. Actually, as in oral history in general, we have at hand the present opinion of the interviewees about what should be thought of about the past.

This is not total or strong constructionism, which would mean that the reality is wholly constructed in discourse and there is nothing outside the texts and no relation between our fieldwork materials and the past, external reality. "Pure" social constructionism has been criticized for ignorance of the material world outside the discourses. Social discourses are relative but not arbitrary and generated by social structures and other factors. (Cromby and Nightingale 1999.)

Folklore studies have traditionally had certain orientations towards relativism and constructionism regarding the relationship of the stories with the reality they are referring to. In folklore studies, the relationship of the legends, or stories in general, to the reality has usually been suspended as background information that can perhaps be used to explain the reason the stories exist. Stories are not valued as historical documents but as representations of folk imagination, attitudes and ways of making issues understandable or explainable. For a long time it has been a well-known fact that historical legends often have a migratory character – the same stories are told in various places at various times but are always locally attached to concrete places and persons.

It is a principal issue to make a clear distinction between the narratives and events behind the narratives. However, sometimes in the actual work it has been difficult to keep in mind that the narratives are not true documents about the past reality but interpretations of the past experiences of the real world.

Finally, it is important to remember that the informants always have the opportunity to control the information given to interviewers – they can choose what to tell and how to tell it. Although the issues discussed were not usually highly political, topics suitable for open discussion were, in the past Soviet society, quite limited, particularly when a foreigner was present, and some of this sad heritage may still reside in the minds of the inhabitants of the former border zone. This fact, in conjunction with the usual ethic norms of research, help to explain the imprecise source notes for the field materials.

Our interviews are, for the large part, structurally construed as personal narratives and life stories. The concept of "personal narrative" is widely used in the study of oral history. Sandra Dolby Stahl has defined this concept on the basis of three features: the story has a dramatic narrative structure, there is an assertion that the narrative is true, and the teller and the main character of the story are one and same person (Stahl 1989: 14–15).

Our material does not only consist of true personal narratives. Besides these, our recordings include answers of various length, and all the interviews are structured on autobiographical narration. In the flow of discussion, there are sometimes personal narratives and even stories with certain fixed content that are transmitted by a chain of tellers, i.e. folklore legends.

The contributors of this book share, in general, the perspective on "text" that Ruth Finnegan holds, for whom the main issue in studies on narratives has been the "somewhat decontextualised cognitive signification" (Finnegan 1998: 7). The way of performing, producing a narrative or stylistic or contextual factors have been left aside, although hardly any of us would simply deny their meaning for the discussions in the fieldwork. Rather, it would be another field of research and there is an abundance of literature particularly in the performance-oriented folklore studies (cf. Honko 1998: 46–49) on this field. It has been up to individual authors whether they consider it purposeful to comment on the meaning and moments of the interview situation for the evaluation or analysis of the material recorded. We are primarily interested in the content – the cognitive signification – of the stories that reflect the experiences, emotions and attitudes of the settlers of the places studied.

Not ignoring the problems studied in the dialogic fieldwork (Vasenkari 1999), neither do we concentrate on this topic. It is, again, a matter of individual decision for each author if he/she has considered it essential to analyse the interview situation and process and the positions of the interviewer and the informant, in order to better understand what is being told. The interview quotations have been published in a simple transcription form and special emphasis in the speech is noted if it was deemed to be significant for the understanding of the text passage.

For the study of place experiences of the local inhabitants, the historical truth is usually not very important, instead the subjective recollections and images people have constructed during their life in connection with the place and which form the meaning the place has for people is crucial. In this sense, our materials, despite their subjectivity and some incongruence with factual history, are reliable for our studies. The existence of these subjective experiences and recollections is an objective, historical fact.

Editorial notes

In the transliteration of Russian and Ukrainian names and words the usual English system is used. In the article of Alla Sokolova, the Ukrainian forms of place names have been used except for some cases where the Russian form has been common. Place names of the former Finnish territory are given in their Finnish form. The illustrations consist of the photos of the authors or archive collections from Finland. From the latter sources, there are interesting materials from the year 1941 of Karelia after Finnish re-occupation that reflect traces of the short Soviet period between 1940–1941. The Soviet territorial administrative terminology has been translated in the usual way; thus, *region* means the Russian term 'oblast' and, conversely, *district* means 'raion'. Further special terms have been explained in the text or footnotes.

REFERENCES

Abrahams, Roger D. 1986: Ordinary and Extraordinary Experience. In: *The Anthropology of Experience*. Ed. by Victor W. Turner and Edward M. Bruner. Urbana and Chicago: University of Illinois Press.
Bruner, Edward 1986: Experience and its expressions. In: *The Anthropology of Experience*. Ed. by Victor W. Turner and Edward M. Bruner. Urbana and Chicago: University of Illinois Press.
Cromby, John and Nightingale, David J. 1999: What's wrong with social constructionism? In: *Social constructionist psychology. A critical analysis of theory and practice*. Buckingham: Open University Press.
Finnegan, Ruth 1998: *Tales of the city: a study on narrative and urban life*. Cambridge: Cambridge University Press.
Honko, Lauri 1998: *Textualising the Siri Epic*. FF Communications No. 264. Helsinki: Suomalainen tiedeakatemia.
Kumar, Krishan 1988: *The rise of modern society: aspects of the social and political development of the West*. Oxford: Basil Blackwell Ltd.
Portelli, Alessandro 1991: *The death of Luigi Trastulli and other stories: form and meaning in oral history*. Albany: State university of New York.
Portelli, Alessandro 1997: *The Battle of Valle Giulia. Oral history and the Art of Dialogue*. Madison: The University of Wisconsin Press.
Rodman, Margaret C. 2003: Empowering Place: Multilocality and Multivocality. In: *The anthropology of space and place. Locating culture*. Ed. by Setha M. Low and Denise Lawrence-Zúñiga. Oxford: Blackwell Publishers Ltd.
Rosaldo, Renato 1986: Ilongot Hunting as Story and Experience. In: *The Anthropology of Experience*. Ed. by Victor W. Turner and Edward M. Bruner. Urbana and Chicago: University of Illinois Press.
Stahl, Sandra Dolby 1989: *Literary folkoristics and the personal narrative*. Bloomington: Indiana University Press.
Thompson, Paul 1978: *The Voice of the Past: oral history*. Oxford: Oxford U. P. 1978.
Tuan, Yi-Fu 2001: *Space and Place. The Perspective of Experience*. Minnesota: University of Minnesota Press.
Vasenkari, Maria 1999: A dialogical notion of field research. In: *Arv. Nordic Yearbook of Folklore*.
Vostochnaya Prussiia glazami Sovetskih pereselencev. Pervyie gody Kaliningradskoi oblasti v vospominaniiah i dokumentah. Ed. by Yu. V. Kostiashkov et al. Sankt-Peterburg: "Belveder" 2002.

ANTTI LAINE

Modernisation in the 1940s and 1950s in the part of Karelia that was annexed from Finland on 13 March 1940

The practical realization of a new kind of society in the USSR meant, first of all, the destruction of old ownership relationships and the introduction of a "New Deal" for the economy. It also meant that new people who found themselves leading an economy and other aspects of social life, who had previously been inexperienced and uneducated, had to be trained to run this new kind of society. This political reformation also meant the liquidation of a substantial amount of know-how, since the reification that took place through the destruction of the political opposition was largely aimed at the educated population of Russia, which was still scarce at the time.

The NEP period that followed the civil war signified, for a short period, the abandonment of strict war communism and permitted capitalistic features in the economy. During this period, the economy of the country began to gradually revive and the figures of the pre-war period for agriculture, as well as in other fields of production, were reached before the next phase. The central question in the economic policy of the Bolsheviks was whether the NEP could create a working foundation for the development of the Soviet economy so that it could challenge the capitalist countries. (Davies 1994: 12.)

The various wings of the Communist Party were committed to the industrialization of the country and the development of a socialist society in the Soviet Union. Since the beginning of 1928 until the German offensive launched on 22 June, 1941, the economy and the way it was realized in various fields was dominated by aspirations to reach and outrun the capitalist countries in production, technology and, above all, military power. The crises in the world policy in Asia and Europe in the early 1930s forced the Soviet Union to increase its military expenses. In the domestic policy, several financial opinion leaders and leading industrialists were displaced during those years. The strength of the Soviet army was increased from 1,5 million men to 5 million in the period between 1937 and the eve of German offensive in 1941. Correspondingly, the armament industry increased by 2,5 times between 1937 and 1940. In 1939, the accelerating armament particularly dominated the economy. (Ibid. 15–18.)

By 1935, the economy had reached the form in which it would remain for almost the next 50 years. Both agriculture and industry were strictly controlled by the state. A small share of agriculture, the so-called state farms, or sovkhozes, functioned under the same principles as the state factories. The majority of the farms, those 25 million farm households that had existed in 1929, had been combined to form 250 000 collective farms; there was one or more of them in each village. The old boundary lines between the farms had been removed and the lands united. The farm machinery that was intended for the collective farms was obtained from the state-owned tractor and machine stations (MTS). There were c. 8000 of them in the whole country. The collective farms were supposed to hand over a considerable part of their yearly production to the state at a fixed price. (Ibid.)

The year 1941 is central in the historical periodisation of the Soviet Union. After Germany had invaded the country, the so-called Great Patriotic War, the battle against the Fascists, began. The beginning of the Second World War on 1 September 1939 does not hold the same significance, although the Soviet Union, between these two dates, fought a war against Finland, which altered the border between the two countries, and also annexed the Baltic countries without a war.

Just on the verge of the war, the European countries were looking for partners to fortify their positions in a constantly tightening political situation. A negotiation contact between Germany and the Soviet Union began when the People's Comissar of Foreign Affairs, Viacheslav Molotov and the ambassador of Germany in Moscow, von Schulenburg, met on 3 August, 1939. This meeting was arranged by the Foreign Minister of Germany, Joachim von Ribbentrop. In this negotiation, the ambassador said that the government of Germany had tried to improve relationships between these two countries. There were no grounds for conflicts between Germany and the Soviet Union in the whole area of the Baltic Sea and the Black sea. Therefore, there were possibilities to reconcile mutual interests. This was a period of exploration which lasted a couple of weeks following the meeting. (Rzheshevskii 1997: 104–105.)

Von Schulenburg said to Molotov on 19 August that because of tense relationships between Germany and Poland it was necessary to solve relationships between Germany and the Soviet Union urgently. At the same time, attack preparations by Germany upon Poland were being finalised and the day of the attack was determined. The Foreign Minister of Germany came to Moscow on 23 August to negotiate a non-aggression pact. On the same day, a ten year treaty was signed and secret supplementary minutes were enclosed. (Ibid. 106–107.)

In these minutes, the following matters were mentioned: in the case that there will be regional-political rearrangements in the area of the Baltic Sea countries (Finland, Estonia, Latvia, Lithuania) the northern border of Lithuania concurrently forms the border between Germany's and the Soviet Union's sphere of interest. In the case that there will be regional-political rearrangements in the areas which belong to Poland, the border of Germany's and the Soviet Union's spheres of interests run about along the lines of the rivers Narev, Veiksel and San. In relation to Southeastern Europe, interests in Bessarabia were stressed by the Soviet Union. Germany stated that it was politically fully uninterested in these areas.

The treaty broke the Soviet Union's treaties which had been made earlier (non-aggression pact 1932) with Poland and some other countries, for example Finland. The incorporation of Finland into the influence district of the Soviet Union meant that since signing the secret supplementary minutes the Soviet leadership had extreme means to force Finland. At the end of September, within the framework of the sphere of interest division, the Soviet Union started to improve its possibilities for war in the northern parts of the Baltic Sea. It started to negotiate about mutual defence questions with the Baltic Sea countries Estonia, Latvia, Lithuania and Finland. (Manninen & Baryshnikov 1997: 111–113).

Since Germany was able to guarantee with this pact that the Soviet Union would not pose a threat for its invasion of Poland, it soon became active. The German invasion of Poland began on 1 September, 1939. As a consequence, Great Britain and France declared war on Germany. The Second World War had begun. After Poland collapsed, the Soviet Union was ready to seize the eastern parts of the country, as had been agreed. Those parts of Poland which were located on the eastern side of the river Bug were incorporated into the Soviet Union because of the treaty and since then they have belonged to the Soviet Union as the western part of Belorussia and the Ukraine. A part of the population of these areas were forced to move to other parts of the Soviet Union as was as a part of the population of the Baltic countries that were incorporated into the Soviet Union in summer 1940.

Fairly soon, the Soviet Union became active in its own sphere of interest, in the Baltic Countries and in Finland, and invited the representatives of each country to negotiate in Moscow. Finland was invited on 5th of October to negotiate about concrete political questions. Beforehand, nobody revealed to the Finns what kind of questions these were. As chairperson of the Finnish Negotiation Committee, the ambassador of Finland to Sweden J.K. Paasikivi, was elected. He had an understanding of the problematic Russia questions and had taken part in peace negotiations in Tartu in 1920. (Ibid.)

When the negotiations were underway demands in the name of the security of Leningrad were presented to the Finns. In these Soviet demands the territorial surrender of the Karelian Isthmus, the islands of the Finnish Gulf and also in the direction of Petsamo were mentioned. In addition, there was a question about a base area which was planned to be built in Hanko and the continuing demilitarisation of the Åland Islands and the Soviet Union's right to supervise it. (Ibid.)

The Foreign Minister of Finland, Eljas Erkko, told negotiators in Moscow: "We are not going to make any assignments to the Soviet Union but on the contrary we are going to fight whatever happens, because Britannia, America and Sweden have promised to support us." The territorial demands were thought to be unjustified, because Finland promised to defend its territory against all attackers. Capitulation would have meant the loss of the defence zone of Finland. Negotiations broke down without results on 14 October and the Finnish delegation came back to Helsinki to receive more instructions. (Ibid. 114–116.)

On a second trip, the Finnish delegation departed on 23 October after they had been given permission to make small concessions. The trip ended without results. At that time the Red Army troops had started to move into East Karelia. Negotiations continued again in Moscow 3.–4.11. when negotiations became stuck. The Russian Foreign Minister, Molotov, expressed a threatening statement: "We civilians, we can not do more in this matter; now it is military circles' turn to say their words." On 9 November the Finnish delegation was authorised to return home. As the Finnish negotiators travelled on November 13 from Moscow, it remained unclear in what form negotiations could be continued. (Ibid. 122–124.)

As early as at the end of 29 October, the war council of the military district of Leningrad gave to the People's Comissar of Defense, Kliment Voroshilov, a plan of action to destroy the land and sea forces of the Finnish army. Operative preparation was supposed to be complete by 5 November. Troops were being continuously mobilised to the border of Finland. On 23 November, the troops of the Leningrad Military District received instructions regarding the political administration of the military district on how to inform the troops about the tense relationship between the Soviet Union and Finland. After the Finnish delegation returned from Moscow to Finland there was an impression that despite a lack of results in negotiations there was less tension and there was no reason to assume that military conflict would break out against the Soviet Union. (Baryshnikov & Manninen 1997: 130–131.)

Immediate preparations for the war had begun already a few days earlier. During those days (11–15 November) decisions were being made concerning the political coating of the offensive. From the Soviet Union's perspective, when the war would break out, the so-called People's Government of Finland would be formed and it would have an army of its own raised from the Red Army. The military part was prepared first. The People's Commissar of Defence, Kliment Voroshilov, gave an order to the war council of the Leningrad Military District on 11 November that they form the 106th Division, which would later become the body of the People's Army, and that recruits of Finnish and Karelian origin under the age of 40 be drafted for it. (Rentola 1994: 161–162.)

Besides clearly military questions, the Soviet government had a general political problem: How to justify the initiation of military action? To be precise, they tried to prove that Finland was guilty of military provocation. In a few days, the relationship between Finland and the Soviet Union became awkward with the help of the media. Radio Moscow stated that the artillery of Finland had fired on the territory of the Soviet Union in the Karelian Isthmus nearby the border village Mainila on 26 November, where four soldiers died and nine were wounded. Soon the Finnish ambassador in Moscow received a note regarding these happenings in Mainila as a hostile action against the Soviet Union. On these grounds it was demanded that the Finnish forces be moved away from the border by 20–25 km so that they would not threaten the security of Leningrad. The Finns refused this demand. Finally, at noon on 29 November the Red Army forces at the border of Finland were informed that a sign would be given to start the attack on 30 November at 00.00 o'clock. The attack eventually took place at 8.30 o'clock. (Baryshnikov & Manninen 1997: 131–137.)

Contrary to Soviet plans, Finland succeeded in maintaining its independence. The Soviet Union, which during the offensive period did not accept Risto Ryti's government as the official Finnish government in the negotiations, made "peace" with the People's Government, which was founded in Terijoki at the outbreak of the war and was led by the emigrè communist Otto Ville Kuusinen, who was living in Moscow; this treaty was signed on 3 December 1939. The aim to crush Finland from the inside did not succeed. On the contrary, that piece of news about the government of Terijoki made Finns fight unanimously towards the independence of the country.

The war between Finland and the Soviet Union 30.11.1939 – 13.3.1940 – the Winter War

Immediately after the war began A. K. Cajander's government broke up. It was thought that in this way it might be possible to settle a new negotiation. The President of The Finnish Bank, Risto Ryti, was appointed as Prime Minister. It was considered that Ryti was able to make "coldblooded" decisions. (Laine 2003: 694–699.)

At the beginning, the politics of peace had a lack of necessary resources when Foreign Minister Molotov pointed to the government that was founded in Terijoki that was led by the emigrè communist Otto Ville Kuusinen. The Soviet Union did not have any kind of conflicts with Kuusinen's government that was said to represent Finnish people the Soviet Union did not have any kind of conflicts. (Ibid.)

After a week of retreat at the Karelian Isthmus the Finns succeeded in halting the Red Army troops at the main battle stations of the Mannerheim line. At Ladoga Karelia the Finnish troops were quite few in number, but they also succeeded in stopping the Red Army on 12 December at the river Kollaa. There the lines stayed in place till the end of the war. The Red Army also attacked the far north but without results. This occurred at the same latitude as Oulu at Suomussalmi, where the Red Army tried to cut Finland in half by attacking towards the west. Finns succeeded to destroy a whole elite motorised division using so-called "motti-tactics". The Finnish "motti-tactics" was a way of attacking with a small amount of men, by encircling and chopping down large motorised troops tied to the narrow roads. Finnish troops attacked and immobilised several Russian divisions who were then unable to fight at Ladoga Karelia and the regions of Suojärvi and Pitkäranta too. Thus, Finns also obtained large amounts of artillery and tanks and other weaponry as war booty.(Ibid.)

During January 1940, the Soviet Union gathered extra troops to the front of Finland. The People's Comissar of Defense, Kliment Voroshilov, became the leader of the war. The new attack started at the Karelian Isthmus at the beginning of February and it concentrated on the front at Summa, where Russians had seven times more artillery than the Finns. With this force they broke the main defence line. The Finnish Commander-in-Chief, Mannerheim gave an order on 27 February to move back to the Viipuri-Tali-Vuoksi line. The Finns succeeded in keeping the city of Viipuri till the end of the war but the Red Army had already managed to make an invasion across the Viipuri gulf from the southwestern side of the city, thus moving ahead to the Viipuri-Hamina road. (Ibid.)

The strength of the Finnish army began to dwindle. Members of government, particularly the Foreign Minister Väinö Tanner tried to achieve negotiation contacts vigorously. The Soviet government also began to nurse hopes for prospective peace with Ryti's government at the beginning of January. Finally, negotiations were opened with the assistance of the Ambassador of the Soviet Union in Stockholm, Aleksandra Kollontay. Tanner met her on 5 and 6 February. The Finnish Foreign Affairs committee was convened on 12 February. It was kept apart from the events. The Finnish Foreign Affairs Committee was not unanimous and some members leant toward Sweden. An official request for help from Sweden was asked for at the same time as insiders of the government informed them of its agreement to negotiate with Moscow. It took a long time to receive an answer from Moscow. The answer finally arrived on 3 March. The Peace Committee that was led by Paasikivi was highly regarded and was sent to Moscow the next day. (Ibid.)

The Conditions of peace with the Soviet Union were more demanding than before the war. Now, they demanded territorial surrenders from Kuusamo and Salla. They also wanted that the border held by Peter the Great, from 1721, be the new border. In Moscow, they listened to the Finns only on a few details regarding this treaty. Finally, the peace treaty was signed on 13 March at 01.00 o'clock. (Ibid.)

Evacuation of the Finnish Karelians and their relocation elsewhere in Finland

When the Red Army crossed the border, Finnish civilians evacuated towards the west. In Suojärvi, where the border line made the so called "bend of Hyrsylä" almost 3000 Finnish citizens fell into Soviet occupation. They stayed in their homes where they could live until the beginning of February 1940. When the Soviet Union accepted the government of Finland led by Risto Ryti – instead of the marionet cabinet headed by O. W. Kuusinen created by the Soviet Union in the occupied territory of the Karelian Isthmus – as a negotiation partner, the population were moved to the work camp of Interposiolok which was located in the district of Prääzä in the Soviet South Karelia. In June 1940 these people were returned to Finland after the peace treaty of Moscow, when the new border was defined.

During the Winter War and after the Moscow Peace Treaty, the inhabitants of Finnish Karelia left as evacuees without deeper considerations. This choice was some kind of shared necessity. Finnish Karelians evacuated long distances even by foot. The people's slight properties, for example, cattle, were transported by trains to the relocation areas. Refugee camps were not included in the refugee politics of Finland, at any stage. The evacuated population, which was called "evacuees" by the public, was accommodated, at the beginning, in schools and other public buildings and at the new location areas in peasant houses. (Hietanen 1989: 240–249.) Finland signed for peace in Moscow at the final moment due to military pressure. Despite this peace surprised almost the whole nation which was unprepared for its necessity. Particularly for the Karelians who had lost their homes in the peace treaty it was a bitter and surprising disappointment. Because of this the political and military leadership of Finland unanimously informed after the peace treaty that it was necessary to organize new places of residence for the evacuated population in a now reduced Finland. (Hietanen 1982: 116–117.)

The first remarkable detailed resolution about the relocation of the evacuated population was made by the Director General of the Finnish Agricultural Board K. J. Ellilä 29.3.1940. In his memo, the main lines of relocation solutions were defined as they were later prescribed in the Prompt Settlement Act. It reflected a tradition of settlement politics from the 1920s and 1930s. The forthcoming farms of the evacuated population had to be big enough for a medium-sized family to earn a reasonable income. The relocation of the evacuated population had to be direct to those areas where there were few farms compared to the already farmed land and land suitable for farming. Ryti's second government made reconstruction their most important business. (Hietanen 1982: 117–122.)

Because of the territorial surrenders, new arable land had to be cleared. Everyone who had owned land in the surrendered areas was entitled to receive new land. In Finland, a new special interest group, Karjalan Liitto, was founded to work for the evacuated people's benefits. Quite soon a law was prepared. The Prompt Settlement Act was confirmed on 28 June 1940. The preparation of this law had been made on time, but a new war interrupted it in summer 1941. (Hietanen 1982: 123–130, 149.)

The total number of the evacuated population was 420 000 which was 11% of the whole population of Finland at that time. The vast majority of them, 410 000, were from Finnish Karelia. According to the Prompt Settlement Act, the evacuated population had to be relocated in areas similar in natural circumstances to their native regions. These people were split-up into land for farms from lands of state, counties and companies and also from larger private farms that were still undeveloped before the new war. About a half of the evacuated population had made their living from agriculture and related industries. The "industrial" population, for their part, were relocated to cities and other industrial communities. The evacuated population were also financially compensated for their lost properties, which was remarkable, particularly for those who had moved from the center of a town. (Hietanen 1989: 240–241.)

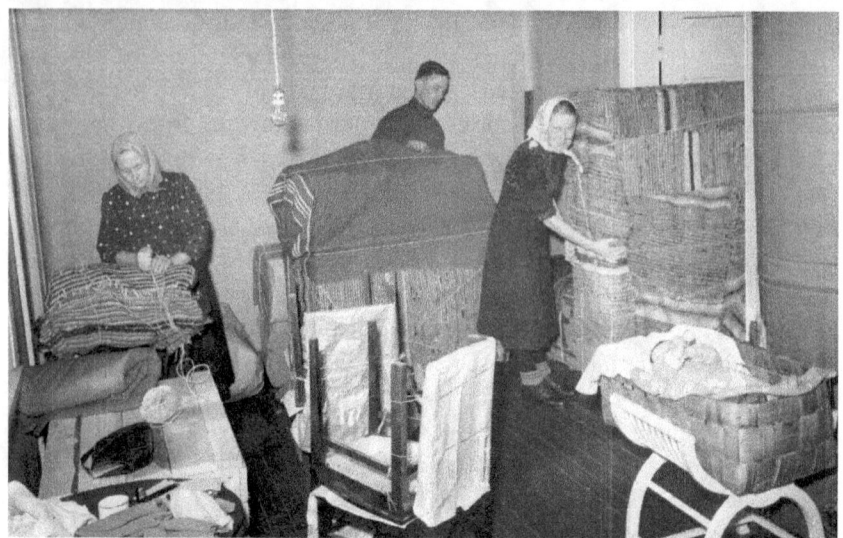

Finnish inhabitants pack their property for evacuation in Kurkijoki, March 1940. The evacuation operations were, in general, relatively well planned and carried out, both in 1940 and 1944, but often limits in transport capacity or other reasons forced Finns to leave something behind. (Photo: Museovirasto)

The Lutheran church of the Kurkijoki parish in 1941, after the withdrawal of the Soviet powers. The church had been used as a club house, with a film projector box in the balcony instead of the organ. In the foreground is a poster presenting paragraph 103 of the constitution of the Karelian-Finnish Soviet Republic. Surprisingly enough, the text is in Finnish, although there were practically no Finnish speaking people in the area during the Soviet period 1940–1941. Apparently, the general political strive to give the new Soviet republic more Finnish character was extended to the newly acquired areas. (Photo: Museovirasto)

Incorporating those parts of Karelia that had been seized from Finland into the Soviet economy

The part of Karelia that was taken from Finland is unique from a war history point of view. The population of this area – 410 000 people – evacuated from the front of the frontier almost totally and those nearly 3000 people who fell under Soviet occupation, mainly due to the hesitation of the Finnish officials responsible for the evacuation, used their opportunity, previously mentioned, in the peace treaty to move to Finland after the war with relatively few exceptions.

On 24 March, the Politburo appointed a commission led by Andrei Zhdanov, the party leader of Leningrad, to prepare the renaming of the republic. On 31 March 1940, the Karelian-Finnish Soviet Socialist Republic (KFSSR) was founded to replace the previous Karelian Autonomous Soviet Socialist Republic. The status of the republic was now that of a Soviet republic among the 11 other Soviet republics that had existed before. The status of a Soviet republic would normally require a million inhabitants, but there were only 300 000 in Karelia – after all, no new population had been gained from the Finnish cessions. On 9 April, the Presidium of the Supreme Soviet of the KFSSR released a statute concerning the border between Soviet Karelia and the Russian Soviet Federated Socialist Republic. In the Karelian Isthmus, a totally new border was erected. This new frontier line was approximately the same as the one that had been demanded by the Soviet Union in the negotiations in Moscow in 1939. (Kilin 2001: 203–204.)

A week after the operation had ceased a commission was sent to the new territories; its task was to inspect the pulp and paper mills. On 21 March, the commission inspected the Lahdenpohja plywood factory and saw mill that was located 40 km from Sortavala. On 26 March, the commission compiled its first inspection report, which concerned the Enso pulp and paper complex. More than a week earlier the government of the Soviet Union had requested that the NKVD repair the most important pulp and paper mills: these included the Enso complex, which was the biggest and most modern in Europe, the Pitkäranta pulp factory, the Johannes pulp and paper mill, the Läskelä paper mill and the Käkisalmi sulphur pulp mill. On the same day, 16 April, the People's Commissar of the Interior, Lavrentii Beriya, ordered that the NKVD organise a special construction unit in the Karelian Isthmus. This so-called GULAG camp organisation was assigned the repair work as its duty. Soon, more than 10 000 prisoners had been brought to work on the renovation. (Ibid.) Käkisalmi was a centre of this sub-camp. The last renovated factory, in Harlu, re-started production at the end of May 1941.

This territorial annexation at once "modernized" the industrial sites of the Republic of Karelia and brought them into world league. Thus, the Soviet Union could increase its production of high-class pulp and at the same time catch up with its underdeveloped knowledge of pulp technology. This knowhow could then be spread to other parts of the country as well. (Ibid.)

The new territories also helped to solve another painful problem. When the Winter War began, the energy crisis of industrial Leningrad was at its worst.

On 9 September 1939, the NKVD of the Leningrad District gave a warning concerning the danger of terminating the energy supply of Leningrad's industrial sector. It was estimated that the shortage in electricity production would be 22 percent in the coming winter. It was also estimated that there was a need to increase the capacity of the power plant system by 400 000 kW after the Winter War. The new annexation provided a substantial relief to this. A couple of years before the war, the Rouhiala power plant had been built in the upper-reaches of the Vuoksi River with a capacity of 100 000 kW. There was also another power plant being built in Enso and it was 60 percent complete. This made it possible for the energy catastrophe to be delayed until later. The decision to connect the Rouhiala power plant with a power line to the Leningrad network was made on 20 April 1940. Thus, the line could be implemented in October. However, it was in late 1940, when the timeworn power-lines that dated back to the days of the Czarist regime still prevented the Soviets from taking advantage of the full capacity of the plant. (Ibid. 205.)

In the beginning of September, Gennadii Kupriianov, the party leader of the Karelian Republic, who had spoken in the negotiations that were held in Petrozavodsk said that "the exploitation of the new territories is a question of top-level politics". His goals were that the work should be organised so that the production units would create more products, the cities and roads and everything else had to look better from the outside, and that agriculture must be more productive than it had been in the hands of the old proprietors. (Ibid. 203.)

In practice, the territories were shared by workers of all means of livelihood as well as soldiers. In the beginning of September, when the exploitation of the area was reconsidered, it was pointed out that the area lacked housing. In the summer of 1940, 86 percent of the houses of Viipuri, 56 percent of the houses of Sortavala and 60 percent of the houses of Käkisalmi were used by military units. A prolonged tug-of-war between the army and the local authorities began; in this argument, both parties appealed to the highest echelons of the country. The vicinity of Leningrad also had an effect, the newcomers who came to Viipuri would discover that people from Leningrad had already taken possession of the houses that had been reserved for them. (Ibid. 206.)

A summary on the financial significance of the new areas for the Soviet Union

According to Yurii Kilin, the areas near Petrozavodsk lost by Finland because of the conditions of peace were very valuable. Clarifying the Leningrad oblast's and forthcoming border questions of the KFSSR were not games between conforming parties. An autonomic republic whose population was under 0,5 million could hardly expect to receive, under conditions of ordinary circumstances, large parts of the former Finnish area. (Kilin 2001: 186–196.)

The city of Leningrad, with its 3 millions inhabitants, had already began a battle over the division of the Finnish area before the end of the war. Already before the peace treaty, the Chair of the Regional Soviet of Leningrad, N. Solovyov, sent to A. A. Zhdanov a draft decision about the Karelian Isthmus. In this draft decision, it was suggested that the Karelian Isthmus should be incorporated into the area of Leningrad. It was all about super-politics: the KFSSR needed more surface area. All in all, the Leningrad region only received about 4000 square kilometres of the border region, in which there were located 200 villages, 5750 houses and about 50 000 hectares of farming land. Finally, after the new war in 1944 the leadership of Leningrad had their way and they incorporated the whole Karelian Isthmus and Viipuri into the area of Leningrad. (Ibid.)

Due to the former Finnish cellulose factories, the Soviet Union was able to rid itself of the underdevelopment that arose during two first five years periods. From a national defense viewpoint, the factories in Pitkäranta and Enso were important. These factories produced high quality cellulose that was used in the production of explosives and gun-powder. The annual output of the Enso factory equalled 50% of the whole output of the Soviet Union. (Ibid.)

In addition, the significance of the agricultural sector that had been incorporated was also great. There were 178 000 hectares of farming land and on that land there was the farming of crops and vegetables. The area of arable land from the former Finland that had been incorporated into the KFSSR exceeded 2,7 times the area of arable land previously available in the KFSSR, even though the whole area annexed to the Soviet Union equalled only one quarter of the territory of the KFSSR.

The new areas as part of the Leningrad Forest Management Area

When the Soviet Union entered into a planned economy, the Soviet Karelia, as a forest republic, was made responsible for large logging operations. It became a large cutting site. In the five-year plans, the number of cuttings was increased enormously. However, there were big problems due to the lack of a work-force and poor transportation.

During the Second World War, the Soviet Union was conducting its third five-year plan, which had begun in 1938. The objectives of the five-year plan in Karelia included a faster rate of industrialization and the development of the paper, pulp and wood processing industries. There were plans to invest 1,5 billion roubles into the Soviet Karelia economy during the third five-year plan; this was equal to what had been invested into the forestry sector of the whole Soviet Union during the first five-year period.

During the third planning period, the emphasis in Soviet Karelia was on the development of the wood processing industry in the North. Collective paper combines were being planned for Pääjärvi and Pudozh, east of Lake Onega, in 1939 and a further two in Repola, in the vicinity of the Finnish border. The areas that were annexed to the Soviet Union in the Moscow Peace Treaty caused great changes in the economy of Karelia. Immediately after signing the peace treaty, preparations began in Moscow to estimate the forestry of the new territories and to make it part of the five-year plan. A report written for the People's Commissariat of Forest Industry observed that because of the geography and the traffic connections and, especially, from the viewpoint of the balance between production and raw material consumption, the Leningrad region, together with the western parts of Karelia and the Vologda region, constituted an economic unit. The central message concentrated on the way the new areas could best fulfill the wood demands of the Leningrad Industrial Center and the City of Leningrad. (Autio 2002: 214–225)

Karelia and the western parts of the Vologda region transported wood to Leningrad, which would also, in the future, depend on transportation from those areas. A complex transportation problem had to be solved.

The consumption of wood in the area was divided as follows:

Fig. 1. Consumption of wood (per cent; F 7637, Op 5, ed. hr 72, p2, RGAE)

The City of Leningrad and the Leningrad region	74
Vologda region	6
Karelia	20

The raw wood resources, on the other hand, were divided as follows:

Fig. 2. Raw wood resources (per cent; F 7637, Op 5, EdPr 72, p2, RGAK)

Leningrad and its region	18,5
Vologda region	14,5
Karelia	67,0

A half of the total quantity (a plan from year 1939 equalled 26, 84 million m^3) of the consumption of wood of the said areas went to the refinement of wood. The city dwellers used 20% of the wood as their firewood. One might think of moving refinement plants close to the sources of raw materials but it was a different situation to other consumers and would also need, in the future, the transportation of wood from Karelia and Vologda. The Leningrad Industrial Centre needed most of the wood. It was responsible for 30% of the whole consumption.

The extra forest resources that the new areas brought with them were incongruent with the consumption of wood. The annual consumption in the former Finnish industrial plants was 6 million m^3. With respect to different sorts of wood, the incongruity was even greater, since 50% of the total consumption was pulp wood, but only one quarter of the different kinds of wood in the area consisted of pulp wood. This meant that in order to provide the Finnish paper and pulp plants in the ceded areas with the raw material they required, it was necessary to organize water transportation and railroad transportation from the areas situated north of the present border. The industry had been cut off from its original raw material supply area. The only raw material resources available to the industry were the forests of Karelia and Vologda on the shores of Lake Ladoga and Lake Onega. In the new forestry areas, Sortavala was clearly short of wood resources. In this area, there were 5 pulp and paper mills, 8 sawmills and 3 plywood factories, with an annual consumption of 4,4 million m^3 while the total volume of the resources was 24,8 million m^3. In the Viipuri Forest Management Area, the total volume was 12,2 million m^3, but it was a limited logging area. The industry in this district consisted of 5 pulp and paper mills and 27 sawmills, with an annual wood consumption of 1,7 million m^3. There was a severe shortage of raw material in the district.

The dimension of the Finnish industrial establishments can be illustrated by comparing against the other plants in the same area. The 27 pulp and paper mills in the Leningrad District, Karelia and Western Vologda used 2,3 million m^3 at full capacity. Correspondingly, the 10 formerly Finnish mills consumed 2,25 million m^3. More than 40% of the wood consumption was concentrated in the western parts of the area.

Resettlement of the new areas

The concrete coupling of the Finnish territories to the Soviet Union began with a decision made by the Politburo on 20 April. It was decided that a high voltage connection would be built from the Rouhiala power plant in Jääski to Leningrad. The energy need in Leningrad was so great that of the 96 000 kW produced by of the plant 45 000 kW would go to Leningrad. The new power line would guarantee so much energy that it would suffice, not only for the industry of Leningrad, but also for the city itself. The power plants in the areas ceded from Finland produced twice as much energy as the rest of the plants in Karelia. (F 17, Op 8, d 16, p 32.)

As early as in the spring of 1940, Stalin was sent a report on the condition of the new areas and an estimate of the development needs for the near future. The report stated that the main areas of business were forestry and the pulp and paper industries. The area contained 13 saw-mills with at least two-framed sawing lines each, two plywood factories (Sortavala, Lahdenpohja), a furniture factory in Helylä (Sortavala) and 11 pulp, paper and cardboard factories. Their total production was 500 000 tons, which meant that Karelia was the biggest pulp producer in the whole Soviet Union. (Laine 1999, 83.)

Since the area had been emptied of the "White Finnish" population and their cattle, the re-launching of the farming industry in 1940 required that at least 20 000 cooperative farm families be transferred from the areas where there was an abundance of people and a lack of land. Plans were made according to which the migration of at least 5000 further families would be needed the following year. The idea was to establish 500 cooperative farms with at least 50 families each; the farms would have 400 hectares of arable land and 200 hectares of pasture. (ibid.)

Overestimated resettlement plans

The report that the Gosplan sent to Stalin stated that as many as 40 000 cooperative farm families should be recruited to the areas that were formerly Finnish. The objective for 1940 was 20 000 families. It was quite quickly noticed that the plans were overly optimistic. In March 1940, the chief of the Migration Centre made a complaint to the Council of the People's Commissars: the target of 40 000 migration families was too high, since the area could only offer housing for 15 000 families. It was necessary to build new houses, which was not a minor task. The reason for the "lack" of housing was that the houses were in the "wrong places" because of the scattered settlement of the Finnish countryside. The dispersed form of Finnish settlement - an isolated house in the middle of the estate - was not suitable for the Soviet agriculture. This is why it was ordered that houses be physically re-located to the centres of the collective farms. Often the demolition work was done and the material was even moved to a new site, but the lack of a work force and extra material prevented the rebuilding of the houses in their new location.

The change from the Finnish form of agriculture was activated through house movement campaigns. For example, in the county of Kurkijoki, which was during the Finnish era a considerable centre of agriculture, 1760 farm houses were moved during the final months of 1940 and at the beginning of 1941. (Tikka & Balashov & Stepakov 2002: 32.)

The People's enthusiasm to settle quickly dwindled. Settlement recruiters received many excuses and explanations. For example, in the summer of 1940, kolkhozes, which were located in the area of the Russian Federation, had to send workers to kolkhozes on the Karelian Isthmus to help in hay work because there were not enough workers in the new kolkhozes. This situation demanded action. The Immigrant Government changed their recommendations to orders. (Tikka & Balashov & Stepakov 2002: 26–27.)

Before the new war, 177 kolkhozes were founded in the new border spheres of the Republic of Karelia: Suojärvi, Sortavala and Kurkijoki. There were 6 sovkhozes in those southern spheres. The surface area of these kolkhozes totalled 47 689 hectares and the sovkhozes totalled 5675 hectares. There were 4 tractor and machine stations which served the kolkhozes and they had 66 tractors. The sovkhozes had 25 tractors. (From the secretary of the Central Committee of KP of KFSSR to the secretary of the Central Committee G. Malenkov 11.1.1945; F 8, Op 1,d 1467, KGANI)

The new war – the areas originally ceded by Finland are completely emptied

The Barbarossa Offensive conducted by Germany against the Soviet Union was soon followed by the invasion of Finnish troops into Karelia, at first to liberate the areas that were lost in the Winter War. However, in the end, the Finnish invasion extended all the way from Lake Syväri to Lake Onega. The Soviet population that had moved into the former Finnish areas during 1940–1941 had to be evacuated almost entirely.

Immediately after the German attack, evacuation in Soviet-Karelia began quickly so that those evacuees who were able to work did so until the enemy approached. In former Finnish areas, there was time to evacuate the population when the actual main attack upon Soviet-Karelia began on 10 July. Sure the first divisions crossed the border at the same latitude as Repola. The evacuation of the new inhabitants in the former Finnish areas succeeded quite well and, of the Soviet inhabitants, only 1400 fell under Finnish occupation. These were separated and moved to Miehikkälä, which belongs to the contemporary area of Finland. In Miehikkälä, a camp was founded for these people. (Laine 1982: 116.) From the southern spheres of the Republic of Karelia and from the shores of Ladoga there 29 905 inhabitants were evacuated to Vologda region (Ibid.)

The areas ceded in the Moscow Peace Treaty had now been reannexed to Finland on 6 December 1941 by the Finnish Parliament. The Soviet Union, on the other hand, regarded the area as occupied by the Fascists, in the same way as the rest of the Soviet Karelia had been occupied by Finns. After the spring of 1942, former inhabitants began to return to their homelands, from which they had to be re-evacuated in the autumn of 1944, when the Finns finally ceded the area according to the terms of the armistice signed on 19 September.

Homecoming

The resettlement of the Soviet population to the former Finnish Karelia was fairly slow. In the beginning of August 1945, 7 965 people had returned to Sortavala and, correspondingly, 5 892 people to the rest of the area. Two months later, the town was already inhabited by 8 420 people and the whole area by 12 500 people. In the whole of Soviet Karelia there were only 267 000 inhabitants by the beginning of October.

In 1945, several sovkhozes and collective farms were founded in the Karelian Isthmus: the Viipuri, Jääski, Käkisalmi, Kanneljärvi, Rautu and Koivisto districts saw the foundation of 54 collective farms (8800 hectares), 29 sovkhozes (8040 hectares) and 136 subsidiary households[1] (424 hectares) altogether. This meant resettlement for 4,730 families: of which 2,130 went to sovkhozes and 2600 to collective farms. 16 were managers, 13 were accountants. (The statute of the Central Committee of the VKP(b): O meropriiatiiah i tseliah po postanovleniiu sel'skogo hoziaistva v raionah

The centre of Räisälä village in summer 1941. Huge concrete statues of Lenin and Stalin as well as the ceremonial gate had been erected during the short Soviet period. (Photo: Räisäläisten-säätiö)

Finnish soldiers and a female civilian pose at the statue of Stalin in Räisälä, 1941. (Photo: Räisäläisten-säätiö)

The centre of Räisälä in 1941–1944. In the centre of Räisälä three houses were destroyed in the battles of the summer of 1941, one of them was the Finnish cooperative store. (Photo: Räisäläisten-säätiö)

Karel'skogo peresheika Leningradskoi oblasti, Fond 17, Op 121, Ed.hr. 415, p.25, RGASPI.)

In the beginning of August 1945, the former Finnish areas of the Republic of Karelia had the following population:

Fig. 3. Amount of inhabitants in built-up areas (F 8, Op 15, delo 327, pp. 40–41, KGANI.)

Towns		Workers' communities	
Sortavala	7965	Salmi	107
Lahdenpohja	1300	Impilahti	432
Pitkäranta	173	Läskelä	69
Suojärvi	1792	Harlu	517
Total	11230	Total	1125

Towns and workers' communities in the whole Soviet Karelia: 104, 543.

Fig. 4. Amount of rural population

Kurkijoki	3668
Pitkäranta	1655
Sortavala	5306
Suojärvi	4659
Total	15288

Total population in the former Finnish areas: 27 645 (F 8, Op 15, delo 327, pp. 40–41, KGANI).

In 1 February 1946 The population in the districts of the Leningrad region on the Karelian Isthmus was as follows:

Fig. 5. Amount of population on the Karelian Isthmus (Tikka, Balashov & Stepakov 2002, 98)

District	Urban	Rural population	Total	In kolkhoses population
Viipuri	1203	4514	5717	2277
Käkisalmi	–	7160	7160	3887
Koivisto	1247	5420	6377	1712
Raivola		8265	8265	808
Rautu		6356	6365	1575
Jääski	7532	1505	9037	1327

Towns	Total
Viipuri	21 445
Käkisalmi	3418
Sestroretsk	8549 (belonged to the USSR already before the war)
Terijoki	3215

(Excluding the military units)

A rough idea about the number of military units on the Karelian Isthmus can be obtained from the population figures of the electoral districts. In the Soviet Union, one voted in the locality where one was doing his military service. The population in the electoral districts in the Karelian Isthmus in 1946 was as follows:

Fig. 6. The number of voters and military personnel on the Karelian Isthmus (Tikka, Balashov & Stepakov 2002, 98)

Leningrad	2 900 000				
Viipuri	37 477		this means altogether 16 032 soldiers, presumably including the family members		
Käkisalmi	4918	military	3142	Towns in the districts	
Viipuri district	13 683	military	7966		
Koivisto district	7147	military	770	Antrea	1296
Käkisalmi district	12 813	military	6746	Enso	4666
Raivola district	8265	military	–	Koivisto	1500
Rautu district	6356	military	–	Uuras	500
Jääski district	16 481	military	7444		

According to the summary above, there were, altogether, 42 100 soldiers and their family members who were not included in the actual population figures in the former Finnish areas of the Karelian Isthmus on 2 February 1946. (Tikka & Balashov & Stepakov 2002: 98.)

During 1946 the industry of the KFSSR received over 15 000 people who were able to work. 5000 people went to work in the forest industry and 1000 people worked in the ministry of building materials. The sovkhozes of the Suojärvi, Pitkäranta, Sortavala and Kurkijoki districts (former Finnish areas) received 3000 people and the fish industry received 200. A plywood factory in Lahdenpohja took on 500 people and 16 338 people were brought to the kolkhozes of the Republic to work there. For the district of Kurkijoki, 4 complete kolkhozes with all their properties were established: seeds, tools, cattle and horses. (Spravka Chief of Immigrant Ward Zaharov, to M. J. Isakov: About end results of conclusions 26.10.1945 n:o 2753 and 15.9.1946 n:o 2119 to serve the return of the evacuated population in 1946, F 1394, Op 6, delo 23/129, NARK.)

At the beginning of 1947, the population of the Karelian Soviet Republic was 361 000 people, which was only 64% of the population that the republic had had in 1940. 48% of this number, i.e. 173 000 people, were fit for work; that equals 55% of the population of the pre-war period.

A special problem for the post-war agricultural planning was the Finnish tradition of private farming and the capitalist system, which had to be fully adapted to the circumstances of the socialist economy; this required a number of specialists. (The vice chairman of the Council of Ministers of the Karelian-Finnish Soviet Socialist Republic M. Isakov to comrade Yegorov from the National Committee of Employees of the USSR, April 17, 1946, F 1394, Op 6, delo 20/108, NARK.)

The so-called khutor houses, or scattered houses, was a form of settlement that was occasionally pointed out to be a problem in the Soviet countryside. The Finnish farmers who practiced cultivation and animal husbandry lived far away from the villages - in any case outside them. The Russian countryside, in turn, was characterized by village settlement, and, since the days of collectivization, the collective farm centres and sovkhozes. Decisions had already been made earlier, but in 1950 the evacuation of small villages was intensified. To speed up the process, university students from Leningrad were ordered to "help in removing" the people from the smaller villages. (Tikka & Balashov & Stepakov 2002: 114.)

During the Great Patriotic War, in 1942, it was prohibited for Germans and Finns, who belonged to the nationalities that were part of the Fascist front, to live in the besieged Leningrad. As a consequence, thousands of Ingrian Finns were evacuated along the "Life Line", the supply route between Leningrad and the Soviet mainland, over lake Ladoga towards Siberia. The majority of the Ingrians living westwards of the city of Leningrad were under German occupation in 1941, and circa 65 000 Ingrians were moved to Finland during German occupation in 1943–1944.

When the war against Finland had concluded on 19 September 1944, the Soviet Union declared that, according to the 13th Article of the Interim Peace Treaty, the Soviet citizens –mainly Ingrians – who had been transported to Finland should be returned. In 1944, c. 45 000 of them were returned and transported far away from their homeland to central Russia. (Nevalainen 1990: 282–292.) On 13 May 1947, it was decided that the Finns and Ingrians who had been evacuated from Leningrad and the Leningrad District in the previous war and returned from Finland were not permitted to live in the Leningrad District; those who already lived there were to be expelled within two weeks. (Tikka & Balashov & Stepakov 2002: 107–108.)

When resettling the Republic of Karelia, the authorities were careful about the previous contacts of the people who were entering to the area.

> Considering that these territories are located in the border areas, where one's first task is the reconstructing of economy, the area must be populated with honest people, who are faithful to the fatherland and who have no connections with the Finnish occupiers. In this way we can create a strong basis for border troops which protect the state border and prevent Finnish spies and saboteurs from entering our fatherland.
>
> (An official letter from G. Kuprijanov to G. M. Malenkov concerning the development of agriculture in the Suojärvi and Pitkäranta districts and reevacuation, October 21st, 1944. F 8, Op 14, d 368, pp. 7-9, KGANI.)

The new forestry plan for the North-West areas was completed in 1951. The plan was much more detailed than the one completed 10 years earlier and it covered the development of the whole field of forestry; also its time perspective was longer. The plan was made by the State Institute for Planning of the Wood Processing and Forest Cutting Establishments, GIPRODREV, and, presumably, the planning had already begun in 1949. The "starting shot" for the plan was the order given by the Minister of Forest and Paper Industry of the USSR in 1947. The plan also included a detailed estimate of the development of the infrastructure, such as new railroad lines, roads and water canals. (Generalnyi plan, Promyshlennogo osvoieniia lesov KFSSR i Karelskogo peresheika, Leningrad 1951, F 7637, Op 5, delo 171, RGAE.)

Much of the plan was eventually left unrealised. Had it come true, the road and railway network in the Republic of Karelia would be much denser than it is today. One could drive from Suojärvi all the way to Kiestinki on a route parallel to the Murmansk railroad but closer to the border. All in all, there would have been considerable investments in the exploitation of the massive forests resources in the western parts of the republic. Could it be that the reason for putting on the brakes depended on the authorities who were responsible for guarding the border? They constantly kept reminding the others of the threat of spies and sabotage. The stormy clouds of the Cold War probably cast their shadows over the traffic plans for the whole of Karelia and withered them up.

In agriculture, the late 1940s and the 1950s meant a gradual transition towards larger units. The main task of the sovkhozes in the Karelian Isthmus was to supply food products for the industrial population of the area and also to guarantee a food supply for the Leningrad metropol. In Ladoga Karelia, in other words in the territory of the KFSSR, small collective farms were first united together and then combined with one of the local sovkhozes, many of which, especially on the northern shores of Lake Ladoga, "were feeding" Leningrad. (An inventory of the development history of the various collective farms in the Ladoga region. The unification was most vivid in the early 1950s. F 3222 (Selsovets) Op 1, NARK.) All in all, it seems that especially in the Ladoga Karelia the unit size of agriculture was small in the framework of "modern" Soviet agriculture.

At the beginning of the 1950s, the Council of Ministers of the Soviet Union made a decision regarding measures to develop the agriculture of the KFSSR. The decision mentioned that the agricultural development of Karelia was clearly behind the development of the national economy of the whole country and cannot guarantee the minimum needs of the population with respect to potatoes, vegetables and dairy products. (Economic material concerning the agriculture of the KFSSR (for official use). The decision of the Council of Ministers of the USSR on the development of agriculture in the KFSSR (1951–1955). F 5675, Op 1, d 463, RGAE.) In practice, the farming units were not even self-sufficient, let alone able to hand-over part of their production for outside consumption.

At the beginning of 1950, 13% of the collective farms in the republic had less than 20 hectares of arable land per worker and 2% of the collective farms possessed only 25–50 hectares of arable land per worker. In addition, in the areas annexed from Finland, there had, so far, been no success in setting up agricultural centres, and the resettlement measures in the collective farms had not been realized. This called for the unification of collective farms, extension of arable land, measures of soil improvement and mechanization of cultivation. It also required migration from other districts. The sovkhozes were not on the same level of development with the agricultural production of the rest of the country either; their production was "negligible". When compared with the first-rate collective farms and state farms, it became evident that it was possible for the republic to be self-sufficient in potatoes, vegetables and daily products, but not in growing grain. (Ibid.) It was decreed that the amount of arable land should be increased and stones be cleared from the fields. In particular, there should be new collective farms and sovkhozes founded on the lands "overrun with grass" during the period between 1951 and 1955.

A completely different characteristic that tied in with the idea of how inviting the area was the fact that so many of the new settlers were willing to move away from the resettlement area. In particular, the Ukrainians wanted to move out. At its worst, this remigration reached a dimension which lead the authorities who were responsible for resettlement to consider sanctions to prevent it.

Säiniö could be mentioned as an example of administrative changes made in former Finnish areas, which was located in the sphere of Viipuri. The provisional government was nominated for the whole area on 9 June 1940. This provisional government took control at the end of year 1940. On 24 December the Säiniö village soviet held a meeting where budget, school and trade committees were established. The village soviet (selsoviet) acted as the government's local deputy. In this area, there were two kolkhozes: Stakhanovets, whose central place was in Säiniö and Gorkogo, whose centre was in Ylä-Säiniö. (F 19, Op 1, delo 1, LOGAV.)

In the above mentioned source it was mentioned that selsovets in the sphere of Viipuri had to combine with the occupation government. The Finnish troops occupied the city of Viipuri on 29 August 1941. After the Winter War the sphere of Viipuri that used to belong to the Republic of Karelia was moved from the KSSNT to the Leningrad region on 24 November 1944. Place names in the Karelian Isthmus were Finnish until 1948. Säiniö was changed to Cherkasovo on 1 October 1948. The names of the places of residences of village soviets changed from Finnish to Russian as following:

Fig. 7. New and old names of village soviets (F R-19, Op 2, d 1, LOGAV)

Gavrilovo	=	Kämäri, Leinola
Zabrovye	=	Näykki, Kuusisto, Vornanen, Seljanmäki
Zobryka	=	Vääräkoski, Ojala
Lebedevka	=	Honkaniemi, Suokanta, Mäkelä, Mäkirinne, Kouvonen

Nizhne-Cherkasovo	=	Ala-Säiniö. Uskela, Kivisilta
Tolokonnikovo	=	Helenotko, Pienpero, Kuusisto, Pellonpää
Cherkasovo	=	Säiniö, Rauhalaitainen, Mikkolanmäki

Settlements of the closed down selsovets of Petrovo, Svetloe, Osinovka and Ulybino were incorporated into the selsovet of Cherkasovo. In February 1960, Stalinets was closed down and incorporated into the kolhozs of Znamya Ilyicha in the Sokolinskoye selsovet. (Ibid.)

The former city of Käkisalmi could me mentioned as an example of changes in the governments of cities. Exactly like Sortavala, Käkisalmi was also named during the provisional government in accordance with the Swedish name Serdobol = Sortavala and Keksgolm = Käkisalmi. On 27 December 1940, a planning committee was organised in the regional administration of Käkisalmi. According to a Russian document, the planning committee had cut off its connection to the occupation committee in August 1941 (a report of the Planning Committee of Priozersk, Fond R-327, LOGAV). In practice, it was about the Russian population getting out of the Finnish attack troops' way.

After a truce agreement when the town of Käkisalmi returned to Soviet control again on 19 September 1944, the Highest Soviet of the Russian Federation moved the Käkisalmi district to the Leningrad region. The name of the district was changed to the Priozersk district and other place names were also changed on 1 October 1949. On 26 December 1962, the Priozersk district was abolished and incorporated into the Vyborg district (Ibid.)

The vicinity of the Finnish border undoubtedly had an influence on decisions concerning the economy of the Republic of Karelia and the Karelian Isthmus, during the Soviet era. This can be noticed both in the everyday economic policies and the restrictions that were set against the people's mobility. The land remained *terra incognita* until the 1990s.

NOTES

1. In Russian "podsobnoye khoziaistvo"

REFERENCES

Autio, Sari 2002: *Suunnitelmatalous Neuvosto-Karjalassa 1928–1941: Paikallistason rooli Neuvostoliiton teollistamisessa*. Bibliotheca Historica 71. Helsinki: SKS.
Davies, R. W. 1994: Changing economic system: An overview. In: R. W. Davies & Mark Harrison & S. G. Wheatcroft (eds.) *The economic transformation of the Soviet Union 1913–1945*. Cambridge: Cambridge University Press.
Hietanen, Silvo 1982: *Siirtoväen pika-asutuslaki 1940. Asutuspoliittinen tausta ja sisältö sekä toimeenpano*. Historiallisia tutkimuksia 117. Helsinki: SHS.
Hietanen, Silvo 1989: Siirtoväkikysymys syntyy – ennakkonäytös vuosina 1939–41. In: Silvo Hietanen: *Kansakunta sodassa I*. Helsinki: Opetusministeriö.
Kilin, Juri 2001: *Suurvallan rajamaa: Neuvosto-Karjala Neuvostovaltion politiikassa*

1920–1941. Rovaniemi.
Laine, Antti 1982: *Suur-Suomen kahdet kasvot. Itä-Karjalan siviiliväestön asema suomalaisessa miehityshallinnossa 1941–1944*. Helsinki: Otava.
Laine, Antti 1999: Suomalaisen Karjalan liittäminen neuvostotalouden osaksi vuoden 1940 jälkeen. In: Kyösti Julki (ed.) *Rajamailla V*. Studia Historica Septentrionalia 35. Rovaniemi.
Laine, Antti 2003: Suomi sodassa. *Suomen historian pikkujättiläinen*. Helsinki: WSOY.
Manninen, Ohto & Baryshnikov, N. I. 1997: Syksyn 1939 neuvottelut. In: Olli Vehviläinen & O. A. Rzheshevskii (eds.) *Yksin suurvaltaa vastassa: talvisodan poliittinen historia*. Helsinki: SHS.
Nevalainen, Pekka 1992: Inkerinmaan ja inkeriläisten vaiheet 1900-luvulla. In: Pekka Nevalainen, Pekka & Sihvo, Hannes (eds.) *Inkeri. Historia, kansa, kulttuuri*. Helsinki: SKS.
Rentola, Kimmo 1994: *Kenen joukoissa seisot? Suomalainen kommunismi ja sota 1939–40*. Helsinki: WSOY.
Rzheshevskii, O. A. 1997: Kesän neuvottelut ja Suomen kohtalo. In: Olli Vehviläinen & O. A. Rzheshevskii (eds.) *Yksin suurvaltaa vastassa: talvisodan poliittinen historia*. Helsinki: SHS.
Suomen historian pikkujättiläinen. Helsinki: WSOY 2003.
The economic transformation of the Soviet Union 1913–1945. Ed. by R. W. Davies & Mark Harrison & S. G. Wheatcroft. Cambridge: Cambridge University Press 1994.
Tikka, Jevgeni & Balashov, Jevgeni & Stepakov, Viktor 2002: *Karjalan kannas sotien jälkeen v.1940–1944–1950*. Sankt-Peterburg: Turussel
Yksin suurvaltaa vastassa: talvisodan poliittinen historia. Olli Vehviläinen & O. A. Rzheshevskii (eds.). Helsinki: SHS 1997.

ABBREVIATIONS

KGANI	Karelskii Gosudarstvennyi Arkhiv Noveishei Istorii (Petrozavodsk)
LOGAV	Leningradskii Oblastnoi Gosudarstvennyi Arkhiv Vyborga
NARK	Natsionalnyi Arkhiv Respubliki Karelii (Petrozavodsk)
RGAE	Rossiiskii Gosudarstvennyi Arkhiv Ekonomiki (Moskva)
RGASPI	Rossiskii Gosudarstvennyi Arkhiv Sotsialno-Politicheskoi Istorii (Moscow)

MARINA HAKKARAINEN

"We were unaware of the history. Just took... our risk"[1]

The past, cultural landscape and identity in migrant communities in Ladoga Karelia and the Karelian Isthmus

On March 13, 1940, at noon, a powerful volley of "Voroshilov artillery" shook the Soviet-Finnish battlefront. Following this volley, machine-guns on the frontline were hurriedly munching up the remnants of cartridge belts, and at noon sharp the war "was left to history" (Stepakov and Balashov 2001: 5). As a result of the Winter war, the Soviet Union annexed territories in the Karelian Isthmus and Ladoga Karelia from Finland, and the Soviet history of these territories began. "New regions" – as appropriated land was called at the beginning (Ibid. 21) – had to be inhabited and developed in the Soviet style of life. People who came to these "new regions" with the first stream of migration in 1940, as well as those who arrived with the second one after WWII formed new communities. With regards to contemporary Russian public discourse about the past and history maintaining the value of centuries-long territorial continuity of societies, the communities in the Karelian Isthmus and Ladoga Karelia regions still continue to be "new". Since they are only "one generation old" or even a little bit "younger" than that, their history is too short, and consequently their past is devoid of valuable depth. A number of times during the ethnographic fieldwork of our research group in former Finnish territories people told us that local inhabitants "lived there only for the present", as far as all of them are migrants, "they did not have a past, nor tradition", and "they were unaware of the history" of the land. So, the absence of long-term links to the place of habitation presupposed the ignorance of local "history" and the lack of a "past" at all.

However, it is difficult to conceive people without a past. It is essential for any human activity, both on conscious and unconscious levels. On both levels, people define or represent themselves as individuals and collective actors in time and space. Consequently, "Self-definition does not occur in a vacuum, but in a world already defined. As such, it invariably fragments the larger identity space of which its subjects were previously a part. This is as true of individual subjects as of societies or of any collective actors. The construction of a past in such terms is a project that selectively organizes events in a relation of continuity with a contemporary subject, thereby creating an appropriated representation of a life leading up to the present, that is, life history fashioned in the act of self-definition. Identity, here, is decisively a question of empowerment. The people without history in this view are the people who have been prevented from identifying themselves for others" (Friedman 1992 b: 837).

By defining or representing themselves, people can constitute their "meaningful past attributed to the structured present" (Friedman 1992 a: 194) in various ways. Construction of a past takes into consideration both social positions of people (see Friedman 1992 a) and particular cultural conventions that structure discourse about the past on many levels (see Tonkin 1992: 6–9).

In any society, there are culturally determined norms and forms of reproduction of a past: the depth of a past can be of relative value; the system of references on which continuity relies can vary; the credibility of a past can rest upon different kinds of authority. Varied forms, genres or terms of representation of a past (oral or written, individual or collective, privately or publicly represented, verbal or non-verbal, narrated as a complete story or dissolved in discourse etc.)[2] create different pasts that may intersect, contradict or support each other[3]. Collectively held (recorded or publicly reproduced), and understood as a process of socially significant changes, a past becomes a history.

Thus, having considered theoretical issues concerning representations of the past prior to our fieldwork in Melnikovo village (former Räisälä, in the Karelian Isthmus) and a small town of Lahdenpoja (Ladoga Karelia), we formulated several questions, which among others, included the following: what kinds of past did the early migrants choose in representing their communities? In what terms did they shape it? What does it mean in regard to their present self-identification, or how "society's sense of past is integral to its self-production through time" (Peel 1984: 111)? The answers to the above questions helped to clarify the issue of how these communities were formed as social units.

"History" and "past"

During our fieldwork in two communities – Melnikovo village and a small town of Lahdenpohja and their surroundings, people often asked us about the purpose of our work. We answered that it was important for us to learn the history of these localities. In our turn, we asked people if they had known anything about the history of just this place at the time of their arrival and what they knew about it at present. From our point of view, the question about history was quite common and most adequate for the situation. However, the theme of history almost always led to emotional tensions. The majority of our informants (they can be called 'ordinary people') tried to avoid speaking about history, and explained their reluctance by putting it down to incompetence, in its own turn caused by a lack of time to delve into such things. Sometimes, questions concerning history provoked irritation coupled with distrust, followed by complete refusal to talk with us. Many people expressed a feeling of regret that they were not familiar with the "true history", that had been "concealed" from "ordinary people".

People, with whom we spoke, evidently had different notions about history. Some of them conceptualized it as a distant past existing prior to their life. For others history was a past that should be told in the language of professional historians. For many people, local history was associated with the wartime conflicts, with questionable moments concerning the acquisition of territories by the new owners and with official ideology imposed from above, and they did not want to be involved in such a discussion. In any case, history was always understood as the past which existed outside of people's life-experience, and as knowledge, the acquisition of which demands special efforts[4] and special competence. Because of their "historical incompetence", many people suggested that we should contact "competent" persons, i.e. local amateur historians. The latter, truly, understood our interest in local history and tried to tell us as much as possible. It should be stressed that local historians are not "ordinary people" in their communities: till nowadays they have held administrative positions.

Local amateur historians take an active part in making the public version of the past, in respect to their localities. They make local history according to two major directions that have been advanced since Soviet times. The first one concerns the ancient past of the territory and may be seen as an effort to compensate for the deficiency of the "deep past" of new socio-territorial formations. The second one relates to the etiology of particular societies. It relates to the events of the Great Patriotic war and their impact upon a particular territory; the heroic aspect of these events is usually stressed, as well as the moment of arrival of the first representatives of Soviet rule to the territories (the military, administration, professionals). Both of these directions can be seen as official ideological projects aimed at incorporating new local communities into the large-scale history of regions and of the Soviet Union as a whole.

However, recently ideological needs have changed and accents have somewhat shifted. A general devaluation of the Soviet ideology is reflected in the comprehension of history designed in the Soviet times. That is why the previous (Soviet) history is partly seen as an "incorrect history", and, as such, should be revised and completed. This general trend more or less affected the work of local history enthusiasts in the communities under discussion. The results of activities performed by local historians become popularized and distributed through local newspapers and other publications, and thus rather quickly become the property of the whole community. At the same time, the public version of history is the knowledge that largely exists apart from the ordinary peoples` experiences and is understood as a part of the history of the State.

Unlike the issues of history, questions about the informants' own past or the past of their locality did not, as a rule, meet with any objections. People readily told us about their reminiscences of different sides of their own lives (individual past) and the life of their localities (communal past), based on personal experience. It should be mentioned that personal experience holds a very significant part in the narratives of the newcomers: to describe previous times people usually chose stories about their life and the life of their families (migration, resettling, working career, everyday life etc.). At the same time, our willingness "to know the history" provided them with a guiding line: people told us about events that could be meaningful for this "history". Thus, in many respects their understanding of "history" (what could be publicly reproduced and socially significant) or their "sense of history" guided them.

For the majority of our informants, stories about migration and circumstances preceding it seemed to be of particular significance[5]. Every earlier migrant, to whom we spoke, had a personal experience story about her or his way and final arrival to a particular community. Personal experience stories told by those who fought on the battlefields, were evacuated, were victims of ethnic repression, by people from families with the prisoners of war and other categories of Soviet people talk about the journey across the vast territories of the Soviet Union in the context of the war years. They are essential for the individual past of those who live in the "new territories", and play a role in etiological stories. Yet, these stories do not only explain the motives of these peoples' presence in a particular community, or maintain the status of its members. The shared experience of war times and migration join individual pasts, the early period of life of local communities, and the history of the state into a single spatial and temporal whole. The past in pre-settling stories appeared dynamic and global in comparison with the past of local communities themselves. Quite expressive stories of migration often end with words: "and then we came here and started to live and to work". Chaotic movement, displacement and separateness during the war years gave place to the stable structures of new communities.

Local past: From foreign territories to the lived-in place

The life of people who came to the new territories just after WWII and constituted the core of the 'old residents' of the communities was closely connected with the material world left by the previous Finnish inhabitants. Food, fodder, implements, tools, clothes, furniture – all of this was essential for people who during the long years of the war starved and suffered from a shortage of various commodities. However, for people who left their places of permanent habitation by force, experience of displacement and homelessness seems to be more disturbing than anything else. The cultural landscape of abandoned territories, and particularly dwelling and public houses left untouched after the war, played an especially significant role in their lives. Thus, one can easily understand why landscape realities are very likely to acquire symbolic meanings of either stability or destruction in communal life.

Both in Melnikovo and Lahdenpohja, the scenery of the communal past is "filled" with material objects belonging to the public space: mills, bridges, churches, factories, and dwelling houses with additional buildings, left behind from the Finnish world. In their stories about the "new territories", the early migrants describe the cultural landscape "inherited" from the Finns and events that happened to dwelling buildings to represent social relations and processes in local communities. The destiny of these buildings may explain significant events on the territory, such as the establishment of the new rule or resistance to it:

> When we came here all houses were brought here from farmsteads within one year. Here are resettlers, resettlers – that's how the kolkhoz was put together! They built the whole village just in one year! Built out of farms ... so as ... when one works, to that one doesn't need to go to a farmstead. So what do you think! [We] came after the war – all the houses are still on their place... on their places! The Finns moved [them] all again to their places. That's how..." (Vasil'evo village, 01, PF-24).

Speaking about general processes in communal life, people also often start describing or enumerating residential houses:

> – Could you tell please, do you know the history of this region? <...>
> – Well, I know that in [nineteen] forty five-forty six there were only small Finnish houses left here, [they were] small, wooden. And later the industry started to develop, and they built five-storey big houses all over ... comfortable. Clearly, life was moving ahead" (Lahdenpohja, 02, MD-7).

The general development of social changes in the communities is often expressed through a listing of changes that happened to original Finnish buildings, cultivated lands or natural objects.

A description of the environment is one of the most privileged means available to conceptualize the state of society and social processes. The chain of major historically successive social events and processes are tightly connected with the restructuring of the cultural landscape: the first impressions of the well-ordered cultural landscape, bringing together of the houses from distant farmsteads and enlargement of fields, the construction of multi-storied houses, the ruination of suburban farms and the disappearance of an idyllic and picturesque view. Changes in an environment embody social changes, marks and traces left in it register the turning points of social changes in the material world.

The beginning of the new world: The order

The experience of newly discovered territories for many newcomers becomes an important theme of their narrative. Many informants paid special attention to descriptions of the cultural landscape that they faced in the new place of dwelling at the beginning of their stay there. Remembering their arrival to the new territories, many informants told us about their first impressions. The stories about newly acquired territories of habitation are characterized by the outside position of newcomers and remind one of the idealized picture portrayed by a stranger, like a traveler or a discoverer, whose life is taking place somewhere outside of it. Narratives about the new territory are as if of this "out-of-place" character; space and time here seem to be static, relative and closed[6]. The panoramic view of the new environment opens before an observer:

> – It was very nice in here! One would go to the forest – it was clean in it. We were even wondering: "What did they cut wood for?"... And the little stones and everything ... in the fields, in the forest, everything put in piles. Everything was so wonderful! A lot of mushrooms, and berries, everything. <...> And there were bathhouses! Well, in general everything that was built was beautiful. The yards were so immense. We were always wondering, that people lived so well" (Melnikovo, 01, Fpf-12).

> "The place was very nice. Very beautiful was the place. Right now looking back from my present age I remember the garden. The garden was everywhere ... near every house: there were lilac and berry bushes, flowers, apple trees. The settlement was beautiful. Clean, green, and the forest was very beautiful, too: no litter, no wind-fallen trees, straight and clean paths, a lot of berries and mushrooms" (Melnikovo, 01, PF-13).

> "I liked this place. Now that I remember – it was clean and orderly near the houses. And gardens... Everything around was planted with greenery... Near the farmsteads lime trees were planted, and lilac bushes were planted – these decorative bushes... There... and there was a smithy. The smithy was here – you can see foundation ... and the forge was there. Later it was dismantled, because it was already old. <...> There were large yards near some houses ... as the farmsteads. For several heads [of cattle] ... yes. And others ... so to speak ... a woodshed, a little shed, some cattle-shed, a little sauna... And there ... there were very large homesteads, the houses were large and farms too... These buildings were very good, they were perfect. There was sewerage there ... well ... arranged for cattle" (Melnikovo, 01, PF-08).

In such stories, the first migrants explicate a number of characteristics of their new world of habitation that are important for them: it was beautiful, clean, well-ordered and rich in natural resources. A well-ordered material world is projected upon the life of the previous inhabitants of these territories, the Finns. The cultural landscape and the objects of the material world constitute a framework within which present dwellers reconstruct the characteristics of previous inhabitants – practicality, an ability to work diligently, and accuracy[7]:

> "...everything was nice ... very nice. If you go to the hill in spring, it is indescribable... Oh, it is the beauty itself, you see! <...> I remember very many farms... There were apple-trees, cherry-trees in every farm ... in those times we still used these gifts, which ... how to say ... remained after the Finns, was left. Apple-trees, cherry-trees, plum trees, everything ... raspberry-bushes. They were planted like this ... in rows. One could see what people specialized in. In every farm it was clear that ... this person specialized in growing of raspberry-bushes ... he had but raspberry-bushes on plantation ... if you go along [you see] rows of raspberry-bushes ... one could pick tons of raspberries... <...> Then... I remember very many mills preserved, you see, very many mills. Near Rastilahti road – I remember two mills very well. I remember one mill in Lumivaara very well ... functioning mills ... there were seven brick plants [there]... <...> You see, the Finns had the bricks under their feet ... everything was here, you see... They were able to build and knew how

to build. They never used land ... never built on the land ... on the rocks – you are welcome..." (Lahdenpohja, 02, MD-8).

Dwellers also reconstruct a picture of the former social order. The order attributed to the "inherited" environment sometimes grows into the picture of an ideal society, in which the previous Finnish people lived: which includes material prosperity of the community – reserves for people and cattle; with gender roles and family relationships arranged in the traditional way; and a perfect order of work and leisure. In this society, people were actively involved in social and religious life (e. g. Melnikovo, 01, PF-1).

Nevertheless, many of our informants think that the well-ordered Finnish society had one significant flaw: people were segregated into two groups – rich landowners possessing big houses and vast territories of arable-lands, and poor laborers living in shanties. This is how the newcomers interpret the existence of big and small buildings on the abandoned territories. The new society of first migrants, represented as egalitarian, i.e. without ethnic, property, and positional or other inequalities, did not have such a flaw. It was able to share the abandoned property among people in equal parts and inhabited big buildings in a just way, dividing them among several families.

Consequently, many informants define the new territories as the "garden of Eden", sometimes using such metaphors as "miracle" (Russ. *divo*), "fairy-tale" (Russ. *skazka*) and "paradise" (Russ. *rai*) in their descriptions. The new territories appear as the main attribute of an idealized past of the first migrants' community. However, the gained paradise possesses characteristics that indicate its complete foreignness for migrants, the majority of whom are bearers of Russian tradition. It is defined as a rather homogeneous space: dwelling houses, sheds, gardens, forests and fields compose a unified wholeness without inner boundaries. The borders between the natural and the cultural spaces are deleted: dwelling and household buildings are situated in the fields and forests, or on islands; forests and remote islands look like cultivated territory. The landscape lacks people.

Deterioration of times

According to our informants' recollections, the best times for their communities changed shortly after their arrival. The ideal order inherited from previous dwellers collided with the inevitable disorder that gradually penetrated all spheres of social and material space:

> – And this beauty, has it kept safe for a long time after...?
> – You see, no. Yes-yes-yes ... in that way. Because you see ... how shall I say ... in short – there are no bad nations, but there are bad people. Yes. And I wouldn't say that there bad nations or something like that. But they can't or don't want to – we just could not comprehend, why. But they ...they ... they did not have any order. Yes, they did not maintain the order. And later ... oh ... in [nineteen] seventies ... when ... district [Party] committees started to do different foolish things – after that

everything disappeared. This way [it was]. When district committees began to command. <...> And now there is no single house here with no office inside. How would one have order [in such a situation]? And … there had been nothing afterwards… Already in [nineteen] seventies nothing existed. Just like that" (Lahdenpohja, 03, MD-1).

Many people told us that under the gradual influence of unavoidable forces of disorder, the locality started to decline. Enlargement of *kolkhozes* and organization of *sovkhozes* in the 1950s and 1960s destroyed the idyllic environment of the first years. In the stories about the past, events of such socialist reorganizations are closely linked to systematic collection of buildings from Finnish farmsteads, to enlargement of fields, to the increase of population. First and foremost, the narratives portray this decline in terms of the ruination of dwelling and public houses, rebuilding or destruction of industrial buildings, roads becoming impassable, fields turning into swamps, and forests becoming overgrown (e. g. Lasanen, 02, MD-15; Melnikovo, 01, PF-17-18; Melnikovo, 01, PF-08). The construction of multi-storied houses which began in the 1960s is seen by many inhabitants as the turning point in community life. The question about the most important changes in their communities during their life is often answered by: *"These big houses have been constructed"* (Lahdenpohja, 02, MD-1). Some people think that the construction of multi-storied buildings testified to the general economic rise and improvement in living conditions (Melnikovo, 01, PF-1; Melnikovo, 01, PF-10). Others, on the contrary, connect this time with a housing crisis (Melnikovo, 01, PF-13). However, in any case, the majority of the inhabitants (particularly the inhabitants of Lahdenpoja) describe this time as the disappearance of the previous world and the Finnish past in nostalgic terms. Very often they refer to the multi-storied houses with discontent, calling them "comfortable" with a bit of irony.

Actually, the social processes in the communities are inseparably linked with the restructuring of the previous Finnish cultural landscape, according to the rules of the new inhabitants. Inhabited places, cultivated lands and natural places collect into larger units. The difference between inhabited and natural spaces grow, new boundaries between them have been established. Later, new urban features intrude upon the rural life of communities. The first migrants express these processes as the destruction of the 'discovered paradise' or 'deterioration of times'.

It should be mentioned that the first migrants keep themselves at a distance from the source of disorder, be it "bad people", "bad nations", "Party district committees", "Russian Ivan-the-fool" (Vasil'evo village, 01, PF-24), an inefficient bureaucratic apparatus, summer residents (Russ. *dachniki*) from St. Petersburg who appeared here recently, or any other unnamed force. The changes to the territory happen as if without the local people's will or participation, for real actors were excluded from the interaction with the landscape constituting a public space[8]. Events of local life occur as if against a given background. In comparison, local people represent themselves as successors of the Finnish order.

Continuity

The strategy of resistance to destruction is represented in terms of continuity between the old Finnish world and the world of the first migrants who immediately succeeded its ideal order. In contrast to destruction and discontinuity in the public space, a continuity between the Finnish past and the migrants' present is usually constructed from the "inside" of the dwelling space, in its private dimension. This happens by means of local mythology and remarks about Finnish dwelling houses and domestic objects.

The idea of inheriting ownership of Finnish houses is the basis for one possible way of constructing this continuity. The sense of 'legal ownership', as could be seen from interviews, is based in many respects not on the authorities' permission, but on the habitual ways of assignation from the previous owners. Legitimate usage of objects left, as well as their symbolic transformation from 'alien' to 'one's own', can be conceptualized in terms of succession from generation to another generation. The previous generation of Finnish inhabitants left the objects and the houses, and the succeeding generation of migrants came to their place and started to use them. According to the stories, the Finns, who are often presented as the real owners of the houses, used to visit their home places in the first period of the migrants' life in the new territories. They controlled the proper usage of houses and objects, and sanctioned their usage in the right way:

> – And there were talks… These houses, which are on the suburbs – the Finns wanted to visit their places. Visited them. [He] says eh… [he] came to the kitchen and said: "Don't pour water on the floor – it will rot. Take care of the floor. Don't pour much water". He warned the owners…
> – Eh … a Finnish man?
> – Yes. He came from… "Don't pour water here. You … the floor will rot. You will spoil the floor. It is wet here". Such story was told. I've heard it…
> – And why did these Finns cross the border?
> – They just wanted to visit their households. They just … they were nostalgic … they wanted so, just to see all that. They had a longing for these places. It is their motherland. And how many [of them] are buried here! They were coming here. It is their place" (Kurkijoki, 02, MD10).

The Finns who visit their houses nowadays actually play the same role of sanctioning or confirming the proper usage of houses, based on their previous ownership:

> "Our house is Finnish, of course. We lived in the Finnish house. The Finns visited me. And one day came… I look – a woman is walking and walking around. <…> Then she came through the gate rather timidly. And she points to herself and to the house. But at the beginning I didn't understand that this house was their… <…> Well … we can't speak to each other. She just came in and said – "it is clean". And it was tidy, my home… When I live alone, I keep the order" (Ihala village, 03, MD-5).

Another way to construct a continuity with the past of the previous generation of dwellers may be conceptualized through the adoption of practical knowledge. To illustrate this, we would like to turn to the story about the economic success of informant`s husband who was *kolkhoz* director in the 1950s:

> – He [informant's husband] very often visited and inspected cellars in Finnish houses. There were barrels with red bilberries, a lot of vegetables... <...> He inspected all these cattle-farms – how the Finns kept their cows, fed them, how it was, in what way their everyday life was arranged. When they stayed at the border, he was watching ... their everyday life. Everybody knew that at six o'clock sharp they would start heating their ovens and to prepare oh... <...> that porridge ... it was in every single house. And around this time men go to fieldwork. Then at the appointed time they come back home and [the family] meets them or they bring lunch right to the field. And the holidays they celebrated from the bottom of their hearts. <...> All of them were dressed up, took two-wheeled carts and went to the church, to the [Protestant] church.
> – And how did he know all that?
> – He observed it in binoculars. And he saw it, when they stayed at the border, he kept watching after everything... They stayed on the old border! And that's why he, of course, was in the know of all these things. <...> And ... he knew their everyday life very well ... and one can say that he saw it with his own eyes and touched with his own hands, saw and touched. And one has to say that such an experience came in handy later, when he started to work ... here in this kolkhoz (Melnikovo, 01, PF-1).

The main message of this narrative is that knowledge about the arrangement of proper society was acquired as a result of immediate contact with it. This knowledge gained by the informant's husband proved to be the most important condition for the creation of a vanguard collective farm out of a backward kolkhoz.

In fact, the first migrants did not have any immediate contacts with the previous inhabitants. A practical knowledge of the Finnish past is usually represented in the form of a knowledge of objects. In this case, the "alien" features of objects left by the Finnish inhabitants (which stressed the boundaries between the material world of the Finns and that of the first migrants) are effaced. According to the majority of our informants, Finnish dwelling houses did not differ much from those that the immigrants lived in before their arrival here. They were comfortable and resembled the Russian ones, that is why one did not have to change anything in them; Finnish implements left in the houses did not differ much from those that the newcomers used in their previous life[9].

The first migrants, as opposed to the later newcomers, constantly demonstrate that they knew the order of life established before their arrival, that they tried to maintain it, and that they lived in the same way as those who had lived there before and "as their parents lived":

> – We walked around ... we were interested in [things] ... roads are clean, forests are clean, forests are not enclosed. Mushroom and -berries, oh! My Lord! There were mushrooms, and berries, and everything just behind

the house. There were few people here ... the forests were clean ... all in all everything was civilized, everything was all right. And we lived in the same way too, didn't litter, didn't ... and after us already – Lord knows! They began ... now they saw. You probably could see it. And they saw the forests. Saw and leave ... and ... if you go to the forest, it is difficult to go through this forest ... but earlier ... we are old dwellers, as our parents were, and we got used ... to keep order" (Ihala village, 03, MD-12).

These attitudes towards the cultural landscape and to objects left there may be seen as a certain link, which the local inhabitants are building from their present to the idealized communal past of the first migrants, as if trying to prolong the Finnish past of these territories. This is how they construct their territorial continuity[10].

Cemeteries

The Finnish past is included into the social space of the first migrants on many levels. In these cases, Finnish and Russian life in the same territories, divided into past and present, becomes a single time and space. Particular spaces where relations between the Finnish past and the Russian present are actualized are cemeteries. The newcomers, when they come to the new territories, kept using the old Finnish cemeteries. Their social structure, in many aspects, represents the structure of the world of the living.

Today, the general structural features of cemeteries both in Melnikovo and Lahdenpohja do not differ from those of many Russian cemeteries in northwestern Russia and beyond it. In the common space of a cemetery, the grave is usually enclosed with a fence, marking the borders of a family grave parcel. Inside, apart from existing graves and the place for the next ones, there is a table and a bench for memorial meals. Arranged this way, a parcel becomes a complete grave complex. The grave parcel can be well taken care of or not – it depends upon whether they are visited by people or not, yet it is presumed that all of them belong to some family. The place outside the parcels belongs to nobody, so no one takes care of it.

The Finnish arrangement of burial places differed from the Russian one, especially in that Finnish grave places were not enclosed with fences as distinct parcels. Nowadays, all Finnish graves are outside the private parts of the cemetery – the parts that one takes care of. One can assume that the newcomers tried not to disturb Finnish graves, since the traditional peasant beliefs do not permit one to disturb old burial places. This is why attempts to re-use Finnish gravestones, mentioned in a number of stories, evoked the present dwellers' indignation and were usually associated with "aliens". However, with time many Finnish gravestones have fallen down by themselves, without anybody's intervention, and, consequently, the graves themselves ceased to be identified as such. As a result, many Finnish gravestones were removed and stored on cemeteries' margins. It is precisely at the cemetery that one can see the old Finnish world has gone, removed from outside of present life. It implicitly exists in the place, but it is not renewed with new graves or through the care of old ones. The new cenotaph placed at the cemetery of Kurkijoki village and dedicated to the Finnish victims of bombing is an exception.

However, there are certain situations when the borders between the Finnish past and the Russian present disappear. This happens on the days of commemoration of the dead, e.g. on Whitsunday, when many people visit the graves of their dead. This is when the Finnish past becomes actualized: the present inhabitants include it into their ritual space of commemoration. Near the old Finnish gravestones, as on the Russian grave parcels, one can see cereals, sometimes a cup with vodka or artificial flowers. Apart from the old private graves, the newcomers' space of commemoration includes public Finnish memorial crosses and stones, which at other times do not attract much attention from local people. With this practice of commemoration, the local past of present inhabitants acquires the depth of the distant past where the Finnish world has particular importance[11].

Sacred places in historical context

Edward Casey writes, that "places not only *are*, they *happen*. (And it is because they happen that they lend themselves so well to narration, whether as history or as story)" (Casey 1996: 27). Narrativization of the local past and communal social processes through the description of environment transforms the "alien" and distant cultural landscape into a place of the actual past. In this way, incorporated into the traditional conceptual scheme of 'deterioration of times', the alien Finnish cultural landscape becomes "historicized" (see also Lovell 1998: 11) and gains a place in the migrants' system of socio-cultural values.

This historicizing of the Finnish cultural landscape that in its primary condition seemed to be undifferentiated destroys its homogeneity. With narrativization and historicization, important spatial objects emerge from the background and become more "visible". In the communities under discussion, these objects possess the status of sacred places. They are sacred not only because it is assumed that they are marked by human experience of some superior power (see Eliade 1994: 25–26), but rather because they "happen" as places both of ritual practices, and as junctures where controversies of different world views and ideologies converge (cf. Friedland and Hecht 1991). In our informants' recollections, these include cemeteries, churches and memorials.

Representing the communal past, inhabitants of the Lahdenpohja district and Melnikovo village often talk about local conflicts in relation to these objects, and particularly to churches and memorials. However, they choose different objects: inhabitants of Lahdenpohja district pay more attention to the Lutheran churches, whereas Melnikovo's people concentrate their interest around memorials. Creating in narratives peculiar sacred places, inhabitants of these communities display their values and orientations toward the large-scale and distant past, constitute their own systems of references and reproduce their localities in connection to a wider historical context[12].

The Lutheran churches of the Lahdenpohja district

The fate of the Lutheran churches (Russ. *kirka, kirkha*) of the Lahdenpohja district – of Jaakkima, of Kurkijoki, and of Lumivaara[13] – does not differ a lot from the destiny of many churches in Russia during the Soviet period: they were converted into club-houses (Russ. *kluby*), storehouses and prisons. Recollections about recent events that happened to the churches of Lahdenpoja district relate to the secular usage and destruction of churches during the Soviet rule and the large-scale context of anti-church actions and anti-religious policy conducted by the Soviet state. Stories about the Lutheran churches of the district contain details characteristic to the Russian traditional stories about the destruction of Orthodox churches and the desecration of holy places during the struggle against religion (see e.g. Dobrovolskaya 1999; Moroz 2000; Shtyrkov 2003). They were stripped of crosses and bells, their benches, "made for ever", were sawn. The reason why Finnish Lutheran churches lack the usual marks of Orthodox Church buildings is often explained by the anti-religious actions of authorities:

> – Empty walls. And ... and ... the cupola was taken away. It was purposely taken away so that it wouldn't look like a church" (Lahdenpohja, 02, MD-3).

> – There were no such ... icons there. There were not. There everything was destroyed. May be painted over or ... a new... I don't know, but there was nothing there in the church (Lasanen, 02, MD-15).

Although, in the opinion of many informants, the majority of whom belong to Russian Orthodox religious tradition, Finnish churches differ from the Orthodox ones, in the stories they often acquire the attributes of the latter. They are architectural dominants of the villages, surrounded with graves of people regarded with sanctity – priests, monks and nuns, they are equipped with enigmatic subterranean passages. At times, stories about Lutheran churches include the element of a miracle or mysterious horror. Churches are seen as sacred places, so their destiny attracts the attention of the local people. This especially concerns the Jaakkima and Kurkijoki churches because they were destroyed. Their disappearance demands explanations and provokes the reproduction of narratives about it.

Fire was the event that served as a main topic of local peoples' narratives about Jaakkima church. Only the walls of the church remained after the fire. According to the stories, the prisoners who reconstructed the veneer factory lived in the church building at the very beginning. Then they were moved to another place – *"[it was] the frontier zone, here prisoners ... it is not the proper place for prisoners. They were moved somewhere"* (Lahdenpohja, 02, MD-6). After the "maximum security prison" for males, a youth training camp was organized there. Later, the building was used to store the "republic's store of provisions". It was impossible to salvage the provision, for "the door was padlocked". Many people think that the fire occurred as a result of arson – it was necessary to conceal illicit usage of food kept under lock. These events were followed by rather dramatic consequences, e.g. the death of hungry children from the nearby orphanage: *"And it was on fire, and there was sugar there ... and there is an orphanage nearby. Even a child went there to look for [food]... He drowned in this sugar. It's just horrible"* (Lahdenpohja, 02, MD-2). The story of Jaakkima church contains a very strong moral condemnation of the authorities, ascribing them all as possible lames: the use of churches as jails for prisoners sentenced for particularly heavy crimes; giving churches over to young people who are not respectful of holy places; utilization of the church for illegal gains. As a result, the church was ruined and innocent children perished. In such narratives, Jakkima church becomes the center of ideological conflict between the local society and authorities.

Kurkijoki church, also ruined by fire some time ago, became the center of different kinds of conflicts. The stories about this church are rather contradictory, but their main point is the struggle between the previous owners, the Finns, and the present inhabitants for the right to possess the church and to exercise religious services in it. Likewise, the story ends with arson. These stories probably reflect religious contradictions between the congregation of the "Finnish church", established by Finnish missionaries in Kurkijoki some time ago, and the followers of the traditional Orthodox faith.

According to the stories, the sacred status of the church of Lumivaara was also infringed upon. The central episode revolved around the removal of its cross, either because of it value (some people thought it was made of gold) or its religious meaning (authorities wanted to devoid the church of the status of a holy place). However, the church resisted: nobody could take its cross off. Thus, in the stories about Lumivaara church there is a conflict between a sacred place and efforts directed towards its profanization.

The stories about the churches in the district of Lahdenpohja (although Lutheran ones) appeal to the values of Russian religious tradition. In the context of the Soviet history of churches, it is a particular manifestation of local peoples' attitudes towards the past of all the state and their place in it. In narratives about Lutheran churches, we can observe all contradictions of the state past: conflicts between secular and religious, between authorities and the people, between history and tradition[14].

Events related to the local Lutheran churches of the Lahdenpohja district immerse one into the general context of the history of local churches in Russia, and indicate the place of local community as a part in Russian religious and historical space. Usually it occurs through descriptions of local sacred places on former Finnish territories, which (as was demonstrated in the case of churches) acquire Russian Orthodox features (e.g. also the arrangement of the Finnish cemetery – Kurkijoki, 02, PF-8). Some people are pretty sure that apart from Lutheran churches, the Orthodox ones also existed in this locality before and were destroyed by the Finns during the last war (e.g. Kurkijoki, 02, PF-16).

The local people of this district do not separate the Orthodox past and Russian history, often describing both the local and the distant past of their region in terms of the Russian religious tradition. In this way, the distant past of the locality is considered as a part of Russian history. In Lahdenpohja, one can rather frequently hear that previously Finland was a part of Russia. Russian possession of the territory is sometimes supported with historical references underlying this connection:

> – Earlier … earlier it was our land. This land belonged to us. It was Lenin, when he became [a ruler] … he gave this land to the Finns. Yes. Well. It was our land … do you know, who started to build the road in the neighborhood, do you know? Peter the Great" (Kurkijoki, 02, PF-11).

People do not talk about Russian history very much – it is outside the sphere of their immediate interests. However, they see their presently existing community and the previous Finnish community as included into Karelia as a part of the previous Russian Empire[15].

The memorials of Melnikovo (Räisälä)

In contrast to the past of the Lutheran churches of Lahdenpohja district, the past of the church in Melnikovo does not feature any tensions or struggle. At first, this church, like all other churches, was used as a storehouse. But according to one inhabitant of Melnikovo, it was saved by God's will:

> – All the territory, everything, just all this locality … it did not belong to the people, nor to … the village council. It belonged to sovkhoz. <…> That is why they couldn't come up with anything better than to make a storehouse in the kirkha <…> And here, there was a good Finnish clubhouse near the garages, two-stored. There were benches there and … probably amateur theatre was there, some performances … there was a cinema hall on the second floor. And suddenly – I don't know the reason why – it burned down. And … [that's how] God saved this kirkha. The "House of the Culture" was organized there" (Melnikovo, 01, PF-17-18).

The church in Melnikovo was preserved in good condition and until now it successfully combines both the secular functions of a clubhouse and the religious functions of a church. While the new building of the Orthodox church is under construction, religious services are celebrated on the second floor of this church. In Melnikovo, the places that attract attention are memorials[16].

Perhaps, there are slightly more public memorial stones and crosses in Lahdenpohja and its surroundings than in Melnikovo and the villages in its vicinity. However, inhabitants of Lahdenpohja do not notice them in their recollections of communal life or descriptions of cultural landscape, and the term *pamjatnik* is involuntarily associated with park sculpture. As they usually locate near the churches, Finnish memorials are seen as additions to them.

On the contrary, two memorials in Melnikovo, a Soviet and a Finnish one, are objects of attention, connected with meaningful local events and symbolize the Soviet and the Finnish parts of the local past.

The first memorial is placed in the present center of the village, in the square, surrounded by market rows and shops. It is dedicated to the Soviet soldiers who perished during WWII. According to one participant of the action, the memorial was erected at the end of the 1970s, as a reminder of bloody battles on this particular territory; and it is replenished with discovered remains even nowadays. In 2001, a new Orthodox church was being built nearby; the combination of the church and the memorial cemetery constitute a place provided with a 'newly created sacred meaning'. It has a number of external attributes of sacred loci – a religious building, a burial place, and a ritualized worship conducted here on the Day of Victory (May 9). The space combines features of Soviet ritualism and traditionalistic trends, although the memorial requires not so much religious veneration, but rather tribute to those who perished. Notwithstanding its historical meaning, this memorial does not really play a significant role in verbal representations of the actual communal past.

The second memorial was erected in the 1990s on the territory of the old Finnish cemetery, not far from the Lutheran church. It combines two memorial functions, it marks the place of the Finnish cemetery of the Räisälä district and it reminds one about those Finnish soldiers who perished during the last three wars – the Civil war, the Winter War and the WWII. This memorial replaced the old one that disappeared during the Soviet time.

In fact, present inhabitants of Melnikovo have difficulties in explaining the exact meaning of this memorial, yet two things are very important for them: the memorial is a burial place left from the Finnish past, and it was and it is a decoration of the local landscape. Stories about the monument recall narratives about disturbed graves and tell about its destiny in the Soviet time: as with some other gravestones from the Finnish cemetery, it was stolen or *"thrown into a ditch"* (Melnikovo, 01, PF-10). They include references to the relationship between the USSR and Finland: hostility, neglect of the Finnish past of the village (destruction of the cemetery and the memorial), and reconciliation (restoration of the traces of this past). Notwithstanding all disagreements about its particular meaning, it is important for the people because it represents the Finnish part of the local past.

Both memorials mark two centers of the village – the new Russian and the old Finnish ones. Both of them represent the past of the village on 'equal ground', which is motivated by local leaders with memorial obligations to the dead, and particularly to people who perished in hostilities. The equal status of these memorials as representations of local military past could be illustrated by the words of one leader of the Melnikovo village:

> – You see ... to pay tribute not to what they were doing, because ... whatever our opinion of this might be, they probably ... did not know themselves what they were doing ... they are victims, they are the victims of the historical process that took place... <...> And their memory should not be desecrated ... Because they found here ... they carried out their duty. At least they thought that they did. The history should not be reflected sporadically, at any place. It should be represented everywhere... And if a memorial appears somewhere, yes, dedicated to Finnish warriors on

this particular territory, here, and if it is reflected in a museum, this is right. It is a good example. If something is being reconstructed, yes, it is a good example. <...> Their nationality does not make any difference. (Melnikovo, 01, PF-31–32).

The parallel existence of public memorials dedicated to the Soviet and the Finnish soldiers on the annexed territories is a widespread phenomenon. The possibility to erect Finnish memorials on the lands of present-day owners, the enemies of the past, is an expression of their reconciliation at the level of official ideology. However, the "social life" of memorials (on verbal and/or actional levels) differs from one locality to another. In Melnikovo, the Finnish memorial acquires a positive social value.

Inhabitants of Melnikovo and its surroundings include their locality into the Finnish past of the territory, and construct a Finnish identification of it on many levels. In particular, local informal leaders choose "Finnishness" to construct an alternative variant of the local history, different from the official one. They revise the war history: in its new variant the Finns and the Russians appear on the same side, the side of "ordinary people" suffering in the war. They are more interested in the previous Finnish arrangement of the territory. They collect photographs and books about the pre-Soviet Finnish past of the village; they record stories about the Finnish past of buildings, and all this becomes the foundation for regional mythology. Local leaders try to find the "proper tradition" and create an ancient and sacred history of the landscape: a mythology both of the holy places (like springs and stones) and buildings is grounded upon the stories about the previous Finnish inhabitants who presumably had been living here since ancient times (e.g. Melnikovo, 01, PF-17-18). This is why the Finns who visit this locality nowadays are often seen as experts.

Melnikovo leaders are building a bridge with which they try to connect the Finnish past and the Russian future: some influential members of the community regard the perspective of economic and cultural development of the district as a reflection of the Finnish past, or, in the words of one local businessman, as the process of returning "ethnic color" to the locality (Melnikovo, 01, PF-31). In this way they consider 'the Finnishess' of the locality as an economic resource. Ordinary people construct the continuity, particularly by expressing loyalty to Finnish buildings. They even collect published materials and photographs brought by previous inhabitants concerning their locality (though it is rare that they are able to read Finnish, or identify places on the pictures).

Conclusions

The inhabitants of the new communities on annexed territories of the Karelian Isthmus and Ladoga Karelia turn to multiple pasts in their recollections. They depend on many parameters: the time of arrival, the motive for migration, the place of dwelling, the social position of people in the locality, the situation of re-telling, the people to whom they tell their stories, etc. However, it is possible to distinguish general trends in the recollections as representation of local identity.

First of all, through their life and family stories the majority of the early newcomers define themselves as forced migrants (escaped starvation in native villages, war destruction, driven away from native lands submerged as a result of the building of new water systems, etc.). Consequently, their communities are represented as communities of newcomers with hard experiences, including the loss of their native lands and a re-gathering on foreign ones. In this case, the past of their families and personal experience is incorporated into large-scale events of state re-organizations and of WWII. In connection with the migration experience, it is important that inhabitants of the "new territories" differ from bearers of Russian peasant tradition living in their localities for several generations, who are usually indifferent to large-scale history (see Shtyrkov 2001: 22)[17]. The latter is known mostly to migrants, although in their stories it may not be assembled into coherent narratives, but constructed out of short-stories, remarks, utterances etc. (cf. Portelli 1997: 4). So, in migration stories, events of the large-scale history become a motive force in the formation of the new communities, their important identifying marker. However, it is not possible to say that they produce communities of migrants (see Razumova): they try to strike roots with the land they discovered, by including the past of the territories into their present.

The past of the local communities on new territories is constructed by its members into traditional cognitive models. Two major conceptual schemes – 'deterioration of times' and continuity with 'paradise lost' (the former embraces the public space of the locality, the latter is represented as peoples' personal efforts) – complement each other in maintaining the equilibrium and status quo of the communities' social reality. Stories about 'paradise lost' are usual for the Russian peasant traditions and comply with traditional comprehension of historical process as 'deterioration of times' (see e.g. Shtyrkov 2001: 20)[18]. In Russian peasant traditions, 'paradise lost' is always placed in one's own earlier experience or in the experience of people one presupposes to know (parents and grandparents, i. e. two-three preceding generations). So this past has the depth of two to three generations, and serves as an actual past, the model of values (Ibid.). The idealised past for the obtained Finnish territories becomes the value reference-point in this scheme.

In this article, I have tried to show that descriptions of obtained Finnish cultural landscape and its changes appear to be an important tool in the representation of the local history (including collective past and societal transformations) of migrant communities on annexed territories, and vice versa - "alien" cultural landscape is developed and mastered through its narrativization and 'historicization'. The collective past of peasant communities cannot be conceived without links to the territory of permanent habitation. So, territorial continuity is created through relationship with the landscape and objects inherited by the newcomers from the generations of former Finnish owners. Immediate contact with the original state of the new territory, recording the changes in the material world around, as well as the construction of succession with it, turns into an important marker for the newcomer's status. Knowledge of the previous beauties of the Finnish cultural landscape, embodying the past order, becomes a means of expression of local patriotism.

Thus, the identity of the newcomers is established upon two positions constituting their actual past: stories of coming into a particular community (they are put aside in this paper) and descriptions of perception of the new Finnish territory. The actual past is expressed on the level of every-day discourse and is a part of every-day life. In both cases, the represented past is devoid of valuable "historical" depth. Language and conceptual schemes used by local people to create their communal past differ a lot from those accepted in the public discourse. In connection to what was said above, it becomes clear why in relation to locality, national and state history, produced by public and official historical discourse, is limited in demand at the local level. Containing large-scale events, it is scarcely capable of meeting the needs of people whose identity is largely grounded in the local past.

However, it would not be correct to say that the actual local past exists in an isolated state. It is built into the wider context of a more remote and large-scale past, the context of which cannot be imposed from the outside, but is reproduced within the frames of locality itself. First, the life experience of people who settled in the annexed territories cannot be limited by the borders of the locality where they presently live. Their experience of war and migration pushes aside special and temporal borders and creates a context that encompasses the present locality. This is why events of war years are inseparable from the people's individual past[19]. Secondly, though inhabitants of Lahdenpoja and Melnikovo, in general, have a similar pool of narrative means for representation of their local pasts (themes, topics, narrative schemes, motives and verbal formulas), they refer to different contexts while speaking about events connected with chosen sacred places. The former built their local events into the general Russian and Karelian past, whereas the latter stress the Finnish history of their region more strongly. Placing of local events into different contexts implies different values, and the value context becomes a remote collective past. Thus, the identity of new local communities is constructed as a correspondence between local and collective distant past, or history. In this case, history becomes an important element in the building of the local identity. In this respect, they also differ from 'traditional peasant' communities[20].

Yet, history requires (presupposes) a special language and means of expression, as well as specific practices of their reproduction and their specific 'placing'. Moreover, making history is often seen as the practice of authorities (like social processes are seen as being in motion without 'ordinary people's' participation). So, the right to reproduce this collective past in a certain way and space belongs to local historians and specialists in the local lore. As was said above, they work over the reproduction of the distant (remote) past, when constructing the ancient history of the region and they work over the expansion of the borderlines of the local past, by reviving the events of military actions within the frames of state history.

One can add that the official version of the local history of the Soviet period, with its focus on the war actions preceding the annexation of territories, does not prove to be of much importance for those who live here. The present-day research of local historians concerned about events of the Winter war do not seem to be very popular among ordinary people. Events that resulted in territorial annexation contradict the sense of continuity they adhere to. On the one hand, local people know about the military origin of their territories. Yet, on the other, people exclude the Finnish war from their communal past and try to distance themselves from it.

NOTES

1. Lahdenpohja, 02, MD-1. (Citations of field materials include: place and year (XXI c.) of recording and the number of field phonogram (PF) or mini-disk (MD)).
2. On genres, oral and written representation of the past, as well as about individual and collective past see Elizabeth Tonkin's Introduction to her book *Narrating Our Pasts* (Tonkin 1994). On genres and dialogic nature of oral history see also: Portelli (Portelli 1997: 3). For oral and material representations of culture and the past see: e. g. J. Cruikshank (Cruikshank 1992). On public and private versions of the past and the multiplicity of its representations, see also Bloch (Bloch 1998 b [1993]). Different ways of relating to the past and "being in history" are described in: Bloch 1998a [1992].
3. Appadurai argues that "although there might be infinite *substantive* variations concerning such norms about the past, there is a minimal set of *formal* constraints on *all* such sets of norms. These formal constraints can be seen as four minimal dimensions concerning which all cultures must make some substantive provision.
    1. *Authority*: this dimension involves some cultural consensus as to the kinds of source, origin or guarantor of 'past' which are required for their credibility.
    2. *Continuity*: involves some cultural consensus as the nature of linkage with the source of authority which is required for the minimal credibility of the 'past'.
    3. *Depth*: involves cultural consensus as to the relative values of different time-depths in the mutual evaluation of the 'pasts' in a given society.
    4. *Interdependence*: implies the necessity of some convention about how closely any past may be interdependent with other 'pasts' to ensure minimal credibility" (Appadurai 1981: 203). See also E. Tonkin (Tonkin 1992: 6–9).
4. This thesis can be illustrated with the following utterance: "You can either detest it, or like, or whatever – history is history. How can one escape it? It is exact science. History must be more accurate than mathematics. Yes" (Melnikovo, 2001, PF-15).
5. In fact, the majority of migration stories refer to the war years. Even for people who came to these territories in 1940–1941, wanderings during WWII and the secondary migration to the same place have more value than the first migration, and push it into the background. Sometimes the story makes it difficult to comprehend that the informant first came to these territories before WWII.
6. In some sense, they remind one of time and space in folklore genres, see e.g. Nekljudov (1972), cf. Bakhtin 2000.
7. These characteristics of the Finns as main features coincide with the image of the Finns in pre-revolutionary Karelia. See: I. Takala 2003.
8. K. Basso writes about different ways of interaction with the landscape: "members of local community involve themselves with their geographical landscape in at least three distinct ways. First, they may simply observe the landscape, attending

for reasons of their own to aspects of its appearance and to sundry goings-on within it. Second, they may utilize the landscape, engaging in a broad range of physical activities that, depending on their duration and extent, may leave portions of the landscape visibly modified. Third, native people may communicate about landscape, formulating descriptions and other representations of it that they share in the course of social gathering" (Basso 1988: 100). In the introduction to the "Anthropology of Landscape" Eric Hirsch stresses the idea of landscape as a process: " 'landscape' entails a relationship between the 'foreground' and 'background' of social life", where "foreground" presents "the concrete actuality of everyday social life ('the way we now are')", "here and now, place", whereas the "background" turns into "perceived potentiality thrown into relief by our foregrounded existence ('the way we might be'), "horizon, space"" (Hirsch 1993: 3–4). In my fieldwork experience in villages of Northwest Russia (Novgorodskaya and Pskovskaya regions), descriptions of landscapes as such are not common among peasants. Rather the definition of landscape appears through description of interaction with it (see also Shtyrkov 2001: 31). In descriptions of the obtained "new territories" the life of cultural landscape as public space is divorced from the life of local inhabitants almost completely.

9. This does not conform to the actual reality – the houses are in many ways re-designed inside, some parts were added. Later newcomers sometimes stress the uselessness of old Finnish things because of their differences from the Russian ones. Actually 'useless things' were destroyed: for example, 'poor houses' such as sheds in the fields, as well as some unidentified wooden implements were used as firewood.

10. It should be mentioned that the 'Finnishness' of the obtained territory penetrates the everyday life of migrant communities on many levels. It is implicitly present in the social space of the newcomers embodied in the material objects, as well as in everyday discourse. For example, many places and objects are attributed to Finns in nominations 'Finnish houses', 'Finnish cemetery', 'Finnish churches', etc. However, it is possible that it actualises in narratives in special conditions, e.g. meetings with previous inhabitants or with ethnographers. It also becomes a resource supporting relationships with the Finns visiting their native places after the 'opening' of the borders. A good example of actualization of continuity with Finnish past on the level of social relations is a widespread practice of 'friendship' between the present owners of the houses and the previous ones. Nowadays, these relations are an important part of life for many present owners of Finnish houses. They not only legitimise the continuity between old and new ownership on the private level, but they become an important resource both symbolic, as well as economic, for Russian families in that as contain the possibility to prove their state – for example, a possibility to visit Finland.

11. This ritual worship of old graves has parallels in other Russian peasant traditions in the form of a widespread practice of commemoration, or worship, of "forgotten parents" (Russ. *zabudushchije roditeli*). S. A. Shtyrkov writes about the latter: "in ancient times they lived on the same land where now present people live, and then disappeared, usually as a result of some cataclysms (for example, foreign invasion, newcomers' arrival, etc.); ancient cemeteries (burial places of forgotten parents) very often are holy places in the villages; *the forgotten* demand commemoration, and if it does not happen they punish the living; attempts to disturb their remains always lead to disastrous consequences; often forgotten parents are alien people (*Chudj, Pany, Latvians* etc.) (Shtyrkov 2001: 114).

12. Here one can quote the work of Arjun Appadurai in the reproduction of neighborhood (and locality): "In so far as neighbourhoods are imagined, produced and maintained against some sort of ground (social, material, environmental) they also require contexts, against which their intelligibility takes shape. This context generative dimension of neighbourhoods is an important matter, because it provides the beginning of a theoretical angle on the relationships between local and global realities" (Appadurai 1995: 209); and further: "through the vagaries of social actions by local subjects, neighbourhood as context produces the context of neighbourhoods. Over

time, this dialectic changes the conditions of production of locality as such" (Ibid. 210).
13. There were more churches on the territory, but the stories about these three are the most representative.
14. Glassie writes about history and tradition: "Overtly, histories are accounts of the past. Their authors, acceding to the demands of narration, customarily seek change, the transformations by which they can get their story told. Change and tradition are commonly coupled, in chat and chapter titles, as antonyms. But tradition is the opposite of only one kind of change: that in which disruption is so complete that the new can not been read as an innovative adaptation of the old. <...> If tradition is a people's creation out of their own pasts, its character is not stasis but continuity; its opposite is not change but oppression, the intrusion of a power that thwarts the course of development. Oppressed people are made to do what others will them to do" (Glassie 1995: 395–396).
15. In many respects, such a point of view has been formed since the Soviet time. See e.g. how is the recommendation list of literature on regional history is arranged in "Goroda Karelii: Lahdenpohja. Rekomendateljnyi ukazatelj literatury", part "Iz istorii goroda I raiona" (Goroda 1991).
16. In our materials the term *memorial* (Russ. *pamiatnik*) has two main meanings: monument on a private grave; and public memorial constructions – in this case the term has strong burial connotations also.
17. So, unifying the migration experience is stressed in their life stories, and the local cultural diversities are hidden. This situation reminds "the model for cross-cultural understanding" of immigrants in America described by Renato Rosaldo: "...immigrants, or at any rate their children and grandchildren, are absorbed into national culture. Above all, this process involves the loss of one's past – autobiography, history, heritage, language, and all the rest of so-called cultural baggage" (Rosaldo 1988: 82). In this sense, the migrants of "new territories" do not have a past or tradition.
18. In Russian peasant traditions the 'deterioration of times' is a culmination of eschatological narratives. In migrant communities of the new territories they are rare. Yet I cannot avoid the temptation and quote one very vivid example: *'I was a child yet, about five years old. Our church was burning. <...> There were no telephones, no radio, nothing, and the church burnt down, so... <...> The priests' wife was literate, and our grandmother was blind and told us, saying: "Remember, you will not survive so long, but your daughter and son will. Not in the native land they will live* [sic!]. *Great wars will break out, there will be a railway, the horses will fly"* – aeroplanes *will fly in the air. And all people laughed: the priests' wife got insane. But she didn't, she was telling too early. And because people could not read, how could they know? <...> But she was literate, she could read the Bible'* (Lahdenpohja, 2002, PF-5).
19. Cf. Bloch 1998 c, Cappelletto 2003.
20. "...through the vagaries of social actions by local subjects, neighbourhood as context produces the context of neighbourhoods. Over time, this dialectic changes the conditions of production of locality as such" (Appadurai 1995: 210).

REFERENCES

Appadurai, Arjun 1981: History as A Scarce Resource. In: *Man. New Series*. Vol. 16, Issue 2, June 1981.
Appadurai, Arjun 1995: The production of locality. In: Richard Fardon (ed.) *Counterworks: Managing the Diversity of Knowledge*. ASA Decennial Conference Series. The Users of Knowledge: Global and Local Relations. New York and London: Routledge.
Bakhtin, Mikhail 2000 (1975): Formy vremeni. I khronotopa v romane. In: Bakhtin, Mikhail. *Epos i roman*. Sankt-Peterburg: Azbuka.

Basso, Keith H. 1988: "Speaking with names": Language and Landscape among the Western Apache. In: *Cultural Anthropology*. Vol. 3, #2, May 1988.

Bloch, Maurice E. F. 1998a (1992): Internal and External Memory. Different Ways of Being in History. In: Maurice Bloch: *How We Think They Think: Anthropological Approaches to Cognition; Memory, and Literacy*. Boulder: Westview Press.

Bloch, Maurice E. F. 1998 b (1993): Time, Narratives and the Multiplicity of Representations of the Past. In: Maurice Bloch: *How We Think They Think: Anthropological Approaches to Cognition; Memory, and Literacy*. Boulder: Westview Press.

Bloch, Maurice E. F. 1998c (1996): Autobiographical Memory and the Historical Memory of the More Distant Past. In: Maurice Bloch: *How We Think They Think: Anthropological Approaches to Cognition; Memory, and Literacy*. Boulder: Westview Press.

Cappelletto, Francesca 2003: Long-term memory of extreme events: from autobiography to history. In: *The Journal of Royal Anthropological Institute*. Vol. 9, #2, June 2003.

Counterworks: Managing the Diversity of Knowledge. Ed. By Richard Fardon. ASA Defennial Conference Series. The Users Knowledge: Global and Local relations. New York & London: Routledge. 1995.

Cruikshank, Julie 1992: Oral tradition and Material Culture: Multiplying Meanings of 'Words' and 'Things'. In: *Anthropology Today*. Vol. 8, Issue 3, June 1992.

Dobrovol'skaya, V. E. 1999: Neskazochnaya proza o razrushenii svyatyn'. *Russkii fol'klor*. T. XXX. SPb.

Eliade, Mircea 1994 (1957): *Svyashchennoye i mirskoye*. Translated from French by N. K. Garbovskii. Moskva: Izd-vo MGU.

Friedland, Roger & Hecht, Richard D. 1991: The Politics of Sacred Place: Jerusalem's Temple Mount / al-haram al-sharif. In: Jamie Scott & Paul Simpson-Housley (eds) *Sacred places and profane spaces: essays in the geographies of Judaism, Christianity, and Islam*. Contributions to the study of religion 30. New York: Greenwood Press.

Friedman, Jonathan 1992a: Myth, History, and Political Identity. In: *Cultural Anthropology*. Vol. 7, #2, May 1992.

Friedman, Jonathan 1992b: The Past in the Future: History and the Politics of Identity. In: *American Anthropologist, New Series*. Vol. 94, Issue 4, Dec. 1992.

Glassie, Henry 1995: Tradition. In: *The Journal of American Folklore*. Vol. 108, Issue 430, Autumn 1995.

Goroda Karelii: Lahdenpohja. Rekomendatelnyi ukazatel literatury 1991. Sostaviteli L. L. Neiken, L. S. Baranovich. Petrozavodsk, 1991 (Gosudarstvennaya publichnaya biblioteka Karel'skoi ASSR, Lahdenpokhskaya tsentralnaya raionnaya biblioteka).

Hirsch, Eric 1995: "Introduction. Landscape: Between Place and Space". In: Eric Hirsch & Michael O'Hanlon (eds) *The Anthropology of Landscape: Perspectives in Place and Space*. Pp. 1–30. Oxford: Claridon Press

Locality and Belonging. Ed. by Nadia Lowell. New York: Routledge. 1998.

Lovell, Nadia 1998: Introduction: Belonging in Need of Emplacement? In: Nadia Lovell (ed.) *Locality and Belonging*. New York: Routledge.

Moroz, A. B. 2000: *Ustnaya istoriya russkoi tserkvi v sovetskii period (narodnyye predaniya o razrushenii tserkvei)*. Uch. Zap. Pravoslavnogo universiteta ap. Ioanna Bogoslova. Vyp. 6. Moskva.

Nekliudov, S. Yu. 1972: Vremya I prostranstvo v byline. In: *Slavyanskii fol'klor*. Moskva.

Peel, J. D. Y. 1984: Making History: The Past in the Ijesho Present. In: *Man, New Series*. Vol. 19, Issue 1, Mar. 1984.

Portelli, Alessandro 1997: *The battle of Valle Giulia: oral history and the art of dialogue*. Madison (Wis.): The University of Wisconsin Press.

Rosaldo, Renato 1988: Ideology, Place, and People without Culture. In: *Cultural Anthropology*, Vol. 3, # 1, Feb. 1988.

Sacred places and profane spaces: essays in the geographies of Judaism, Christianity, and Islam. Ed. by Jamie Scott & Paul Simpson-Housley. Contributions to the study of religion 30. New York: Greenwood Press.

Shtyrkov, S. A. 2001: *Predaniya ob inozemnom nashestvii: krestjanskii narrativ i mifologiya lanshafta (na materialakh severovostochnoi Novgorodchiny).* Dissertatsiya na soiskaniye uchenoi stepeni kandidata istoricheskikh nauk. (Na pravakh rukopisi). Evropeiskii universitet v Sankt-Peterburge.

Shtyrkov, S. A. 2003: Rasskazy ob oskvernenii svyatyn'. In: *Sovremennyi fol'klor Novgorodskoi oblasti.* Vyp. 3. In print.

Stepakov, Viktor and Yevgenii Balashov 2001: *V "Novykh raionakh": Iz istorii osvoyeniya Karel'skogo peresheika 1940–1941, 1944–1950 gg.* Sankt-Peterburg: Nordmedizdat.

Takala, Irina 2003: Finny v vospriyatii zhitelei sovetskoi Karelii (1920–1930-e gg.). Paper on the seminar of Academy of Finland international project "Image of Russia – Image of Finland", Helsinki, 29 August 2003.

The Anthropology of Landscape: Perspectives in Place and Space. Ed. by Eric Hirsch & Michael O'Handon. Oxford: Claridon Press. 1995.

Tonkin, Elizabeth 1995 (1992): *Narrating Our Pasts: The Social Construction of Oral History.* Cambridge Studies in Oral and Literature Culture 22. Cambridge: Cambridge University press.

Fieldwork materials (PF and MD) from Melnikovo, Karelian isthmus, Leningrad region, in 2001, from Lahdenpohja and Kurkijoki, Republic of Karelia, in 2002 and 2003

EKATERINA MELNIKOVA

Recollections of "native land" in oral tradition of Russian settlers to Karelia

> *It proposed that human beings, by that act of making witness, warranted times and places for their existence other than the time and place they were living through.*
> R. L. Doctorow. Ragtime

The main concern of this article is to reveal the role of premigrational experience in the contemporary oral tradition of Russian settlers in Karelia. This work examines interviews with contemporary inhabitants of the city of Lahdenpohja and its suburbs, which were obtained during the fieldwork of 2002–2003 that was organized by the University of Joensuu (Finland) and the European University at St. Petersburg (Russia).

Antti Laine has provided, in his article, a broad historical review of the process of Karelia's development after this territory was annexed to the Soviet Union in 1940 and 1944. I would only like to stress here some aspects of settlement that are significant for my work. The migration to the new lands, initiated by the soviet government, was arranged in a short space of time[1]. Consequently, during the last half of the 1940s and the beginning of the 1950s several local communities consisted predominantly of migrants: people arrived from different regions, usually not familiar each with other, for the majority of whom Karelia was a perfectly new place. During the first post-war years the sole common feature for all the Russian migrants in Karelia was their displacement and alienation from their place of birth. During the ensuing decades, these former migrants began to experience both the local landscape and social environment. Most of the people with whom we succeeded to talk consider Karelia as their home and identify themselves as representatives of a "new" local community. Nevertheless, even now their recollections of premigrational life play a significant role in their stories.

The specifics of recollections in context with the experience of migrants is connected to their displacement that had once (or several times) happened. Thus, 'the past' that is recalled is associated, for the speakers, with two or more different places. Discussion of the migrants` community presumes speaking not about "sense of place" (see: Basso 1996) rather about senses of *places*, all of which are used for the construction of social reality and become markers of the local identity of people.

Representations of premigrational experience

According to the main issue of this article, I attempt here to find various forms of representations of premigrational past as they are portrayed by the contemporary inhabitants of Lahdenpohja and its suburbs, all of whom had migrated to Karelia during the 1940s and 1950s. In the words of E. Tonkin "in order to think about the past, one must represent aspects of it to oneself, or to another ... References to past events are continual, and judgments about them, explicit as well as assumed, occur in everyday conversation" (Tonkin 1992: 2). Through an analysis of such representations we can reveal a significance regarding the premigrational past when considering the present social environment as experienced by settlers.

I name the representations of past-before-Lahdenpohja as recollections of *rodina*, "homeland", since the sense of place has a central value for them. If applied to an indigenous society that functions in the course of several generations in the local territory this term would sound paradoxical or even senseless. In his famous paper, K. Basso emphasized that "people are forever presenting each other with culturally mediated images of where and how they dwell. In large ways and small, they are forever performing acts that reproduce and express their own sense of place – and also, inextricably, their own understandings of who and what they are" (Basso 1996: 57). From this point of view, any recollection, any oral history expresses a sense of place and may be considered as a recollection of homeland.

The act of movement that is common to all the members of society makes a picture more complex. 'The past' itself is divided for the members of such a community into various partitions in accordance with their movements. It has as many borders as there were resettlements in the life of migrants. In a recent paper by R. Lévy Zumwalt and I. J. Lévy, they carry out an analysis of their own recollections of their once abandoned Atlanta. They argue that such stories allow tellers to "make Atlanta home" after the subsequent return (Lévy, Zumwalt & Lévy 2002). This case presents an example of displacement, where the connectedness with a certain place needs to be both confirmed and demonstrated. Family narratives in this context allow the *creation* of such a connection (ibid. 67). In the situation under focus in my work, people did not return to their birthplace and their recollections do not evoke the creation of present placed-ness but support "other placed-ness".

But it must be noticed that the category of "premigrational past" is solely instrumental for this research. It provides us with the opportunity to examine the process of adaptation of migrants to a new social environment. Premigrational experience becomes apparent in oral stories in various forms. In some cases, 'the past' occurs as a topic of tale and may be discussed in everyday conversation. In others, "recollections" are implicit and can be observed only through studying local nicknames and terms of group identification. For some interviewees, the category of "past before Lahdenpohja" is not relevant. The border between the past before Karelia and the past associated with it is not always as sharp as we could suppose and sometimes there is no such border at all.

Explicit forms of recollections

By "explicit forms of recollections" I refer to oral representations of premigrational past where 'the past' arises as a topic for conversation. Very often during our interviews we ourselves asked people to recall their life before Lahdenpohja, by using specific questions:

> – Haven't you ever missed for Vologda region? Didn't you wish to return there?
> – Well, we... How we didn't miss... It flooded. We visited there. When came here, then what indeed... It was a large church at our place, so, the water did overflow... (PF 10, 2002, Lahdenpohja, f. 1927, Vologda region)[2].

Here the researcher offers an informant the opportunity to recall his life before migration and the interlocutor willingly accepts the offer. The majority of the people whom we spoke to describe their birthplace with pleasure. Any mention of it was usually taken as an invitation for an extended recollection:

> – Voznesenie [*narrator's place of birth*] – it was a city also?
> – But it wasn't called a city yet, but it was planned before the war to be named – city. Village it was called, village Voznesenie, there were already 5 floor houses, and large, large village was, very large, they already wanted to call it city. There was river Svir, just at the river Svir (PF 6, 2002, Lahdenpohja, f. 1924, Leningrad region.)

Another context when the past is explicitly represented is through comparison. Often the interviewer him/herself offers to compare any realities of life in Karelia with those associated with premigrational place:

> – Well, did the Finnish house differ from the Yaroslavl one?
> – Oh, at Yaroslavl there were so good houses at our place. You know! Two-storeyed houses were. At the beginning they built two-storeyed. And then, when we left – it was already my mothers sister who wrote – five-storey began to build. But at the beginning two-storied were. But we lived not in the very city, we lived within 60 km from city. There was sovhoz at our place that was called Volna, Tutaev district. And Tutaev, it was within 4 km from us, we had to go along Volga. And Yaroslavl was the very city – 60 km. As much as Lahdenpohja is from here Yaroslavl was from our place, 60 km. Very beautiful city. Mama went there when she was younger, fifty years she was I think. She hadn't pensioned off yet. She went two times. I had babies, I wasn't able to leave anywhere already. Little babies were, children (PF 11, 2003, Kurkijoki, f., 1939, Yaroslavl region).

In this case, the interviewer had inspired the recollection. But comparison itself is an essential device used by informants to outwardly describe things. Often they resort to it without any leading question:

> – When your brother invited you here, what did he tell you about these places?
> – Well... told that Karelia... That there is veneer factory here, that it is

possible to work here. We... Karelia, sure... We... I lived in Belorussia. It was a wilderness there, there is field, only fields. And here, sure... I came – forest, nature is so marvelous (PF 14, 2003, Lahdenpohja, f. 1930, Minsk region).

The landscape that the migrants experienced after removal was not only new for them, it also bore a lot of traces of the former inhabitants (see the article of Pekka Hakamies in this volume). Though migrants were not able to communicate with Finns they knew about them as former owners of the land. The contrast between settlers and Finns became one of the identity markers of these people. Although their first acquaintance with Karelia elapsed several decades ago for the majority of our informants, the opposition "Finnish – not Finnish" still exists. As they speak about the peculiar, curious things that they found after their arrival our informants use the same speech modes. This shows that the topic is discussed not only with a researcher but among the members of community as well. The main instrument for the testimonial of strange objects is reference to premigrational experience, not to their contemporary realities of local life:

> – When you arrived didn't you find any strange constructions or things, that you didn't understand?
> – No. What we found was the same as at our place. We had a house at hutor, where our aunt lived, so we hold it. The same things as at our place, as where we live in the village. We have the same pots, such... oven fork it is called, pots... the same spades – everything was the same. There was no anything strange. Even for grain threshing – millstone – we have the same in the village, and here the same.
> – And didn't you find spinning wheels?
> – Spinning wheels we found. But we have the same as here. But here there were more foot-operated, by feet, and such hand-operated spinning wheels. But we have hand spinning wheels most of all there, at our place. *Karelians, they have usually foot operated, there are many... Karelians have, so, Finns and Karelians.* But we that live farther from Karelians – beyond Onega, well, beyond Svir – we had hand-operated most of all (PF 6, 2002, Lahdenpohja, f. 1924, Leningrad region).

The comparison of "Finnish" things with "their own" appears as the most frequent rhetorical mode in the migrants' stories. And, although the peasants had arrived from different regions, thus consequently they refer to different past realities, the confrontation "theirs – ours" remains common for local tradition. An appeal to an experience that has a clear locality can be easily changed with reference to any "other" experience:

> Well, it just ... that church was like a shed. They not ... they seem no to do in such a way. And Swedes made[3]. Here at the hill there is made a church. Is it a church really? Like a shed. A church is *usually* with dome. And with such ... you know, everywhere – by TV ... and you go to see, so know, that a church, it is like a church. And here the Swedes made. It is just like a shed! Inside it is fine. Well. But generally. And Finn had the same. I haven't seen that Finn would have a church with a dome. So... (PF 13, 2002, Lahdenpohja, f. 1926, Vologda region).

In her argumentation the informant appeals not to her own past experience but rather to a general, common knowledge. But the comparison, as an instrument of description remains.

One of particular feature of such rhetorical constructions is the constant usage of terms like "at our place" and "our". But in most cases these terms do not express a contemporary locality and social status but those of the informant's birthplace and childhood:

> How they didn't differ? At our place, *where I lived at motherland*, there were loghouses. Or at Medvezhegorsk there were brick (PF 4, 2002, Lahdenpohja, f. 1919, Vologda region).

In the fore quoted interviews, the term "our" connects the informant with a certain community which existed in the Past in a particular territory. N. Lovell has pointed to similar instances in the Introduction to the volume *Locality and Belonging*: "Locality and belonging may be moulded and defined as much by actual territorial emplacement as by memoirs of belonging to particular landscapes whose physical reality is enacted only through acts of collective remembering" (Lovell 1998: 1). Our case is similar. But I would argue that the past locality of an informant is not realized by stories, rather it is constructed by them. Let us observe these situations in more detail.

Implicit forms of recollections

By "implicit forms of recollections" I mean those instances when the informant does not describe premigrational life but implies it by his/her words. As implicit forms of recollection I include various group indications, traced to the name of a place or places abandoned by migrants; for example terms like "our", which is connected to a past locality of a person. Here are some examples:

> There were such kolkhozes[4]. So, at environs. For example *at our place* there was kolkhoz Kirova. "Ninth of December" – *ours* were as well, then. "Settler", then, and others, others. They are all ours... I mean that we had a large kolkhoz, and small arose around (PF 14, 2002, Lahdenpohja, m. 1923, Vologda region).

Whilst talking about kolkhozy that appeared around Lahdenpohja, this informant uses the word "our", meaning natives of the Vologda region, where he himself arrived from. We will now see the reaction of an informant, who is also from Vologda, to the widespread exo-term *vologodskiie*:

> Devil knows it! Well. They said: "Ouch, *Vologodskiie*!" And what *Vologodskiie*? *We were Cherepane*. Then I don't know for fighters there were. Vologda, you know, is large too! We were precisely from Leningrad region, Cherepovetsk district. And then, I don't know why, it was renamed to Vologda region, Cherepovetsk district. We are *Cherepane* (PF 13, 2002, Lahdenpohja, f. 1926, Vologda region).

The woman knows that she is usually referred to as "Vologda", but she prefers a narrower identity – "Cherepane", i.e. natives of the Cherepovetsk district. Names such as *Chuvashi, Belorussians, Karelians, Kostromskiie, Yaroslavskiie* and *Vologodskiie*, both as others- and self- identification terms, are very widespread in this community.

These names reflect the locality of the main migration streams to Karelia. According to the decree of the Emigrant Department of the Council of Ministers, in the 1940s and the 1950s a multitude of settlers from the Belorussian and Ukrainian Soviet republics and Mordvinian, Tatarian and Chuvash autonomous republics, some regions of North-West Russia and Central Russia were recruited or forcibly moved to the recently formed Karelian-Finnish SSR (Stepakov & Balashov 2001: 33, 65). A lot of peasants from the Vologda region were moved to Karelia after the construction of the Rybinsk reservoir, as their villages were flooded.

It was common practice to form a new kolkhoz consisting predominantly of migrants from the same region. Several kolkhozes were completely removed to Karelia with their names and social structure intact. Thus, during the 1940s and the 1950s several local communities appeared in this territory. Through the interaction of migrants among "their" communities and with the members of "others" they constructed their local identity, or more precisely their identities.

Past locality

The stream way of dwelling allowed one to identify migrants according to their membership of the initial, departure region: *Vologodskiie* people (those who came from the Vologda region), *Yaroslavskiie* people (who came from the Yaroslavl region), Belorussians (those who came from Belorussia) and so on. The differences between migrants were constructed in conformity with such divisions. Specific speech manners, dress styles and ways of behaviour were usually described as markers of distinctions between settlers from different regions.

– Did you always know that a person was from Vologda?
– Well, we arrived, it was Vologda here most of all. From Vologda there were people.
– And was it possible to distinguish them anyhow? When you saw them in the street, for example?
– Yes, all were equal, but their speech ... they speak at Vologda in such a way... A lot from Yaroslavl, for example, spoke in such a manner. Then, from Kalinin region (our mamma was from Kalinin), they also have something special. But Vologda, especially it, they spoke usually with 'o', mostly with 'o'. And our Yaroslavl mostly with 'a', turned out with 'a'. And they with 'o'[5] <...> – in such a manner everything was. It was so interesting, you know. I see, Vologda began to speak again (PF 11, 2003, Kurkijoki, f. 1939, Yaroslavl region).

> Well, how… First of all it was striking the clothing of Chuvash. They wore skirts with gathers-gathers-gathers, like Gypsies. Exactly like Gypsies. And Russians didn't have such things. We had different skirts, beads or something like. And they had another. Then Belorussians, they didn't. Belorussians dress like Russians, and Ukrainians in this manner (PF 5, 2002, Lahdenpohja, f. 1924, Leningrad region).

A set of features inscribed to a particular group was stable among different interviews, hence they were obviously many times discussed by the migrants. The divisions of the migrants into specific past locality communities was shaped by group indicators and by ascribed differences between them. The very indicative fact is a correlation between external and self-identifications. The above characteristics of "Vologodskiie", given by a migrant not from Vologda region repeats almost word for word the testimonial made by "Vologodskiie" themselves:

> – They didn't tease you for your language?
> – Well, seventeenth republic.
> – They said?
> – No, we ourselves. Where are you from? From seventeenth republic[6].
> – And why, did your speech differ?
> – We spoke mostly with 'o'. Later me myself … I was little when I was taken, but communicated still among Vologodskiie, then. Well, later I tried to correct at school and at technical school (PF 13, 2003, Lahdenpohja, f. 1933, Vologda region).

We might ask if, indeed, migrants, from different regions, actually had all these features. But this question does not seem crucial. If there were no such things they would undoubtedly be constructed. The essential issue is connected to the possibility of these identity terms functioning among peasants before resettlement. It is obvious that people knew the local terms derived from the name of the region before removal. And it is not difficult to imagine a situation where a person would be called Belorussian, Vologodskiie etc. But it seems improbable for people living during a long period of time in the same territory to operate with such terms in everyday communication. Past placedness of migrants might become known to neighbours through official announcements, it appeared as a basis for further construction of history and distinguishing features.

But relative past placedness was not only used as an instrument for new social reality articulation. It also influenced the way the 'past' was constructed. Such a mode of identification provided people with a sense of their "homeland", it supported a connectedness with their birthplace. Peasants who used to apply past locality terms often recall their *rodina*[7]:

> And then, they brought us back to *rodina* … there, to the city Cherepovetsk. So. *We are Cherepane ourselves*. We were brought there, to Cherepovetsk (PF 10, 2002, Lahdenpohja, f. 1927, Vologda region).

> When the war began, we went here, back, *to ours, to our region*. Until the villages were flooded. *Our village* was flooded <…>. I wish I went

> there to live now. If I were 30 I would go there <...>. I live here since 1945, but I am still longing *to rodina* (PF 11, 2002, Kurkijoki, m. 1925, Vologda region).

> – At your place, where you have lived beforehand, there was no well at every court?
> – At *rodina*? But there was a lake at our place, we took water from the lake. Two held with yoke, and in winter – in sledge. Eleven months it is winter, and the rest it is summer. But now it is conversely. You see what a heat is (PF 5, 2002, Lahdenpohja, f. 1919, Vologda region).

A lot of peasants wish to visit their homeland, some of them desire to return there. But what is curious it is the fact that the application of term 'rodina' to the place of birth usually appears side by side with its usage in reference to Karelia (see the paper of O. Filicheva in this volume). Self-identification based upon past locality co-exists with self-inclusion into a broader community of present Russian settlers in Karelia.

Present locality

During the interviews, our interlocutors sometimes refused to describe or even acknowledge the distinctions between migrants from different regions. Though the informant uses the terms of local identity he/she insists on the lack of any differences between their bearers. Here is one example:

> – Belorussians, did they distinguish Vologda people?
> – No, nor Karelians. There were a lot of Karelians here. Neither Karelian, nor Belorussian, nor Tatar – nobody we distinguished (PF 14, 2003, Lahdenpohja, f. 1930, Minsk region).

One of local inhabitants told us that both *Vologodskiie*, and *Kostromskiie* lived and different people came here. But then after we had asked her if it was possible to distinguish between them, she said: "How could we find out? If you work at the factory or something like, so you'll know. But how to recognize?" A few minutes later she finally added: "So *it is heard*, of course. Both Tatar and Chuvash – whoever is here". (PF 4, 2002, Lahdenpohja.)

An unwillingness to discuss the distinctions of migrants may be explained by a concern of the informant that he/she might be considered malevolent towards some of their neighbours. Any hint of former conflicts between settlers that an informant catches in the researcher's question causes his/her immediate reaction:

> – And Chuvash, for example, what language did they speak?
> – Among themselves they spoke Chuvash language, but with us they had a talk in Russian. Not perfectly correct, but ...
> – *Weren't they teased for this?*
> – What, why would we tease. On the contrary, we lived all right altogether. What for to tease them. *As we'll be teased as they will be* (PF 13, 2003, Lahdenpohja, f. 1933, Vologda region).

The final argument expresses something like a private convention between migrants: "in spite of the fact we differ we are the same as they". The sign of "resettlement to Lahdenpohja" becomes the sole but sufficient marker for the local migrant community. Its main characteristic is performed as a perfectly harmonious interaction that is always described in terms of mutual tolerance: "All were friendly, somehow, altogether. For example the milkmaids were both Chuvash and Tatar. But how friendly all of us were. Didn't regard somehow as that one was Tatar or whoever." (PF 12, 2003, Kurkijoki.)

Past and present local identities have equal value for the majority of peasants who moved to Karelia within a large migration stream. Membership to a past local group is usually performed in private conversation when the interlocutor does not feel any threat of being suspected for being disloyal to migrants. When the interview seems to be more official he/she stresses his/her present local identity.

We can find rather different representations in stories of lone migrants who arrived in Karelia either after a long period of evacuation, or on account of being assigned from a former job or because they were assigned at the institute. Such individuals, as a rule, came to Karelia without relatives or friends, got fixed up in a veneer factory or administrative establishment and remained in the same city.

Recollections of lone migrants

These individuals used to stress in their stories how they belong to the urban milieu and their own desires to live and work in the city. When we discovered that our interlocutor was born in the Vologda region we asked her a traditional question about which kolkhoz she came from. The woman was surprised and immediately said to us that she has never worked in a kolkhoz:

> No, I haven't ever lived in kolkhoz. The husband was railwayman, he graduated from railway institute in Leningrad. And I myself learned to be a tractor operator. Firstly worked as day nursery manageress, well, *had no desire to live in village*. Then worked as tax agent, there were individual farmers in the kolkhozes of the region. And then with komsomol assignment I learned for tractor operator for 8 months in Leningrad region, in Pestovo, from timber industry. But it didn't happen to work. I married, had a practice in Ladva <…> I wanted to the city (PF 4, 2002, Lahdenpohja, f. 1919, Vologda region).

The lone migrants generalize the life in villages at kolkhozes with the term "there", and "here" means "in the city". It is Lahdenpohja that has significance for them as their locality:

> Well, probably, somewhere there, there in villages, may be at khutors. They might be afraid [of Finns]. (PF 4, 2002, Lahdenpohja, f. 1925, Vologda region.)

Although past locality still retains its value for most of the peasants, it is not significant for city-dwellers. In the interview quoted below, the woman agreed with the fact that her countrymen live near to her rather she told about them of her own will:

> – Don't you remember which places did the large groups of people came here from?
> – *No, there were no such.*
> – But they say there were a lot of vologodskikh here?
> – Well, *Vologodskiie*. There was a kind of flood or something like, people were coming also from Volo … there were a lot of Vologda people, *they are my countrymen*. I myself am from Vologda. So they came. There were relatives or what. So they came here, of course. There are, there are, there are a lot of *Vologodskiie* here (ibid.).

It is obvious that the present locality has higher status for our informant than the past one. She prefers to talk about her life in Lahdenpohja, not about her birthplace or the life before the migration. When answering the first question about the place of departure to Karelia, our interlocutor told us about her previous job location, in contrast to other migrants who always mentioned their place of birth: "I came here from … I worked in Karelia … with assignment from Prionezhskii district. In 1951 I was moved here through Karelian Council of Ministers" (Ibid.).

The recollections of "peasants" always perform a sense of place or locality. The past in the testimonies of "lone migrants" chiefly express a sense of movement. For most of them Lahdenpohja became their first experience of settlement, it appeared as the end of a long road from one place to another. The past is represented in terms of movement in their stories, and life in Lahdenpohja is the only subject for description as a static state. I will cite an extract from an interview with a woman who left her home in the Vologda region when she was a child. Escaping from the war, her father and she found themselves in Karelia, and finally in Lahdenpohja:

> – I was born in Vologda, but all my life I live in Karelia. <…>
> – And what was the village there?
> – The village Timokhino. But all the time I live in Karelia.
> – What age were you when you left it?
> – Well. We left it… <…>, I was 6. We lived in the village Kovda. But probably now **there is no such a village**, I think. But our father had been working in forest<…> Foreman. And he was brought there to work. To Kovda. In Kovda, then, there were only three houses. **There were neither roads, nor anything. There was nothing, absolutely nothing there was**. Only the timber that was felled. They felled the timber, took out. *There was a river. The river was passing through. And we fished salmon and lancet fish in that river. Just with hands! You see. How much fish there was. Because there were no people. And the water was clear still, because the wood hadn't been felled yet.* <…> It is already Karelia. Well. And we, so, lived right there. Then, so … what year … then he was moved to the station Ambarnyi, Loukhskii region. This is Karelia as well. But already … <…> The station Loukhi there is also. And we, so, there,

at that Loukhskii region … my father worked in forest again. But **there everything has also broken down now, sure. And at that time there was nothing either. There was nothing**. Worked. They stored the timber up, then sew the boards. Well. And we had lived there till what year… We had lived there … till … in 1937 they took our uncle there. <…>. And with ends. So what. <…> So, and we had lived there. Then we … till what year we had lived… I went to school there. We had lived there till 1939. In 1939 the father was at Finnish [war]. Well. Returned from there. Then. And we moved to Chupa <…> The station Chupa. Of Loukhskii district as well. So then. But closer to here, to the South. Loukhi were to the North. Well, there we have, so, there me… <…> Here we came… in 1940 we came here. <u>Oh, girls, how it was beautiful here! It was a paradise. Oh! What a beauty there was. There was a lilac all around</u>. And we in 1940 – I had elder sisters, they were adults already – and we went to Valaam. <u>It was something! It was</u> … even, I am not able even to say. I am not able even to … if there was any misfortune, I would cry, would be able say. But such a pleasure, such a beauty. I am not able to describe, so can't. So you see, <u>it was made in such a manner!</u> (PF 7, 2002, Lahdenpohja, f. 1927, Vologda region).

This informant is very talkative. She likes to speak and any question of the interviewer led her to perform a detailed story. During our conversations that lasted a few hours, the woman repeatedly recalled her past, which is associated, for her, with escape from the war and numerous removals. But, as with previous lone persons, she emphasizes her present locality: "But all my life I live in Karelia" – she insists. The parts of the text that are printed in bold type present the testimonials of places where she lived before Lahdenpohja. Those places that are empty and that do not exist according to her words. We see a long chain of names, associated with relative dates. I underlined the fragments where our informant describes her first impressions of Lahdenpohja. Here is the only space for the verb "was". In this description, she uses traditional expressions for this community: "beauty and lilac" (see the article of Marina Hakkarainen in this book). But these recollections are not particularly associated with Lahdenpohja for her, but with Karelia in general. Valaam, Salmi, Lahdenpohja – all these places provide her with a new locality and new status.

One fragment of the story I highlighted with Italics. Here arises an idyllic picture of a native village. The model of description that she used is widespread among "indigenous" peasants. Usually only time is marked in such narratives: "it was well before, it is bad now". Such narratives allow peasants to adapt changes in outward things. The specific feature of the previous testimony is the clear locality of a "golden era": "it was the village Kovda of Kaduiskii district of Vologda region where it was well".

This informant, like other "lone migrants", never mentioned a desire to visit 'rodina'. Probably because such a category is not relevant to her experience. Nobody applies the term of "past locality" to such migrants, though many of them arrived from the same regions as the peasants who lived in kolkhozes.

Such diversity in the ways of identification among peasants and city dwellers might be quite clear before the 1990s. We could suppose that within the migrant society of Lahdenpohja and its suburbs there particular communities were distinguished: those of peasants defined by their past locality and then city dwellers. But the situation must have changed after the collapse of the USSR and the abolishment of kolkhozes. Social links in the communities of migrants who associated themselves with the past local group weakened. Some of such communities disappeared since the majority of the inhabitants moved to the town. If before the 1990s past local identities had the instrumental value of being the device of group communication, nowadays there are no local groups that would be identified in such a manner. Nonetheless, past local identity still remains for former migrants. For now representations of past locality in the stories of our informants imply not only a collective sense of "premigrational" place but also their individual sense of belonging to the present local group. When they say "Vologodskiie" or "Belorussians" people identify each other according to their present local identity rather than to their departure area:

– And where did you come from?
– Vologda [laughs]. The very foreign…
– What does it mean, the very?
– Foreign, of course. Vologodskiie, they are interesting [laughs].
– And why are they interesting?
– Then everyone says … the way they call Vologodskiie – the seventeenth republic (PF 12, 2003, Kurkijoki, f. 1922, Vologda region).

This dialogue begins with the researcher's question about the woman's place of departure. In answering, she articulates a group nomination "Vologodskiie". But in this context the term refers not to the people who many years ago lived at her motherland but to those who surrounded her in Kurkijoki kolkhoz. Despite the fact that this kolkhoz no longer exists such a nomination is still significant for her.

The process of constructing social reality is on-going and changes with respect to the new experiences of migrants. Past placed-ness of settlers served for their adapting in Karelia promoting the ways for self- and others-identification. But probably soon it will lose its value and we'll see people who have never been in Vologda region but who would call themselves as "vologodskiie" and would be described by others as such.

NOTES

1. P. Polyan has defined this form of migration as "compensating" one that was aimed to fill the territorial gaps that arose through state politics. As he writes, the main instruments for its realisation were usually "planned resettlement", "evacuation" and "intraregional removal" (Polyan 2001). All these forms were used in migration process to Karelia.
2. I enclose in brackets the following information: year of interview, no. of record (all the records are kept at University of Joensuu (Finland)), place of interview, informants sex (f. – female, m. – male), informants year of birth and birthplace.
3. She means the Pentecostal church that was recently built in Lahdenpohja.

4. 'Collective farm'
5. This reflects the pronunciation difference between Northern and Southern dialect groups of the Russian language. One of the characteristics of Northern dialects is the so-called 'okanie', which means the distinguishing of vowels 'o' and 'a' in the first unaccented syllable after a hard consonant (e.g.: Southern dialects: *karóva*, Northern dialects: *koróva*).
6. Till 1956 the USSR included 16 republics (in 1956 Karelian-Finnish SSR was transformed into the Karelian autonomous SSR within RSFSR).
7. This term has broad semantic meaning and corresponds not only to the birthplace of the informant but rather to that region that is considered by him/her as native. It can be applied both to a very small territory (particular village) and to very wide one (the state).

REFERENCES

Basso, Keith H. 1996: Wisdom Sits in Places: Notes on a Western Apache Landscape. In: Steven Feld & Keith H. Basso (eds.): *Senses of Place*. Santa Fe: School of American Press.

Lévy, Zumwalt R. & Lévy I. J. 2002: Making Atlanta Home: Recollection of Place through Narrative. In: *Folklore Forum*. Vol.33. N.1/2.

Lovell, N. 1998: Introduction. In: N. Lovell (ed.) *Locality and Belonging*. European Association of Social Anthropologists. London: Routledge.

Poljan, P. 2001: *Ne po svoyei vole ... Istoriia i geografiia prinuditelnykh migratsii v SSSR*. Moskva.

Senses of Place. Ed. By Steven Feld & Keith H. Basso. Santa Fe: School of American Research Press 1996.

Stepakov, V. & Balashov, E. 2001: *V "Novykh raionakh". Iz istorii osvoyeniia Karelskogo peresheika. 1940–1941, 1944–1950 gg*. Sankt-Petersburg: "Nordmedizdat".

Tonkin, E. 1992: *Narrating our pasts: the social construction of oral history*. Cambridge studies in oral and literate culture 22. Cambridge: Cambridge University Press.

Fieldwork materials (PF and MD) from Melnikovo, Karelian isthmus, Leningrad region, in 2001, from Lahdenpohja and Kurkijoki, Republic of Karelia, in 2002 and 2003

OKSANA FILICHEVA

"One is drawn to one's birthplace" or "the place where one feels at home is one's motherland"

Concepts of homeland by migrants from Ladoga Karelia

> Homeland – a native land;
> one's birthplace;
> a land, a country, a city, a village,
> where one was born.
>
> (Dal', 1996, p. 11)

The phrase in the title – "One is drawn to one's birthplace" – was used by one of the informants to explain why she had returned to Karelia after having been evacuated during World War Two (PF 4, 2002, Lahdenpohja). After numerous dislocations throughout the war, she had decided to return to her birthplace, Karelia. She even refused to move in with her daughter, who lived in the Ukraine.

However, although there is a 'traditional' understanding of one's native land as being a place where one was born to which one should be naturally drawn, existing material gathered during expeditions to the Lahdenpohja region (2002–2003) compels us to doubt this assertion. When Russian migrants are questioned by researchers about their places of birth and whether they would like to return there, they usually reply in the following manner:

> – Wouldn't you like to go back there [to your birthplace]?
> – Well… [no].
> – Why not?
> – I'm not drawn to the Vologodskaya area, I've got used to this place, I've been living here since 1948. It feels like my homeland here, I have become accustomed to this place… I want to…I stay two-three days somewhere and then I want to come back here. (PF 12, 2003, Kurkijoki.)

In the mid-twentieth century, the Soviet Union had twice occupied a part of Karelia that belonged to Finland. Each time the occupation was accompanied by the arrival and settlement of a Russian-speaking population. The first occupation took place in 1940, after the so-called White-Finnish war[1], and the second in 1944, both during World War Two. In 1942, after the retreat of the Soviet troops, the native Finns were able to return to their homes. In

1944, they were to leave their property one more time after the war between the Soviet Union and Finland finished on 19 September of the same year. Once again, the Karelian Isthmus and Ladoga Karelia had become part of the USSR[2].

It is well known that during the Soviet period the government exercised an internal migration policy. One of the results of this policy was the transportation of several kolkhozes from the Vologodskaya area and Chuvashskaya SSR, in the 1940s, to the newly-acquired Karelian territory. This transportation was a consequence of the construction of the Rybinsk reservoir and the subsequent flooding of nearby villages. In addition to this, the government also carried out a 'recruitment' programme, which included people from the regions destroyed during World War Two, such as Belorussia and Central Russia.

During the first phase of migration (1940–1941), the number of volunteers amongst peasants to move to the 'new area' was low, so the government issued orders which forced people to move. It should be noted that the government had devised a whole range of privileges that the newcomers could enjoy at their new place of settlement (Stepakov and Balashov 2001: 36).

The amount of people who wanted to move to Karelia during the course of the second phase of migration (1945–1953) was abundant. Consequently, this second re-settlement did not require the strict government measures used during the first phase. In post-war times, the Ukrainian and Belorussian population was in desperate need of accommodation, thus people willingly left their ravaged land for the riches of Karelia, as advertised by the recruitment officials.

People were recruited on both individual and family principles. Some would migrate at a later stage, following their relatives in the hope of better living conditions and a job. This situation differed from the main waves of migration of the 1940s, when people were transported to the new territory on a kolkhoz principle (i.e. everybody who lived and worked in a particular kolkhoz would be re-settled).

Many Russian migrants, who first came to the former Finnish territory in 1940, returned to Karelia after evacuation during World War Two. It was common for them to move back into the houses they had occupied before the war on the basis of their main document, a migration card:

> – You were the first to come here in 1940? So there was nobody here ... in Lasanen before you?
> – No, no [there wasn't]. We got here first.
> – So when you returned here in 1945, you were already familiar with this area?
> Informant: Of course, of course. Not only did we have to return, but we wanted to return here. We liked this area very much... Because the territory was ... it was passed into the Soviet hands again, it changed hands. So we were transported here once more in those wagons, in goods trucks...
> – Did you have any documents showing that you were from this... [area]?
> – A migration card. Yes, the migration... It was our document, the migration card...

– Can you recall how many families came here then?
– Oh … the whole kolkhoz it was. (MD 10, 2003, Kurkijoki.)

Therefore, a community was created in the former Finnish Karelia which had no common past, history or traditions. These people were not only challenged to master an alien landscape, but also to adapt to a new social and cultural environment.

This work is based on the materials collected during ethnological expeditions into the former Finnish Karelia during the period 2001–2003. The main aim of this field research was to determine how the settlers accustomed themselves to the new territories. In accordance with the aim of this research, the chosen informants were people over the age of fifty, who were brought to Karelia by their parents or who moved there independently at an age when one is capable of working. The majority of them were of peasant origin, although there were some workers and civil servants, who came to Karelia in search of a job or by assignment from their previous working places. The experiences of these people of life before migration, as well as their motivations and the history of their re-settlement, differ. Once they had arrived at Karelia, they found themselves in differing circumstances. Therefore, the migrants also had a differentiated experience whilst familiarising themselves with the new territory. A unifying factor for this group of migrants is the actual that they moved to Karelia as their permanent residential area; i.e. their present place of residence is the main characteristic which unites them into a distinguishable group.

In the present collection, Ekaterina Melnikova, in her article "Recollections of 'native land' in oral testimonies of Russian settlers of Karelia", studies descriptions of *rodina* ('native land') in order to establish their role and functions in the folklore of the local population (Melnikova, forthcoming). Using similar material, I pursue different ends. Firstly, I want to discover which places the migrants are inclined to call their *rodina*, homeland – Karelia, where they have been living for most of their lives, or the place where they were born? And secondly, I am interested in the categories used by the informants when talking about Karelia as their 'homeland'. How do they justify their sense of belonging and their claim to the right to be in this territory? In other words, which criteria matter most for the migrants when they construct a concept of a homeland and try to explain their affiliation to this land?

Within the framework of these specific aims, I intend to find answers to the following questions:

- what are the conditions which govern the informants' 'choices of homeland'? Are these choices connected with life experiences/biographies?
- is there a connection between biographical facts (the places where people originally come from and the period of migration, etc.) and the way in which informants talk about Karelia, and whether or not it has become their 'home'? If there is such a connection, how does it manifest itself?

By focussing on an individual experience of an ordinary person it allows us to go beyond the factual description of the history of the colonisation of the former Finnish Karelia that is based on statistical and documentary data. One of the most important characteristics of oral sources is, according to A. Portelli, 'the subjectivity of the narrator' (Portelli 2003: 40), which allows the researcher to not only learn about an event, but also about its meaning for the narrator. In our case, the event is a migration to a new territory and the meaning of it is the informant's attitude towards his/her present place of residence. If one conducts a complex investigation, writes Portelli, one would be able to 'construct a certain 'slice' of the subjective perception of a particular social group' (ibid.) and thus discover how the migrants evaluate their residence in the Karelian territory.

Simultaneously, a study of the migrants' individual experiences gives us an opportunity to establish the circumstances which have influenced the formation of attitudes towards their new place of settlement. P. Thompson, who researches the topic of 'family tradition' and the ways of transmitting information between generations, has pointed out the importance of studying individual cases. These allow us to determine the motives behind the process of social migration (Thompson 2003: 120).

A few words must be said about the methods employed for obtaining empirical data for this analysis. During the course of the interviews, some of the migrants would broach the topic of 'homeland' themselves, expressing their attitude towards Karelia, as well as their birthplaces, but this did not happen often. The questionnaire, which was devised for fieldwork in this territory, included questions, which would provoke the informants to express their attitude towards Karelia and to formulate their notion of a place they could call their 'homeland'. Some of the questions were:

- what were your first impressions of Karelia? Did you like it or not?
- have you visited your birthplace again and did you want to go back there? Why?
- which place could you call your homeland?

Significantly, in most of the cases, the question of whether or not the informants would like to go back to their birthplaces provoked extensive responses. Whilst answering this question, the informants would express their attitudes towards their new habitat, as well as their original birthplace, the migration process and, finally, they would talk about their understanding of a 'homeland', without any leading questions from the researcher.

The role of biography in the forming of an attitude towards a 'new homeland'

In the process of correlating the informants' biographical data with their expressed willingness/unwillingness to return to the places where they were born, certain biographical factors become more important than others in shaping settlers' attitudes towards Karelia. These factors are: **the period of**

migration, **the place of birth** and **the age of the migrant** at the time when he/she arrived at the Ladoga Karelia.

The migrants who came to Karelia had different settlement opportunities, depending on the time (before or after the war) they had arrived. Those who came to Karelia immediately after World War Two had access to a whole range of resources abandoned by the native Finnish population: good houses, furniture, crockery, food supplies, etc. Those migrants, who arrived at a later stage, had little choice in dwelling; as to furniture and other household items, according to the migrants themselves, 'they did not find anything'. Boris Tikka, in his *Memoirs about childhood in Koivisto*, writes that 'at first, all the inhabitants were actively utilising everything which was abandoned by Finns', but then, he notes, 'somehow imperceptibly and rather quickly things started to disappear or deteriorate' (In Stepakov and Balashov 2001: 86).

Even though, according to the accounts of many informants, their first impression of Karelia was negative because of the country's peculiar and unusual landscape, the experience of better living conditions than those of the regions they came from made their attitudes more positive. These informants do not want to go back to their birthplaces; they talk about themselves as being accustomed to Karelia; and consider this region as 'theirs'. At the same time, if the circumstances of the settlement were unfavourable, the informants emphasise memories of their pre-settlement past as an ideal time and place, a homeland, to which one wants to return.

I shall illustrate my point with the following example. Two informants, who live in the same village, an ex-regional centre of Kurkijoki, give different answers to the question of whether they would like to go back to the places where they were born[3]. Nevertheless, their first impressions of the new places were the same – negative. However, with time, the attitude of the second informant has changed, whereas the first informant has maintained her original attitude towards her new place of residence.

Informant 1:

– Did you want to go back?
– Informant: To Yaroslavl'? … I would like to have a look at it. Yes, girls, I would like to. I've said, 'Even on my death bed, I will go [to the place] where I was born'. I was born on the banks of the Volga, the Tutaievskii region, Volna village. Our house was on the Volga's bank and it had two storeys. It was so beautiful. (PF 11, 2003, Kurkijoki.)

Informant 2:

– Did you want to go back there [to your birthplace]?
– Well… [no].
– Why not?
– I'm not drawn to the Vologodskaya area, I've got used to this place, I've been living here since 1948. It feels like my homeland here, I got accustomed to this place… I want to…I stay two-three days somewhere and then I want to go back here. (PF 12, 2003, Kurkijoki.)

Informant 1 demonstrates that her first impression has not changed with time and she has not been able to adapt to her new place of residence. In her account of events, she has an image of an ideal past, when she was happier than in the new place. Although, as the interviewer managed to discover from further conversation with this informant, life in her place of birth was not as ideal as she initially tried to present it:

> – So, when you came over here and moved into a Finnish house, how was it different from your home in Yaroslavl'?
> – Oh, the house wasn't big at all – just a kitchen and a room – not much at all. But [in Yaroslavl'] we lived in a two-storey house. We definitely had a better building; back home, we had a similar lodging – a room and a kitchen, but the corridors were spacious... We were doing better there, the lodging was much better. As I said to my mother later, 'we shouldn't have come here' – I said – 'it would have been better for us there'. And my mother said, 'well' – she said – 'once we've come here, there is no point in going back'. (PF 11, 2003, Kurkijoki.)

This example convincingly demonstrates, that time and again, memory is not 'a passive storage house of facts, but is an active process of interpreting the world' (Portelli 2003: 44). The fact that the informant idealises her pre-migration to Karelia life, distorting real facts (something that became apparent after a number of leading questions), is of particular interest here. Her account reveals an effort made by the informant to 'interpret one's past, give one's life a certain shape and form' (Portelli 2003: 44). The need to distort the past in this way might be explained by the influence of various circumstances. In this particular case, a desire to compensate for failures in a new place seems to play a significant role.

The second informant was motivated towards adopting a positive attitude towards Karelia because her sister had come to the region during the first wave of migration and had been able to enjoy the advantages of her new place of residence. Moreover, being a close relative, the informant was given a certain share of household resources and the conditions of her settlement were favourable. As a result, she has changed her attitude towards Karelia:

> – You see, it was very good here, the earnings were very good. Yes. This was a Kurkijoki sovkhoz, a very rich one it was. For my work I was receiving labour days, each of them would get you 200 grams of bread. So we came here, started working, got an opportunity to buy clothes for ourselves, began to live a prosperous life. My two sisters lived here, too. One had come in 1945 and the other one – in 1947... Nothing could be grown in the garden back there, so we would only plant potatoes, cucumbers and cabbage. But here – look at the garden – so much greenery – splendid! And what soil it is here – it is so much better than the soil we had back home. I haven't manured the ground for three years now, and the potatoes are still growing – splendid! Very... (PF 12, 2003, Kurkijoki.)

Thus, time of arrival at the new territory was important when it came to the distribution of resources amongst the migrants. It is, therefore, one of the definitive factors which determines the attitudes of the inhabitants towards their places of residence.

Other factors which have influenced the shaping of attitudes towards new places of settlement were the places and circumstances the migrants left behind. A significant portion of informants was transported from the flooded part of the Vologodskaya area and the regions of Belorussia and Central Russia, which were devastated during World War Two. These informants might have wished to go back to their homeland, if they had not already been deprived of it.

> – Has anybody from this area gone back to Belorussia?
> – They have, they have. Some have gone back to Belorussia and those who had a home to return to would leave, too.
> – All the years that you've lived here – haven't you ever wanted to go back to Belorussia?
> – I don't know. I … we had lived here before the war, but once we came here, I… They had moved to another village, our farmstead had been ploughed up. There was nothing left, all the bunkers were destroyed, levelled to the ground…
> – If you had a place to return to, would you go back there?
> – Perhaps, we would have gone back straightaway, but we had nowhere to return to – we had nothing left – nobody had anything. (PF 8, 2003, Lahdenpohja.)

> – Wasn't your village in the Vologodskaya area flooded?
> – Yes, it was. Out of 150 houses there were only twenty or thirty left in the centre. Not completely, but the water was everywhere. You could only move around by boat and…
> – So when you came here – did you like this place?
> – I don't know whether we liked it or not. Naturally, we didn't want to move, my mother was brought out of the house half-conscious… We had just built a new house, too, it was nice and big. They said if we didn't leave, the village would be flooded anyway and there would be nowhere to live…
> – And later on, when you were living here, didn't you want to go back?
> – There was no point – there was nothing left there at all – everything was flooded, there was nothing there – not even the village. Some people wanted to go back – but what's the point? (Pf 13, 2003, Lahdenpohja.)

As one can see, some of the informants have lost all ties with the places where they were born. If asked whether they would like to go back, these informants quite often say that they would have liked to, if they had had a place or relatives to return to. It appears that, in reality, this group has no place which they would have considered their homeland. Meanwhile, their opinions about Karelia do not have any negative content, their attitude towards it is neutral. It could be suggested that the new territory had become a 'forced homeland' for them.

On the basis of the collected material it seems viable to suggest that for those migrants who were brought to the former Finnish territory in their childhood a juxtaposition or comparison between their birthplace and the place they moved to is not a topical issue. Unlike other informants, this group is not ready to formulate an attitude towards Karelia without being directly questioned on the matter. For these people, living in the region comes as something entirely natural:

> – The first time I ... well, my parents brought me here, was in 1940. I was three years old. When the war began, I was four. Then during the war we were transported back to where we had come from. I remember, in scraps, how we were bombed and had to hide in the forest. And then... After the war, in 1946, my parents enlisted themselves to come back here again, as part of the recruitment programme. We were living on a farmstead here...
> – Could you tell me whether you have ever – all the time that you've lived here – ever wanted to go back to Chuvashia?
> – Not really, I've been living here since I can remember. (PF 7, 2003, Lahdenpohja.)

If this group of migrants were directly asked what place they consider as their homeland, it is highly probable that they would give a laconic answer that their homeland 'is here'. Meanwhile, this kind of question confuses people. It prompts them to think that if such a question is asked, then somebody has doubts about their rights to this territory. In order to prove their indubitable rights to the land, the migrants talk about the length of time that they have spent in the area. Thus, Karelia is their homeland because it is the place where they have lived all their lives:

> – Could you please tell me how you understand the word 'homeland'? Where is your homeland now, do you think?
> – (Informant 1) Oh...
> – (Informant 2) It's here. We grew up here. From a tender age. And a homeland is where you've lived for most of your life.
> – (Informant 1) Since we've lived here all our lives, then...
> – (Informant 2) How can you call that place in Russia a home, or this place, a former Finnish territory? A person is ... usually home is where one can be said to have lived the whole of one's life. Isn't it?
> – (Informant 1) We've lived here all our lives, so that means that it's our homeland here.
> – (Informant 2) So now this is it ... it's ours, it can be called our homeland. (MD 4, 2002, Lahdenpohja.)

It is possible to suggest, that this group of migrants has fully adapted to its new social and cultural environment. One of the pieces of evidence for this statement would be the migrants' attitude towards their 'mother tongue', which they do not try to preserve or pass on to the succeeding generations:

> – Do you remember the Chuvash language, your native tongue?
> – Yes, I remember it. I understand everything, but ... but I speak it so poorly, but once somebody is talking to me, my tongue loosens...
> – What language do you speak to your kids?
> – We speak Russian.
> – Russian. But do they know Chuvash?

> – No, they don't. Well, the eldest can perhaps understand it, but these ones don't understand a thing.
> – Would you like them to know the language?
> – Well, it just turned out this way – all of them, everybody here speaks … they go to school with Russian kids, so…
> – Didn't you speak Chuvash at home?
> – No. (PF 7, 2003, Lahdenpohja.)

Construction of the concept of 'homeland'

Amongst the inhabitants interviewed, quite a large group call Karelia their 'homeland'. When these people try to explain why their present and permanent place of residence can be called their homeland, and not the place where they were born, they adduce arguments, which, in their mind, prove their right to this land. I would like to focus on some of these arguments, which give the researcher an idea about what constitutes the concept of homeland and its attributes from the migrants' point of view.

The region studied by us does not have an old generation of natives born in this area. Nevertheless, the informants refer to this notion, as it seems important for them. They speak of a certain group of people (which usually includes themselves) as the 'old, native residents'. It seems that this notion gives them yet another opportunity to confirm their right, as 'old residents', to Karelian land, and points towards their aspiration to have a collective past, a history. The duration of residence is a defining factor for classifying a person as an 'old resident' of this region:

> – Yes… Could you tell me... who are the native people and how would you distinguish … between the native and non-native people who live here?
> – Er … how would I put it… I can't tell you. Er … when we go out, go into town and meet other people, we go – 'Oh, hello!' – 'Hello!' So we know, we already know, that we are here … well, that we've been living here for a long time. And if… Yes, sure… I'm telling you – I can't think of anything appropriate at the moment. There are a lot of people like that here. Many of them. They've been living here for a long time. Since 1945, and … not so many since 1945, but there are a lot of people who came in 1946 and in 1947, yes. We've been here … so many years that … somehow we all know each other by now. Whenever we meet – we already know that … we can consider ourselves native to here. (MD 2, 2002, Lahdenpohja.)

In the 1990s, 'new' migrants arrived at Ladoga Karelia. This allowed the 'old, native residents' to confirm and secure their indigenous status within the area. Whereas the difference between the first waves of migration and the succeeding ones was not particularly significant, the latest waves have given an opportunity to the originally disjointed society to unite itself under the category of 'we', the natives, against 'them', the newcomers. This unification gives 'the natives' yet another incentive for considering themselves as people who have the most rights to this territory:

> – Who do you think are the native people here?
> – Native... Well, we've been... We call those people native who came here during the first years [of migration] – they could be called native. And some people have just come here recently. They've been living here only for a year or two. So they are... But we consider ourselves native. We've already... warmed this land up. (MD 5, 2002, Lahdenpohja.)

It should be noted that kinship ties formed in a new territory help migrants in the process of defining themselves as native residents – people who belong to this land and can consider it their own. One of the manifestations of kinship ties is children, who were born in the region and live here:

> – I have another question – you've been living here for a long, long time. What do you think is your native land? Where is your home?
> – (laughing): My homeland is more [or less] here now. At home, I haven't lived long. I've spent most of my life in Karelia. My kids have grown up here...
> – Did you go to the Vologodskaya area?
> – No, I never did.
> – After you had moved here?
> – No. After we'd moved here, I never went back there. I never did. (MD 9, 2003, Lumivaara.)

The establishment of kinship ties is also important to those migrants for whom Karelia has become a 'forced homeland'. Family relations help these people to accept their situation and the place in which they live. For example, this informant would have liked to have returned to the Ukraine, where she was born, if she had had any relatives there:

> – Haven't you ever wanted to go back there? To the Kievskaya area?
> Informant: Me? Yes, I have. But then I got married, had kids, the family, so ... how would I be able to go? (MD 6, 2003.)

Another factor, which occurred in all the interviews and which seemed to be almost the main attribute of 'nativeness' and Karelia as a 'homeland' was the graves of the relatives who passed away and were buried in this land:

> Researcher: Would you like to go back there, to Belorussia, nowadays?
> Informant: No, not now... How can I go back now? All my life has been spent here. I came here when I was eighteen and where would I go now? My home is here. My children live here, so do my grandchildren. My husband is buried here, my son is buried here, too: my roots are now in this land. What's the use of going there – I've got nobody left. My homeland is here now. (PF 14, 2003, Lahdenpohja.)

The graves of one's relatives are undoubtedly an important component of the traditional understanding of a motherland. Thus, it is only natural that this component is used by the migrants in the construction of the concept of a homeland at their new place of residence. At the same time, a graveyard is one of the 'landmarks, which may have features of high visibility and public significance, such as monuments, shrines, a hallowed battlefield or a cemetery' (Tuan 2001: 159). It can also 'serve to enhance people's sense of identity, encourage awareness of loyalty to place' (Ibid.). The acquisition of such symbols seems to give people a right for the symbolic acquisition of the territory, which was written about by Zh. Kormina in her study of the functions of sacred places in the countryside (Kormina, forthcoming). This seems to be of a particular relevance for migrants. The possession of the graves makes it possible for people to relate to a cemetery as one of the symbols of one`s homeland. Through this symbol, people can represent their local identity or, as it happens in our case, construct it.

*   *   *

The present inhabitants of the former Finnish Karelia have differing attitudes towards their place of residence. Some of them adhere to the traditional concept of homeland (as a place where one was born), so for them Karelia has failed to become a 'home'. Other migrants do not even entertain the thought of their home being any other place than Karelia. It seems to me that the explanations for such dissimilar attitudes can be found in the biographical circumstances of each informant. I very much hope that this brief comparison of the informants' opinions has helped to reveal certain common threads in the formation of the notion of a 'native land'. Thus, in this present work I have attempted to: a) discover which biographical facts had the most influence on this formation, and b) to reveal certain attributes of a homeland which are topically important for immigrants.

NOTES

1. On the 31 March, 1940, the Soviet government had issued a bill on the 'Transformation of the Karelian Autonomous Soviet Socialist Republic into a United Karelo-Finnish Soviet Socialist Republic'. On the basis of this bill, a considerable part of the Finnish territory, which was annexed by the USSR according to the peace treaty of 12 March, 1940, was to become part of KASSR.
2. For a detailed account of the colonisation of this region by Russian settlers, please see the article by Antti Laine, "Modernisation in the 1940s and 1950s in the part of Karelia that was annexed from Finland on 13 March, 1940".
3. I've chosen this pair of informants as an example despite the fact that the informant, who considers Karelia to be her homeland and does not want to return to her birthplace, arrived at the region later than the other informant. This circumstance does not change the crux of the matter, as the informant came to Karelia to join her sister, who had arrived there earlier, during the first wave of migration. Thus, the informant is familiar with the body of texts which describe the realities of that time (good housing, wealth of the farmsteads, abandoned Finnish property). Moreover, this knowledge is actual for the informant – she appropriates it, making it her own experience:

    - Researcher: You're saying that your sister had invited you to come. When did she come here herself?

- Informant: She came here after the ending, after the war had finished in 1945, so she came here straight afterwards. Everything was Finnish – sheds, stacks of hey, there was a great deal of Finnish wealth here.
- Researcher: Did she tell you this?
- Informant: When we came, everything was still here. (PF 12, 2003, Kurkijoki.)

Therefore, her experience could be equated with the experience of the first migrants.

REFERENCES

Dal, V. 1996: *Tolkovyi slovar zhivogo velikorusskogo iazyka. T. IV*. SPb.: Diamant.
Kormina, Zh. (forthcoming): Religioznost v russkoi provincii: k voprosu o funkcii selskich svatin. St. Petersburg.
Khrestomatiia po ustnoi istorii. Ed. M. Loskutova. SPb.: Izdatelstvo Evropeiskogo Universiteta v Sankt-Peterburge 2003.
Portelli, A. 2003: Osobennosti ustnoi istorii. In: *Khrestomatiia po ustnoi istorii*. Ed. M. Loskutova. SPb.:Izdatelstvo Evropeiskogo Universiteta v Sankt-Peterburge 2003.
Stepakov, V. & Balashov, E. 2001: V *"novykh raionakh". Iz istorii osvoyeniia Karelskogo peresheika 1940–1941, 1944–1950 gg*. St. Petersburg: Nordmedizdat.
Thompson, P. 2003: Semeinyi mif, modeli povedeniia v sudbakh cheloveka. In: *Khrestomatiia po ustnoi istorii*. SPb.: Izd-vo Evropeiskogo. Universiteta v Sankt-Peterburge.
Tuan, Yi-Fu 2001: *Space and place: the perspective of experience*. Minneapolis: The University of Minnesota Press.

Fieldwork materials (PF and MD) from Melnikovo, Karelian isthmus, Leningrad region, in 2001, from Lahdenpohja and Kurkijoki, Republic of Karelia, in 2002 and 2003

PEKKA HAKAMIES

New culture on new territories
The Karelian Isthmus and Ladoga Karelia
in post-war years

The Soviet Union gained, as a result of the Second World War, a considerable portion of Finnish territory in the province of Karelia: the Karelian Isthmus and the western and northern coast of Lake Ladoga. This happened twice, first in March, 1940 after the so-called winter war and a second time in September, 1944 when Finland withdrew from the war as a co-belligerent of Germany. Each time the territory had to be sovietized without delay. That meant that it had to be newly inhabited as the Finnish population was totally evacuated. All new resources had to be exploited, administration and a whole society had to be built, and new inhabitants had to be settled. In addition the history, especially the recent past, had to be explained to the inhabitants in a suitable manner – this was easier the second time when the Soviet army was formally liberating its own territory from enemy occupation.

The new inhabitants soon discovered that the region was quite different from what they were familiar with. Nature with its many lakes, hills and rocks was different, but the greatest difference was found in the way of dwelling. Finns usually left their houses undamaged and if the battles had not devastated the area, the Russians[1] found intact houses, other buildings, perhaps furniture, clothing, tools or other items and an infrastructure in a very good condition in comparison to Soviet standards of that period.

My research task has been to study how the Russian immigrants experienced all that they found on the new territory, how they adapted to the environment and local conditions, how they transformed the Finnish infrastructure into one which was suitable for the Soviet system and Russian cultural traditions and how a new culture was created when no local traditions were available. As an exception to normal migration and adaptation, in this case the Russians had to acquire the territory on their own without any participation from the earlier inhabitants as no Finns were present to tell them anything about the places and past.

Constructing places

One element of this cultural adaptation has been the mental construction of the surrounding territory, the naming of it, and in this way the gradual creation of places in the minds of the new inhabitants. Edward S. Casey has contemplated the relationship between place and space and criticized the "natural view", as he calls it, according to which an initially "sheer physical terrain", plain space, is gradually transformed by culture and its bearers into places with particular history. Casey argues, relying on phenomenology, that place is an already plenary presence constituted by cultural institutions and practices. (Casey 1996: 14, 46.) However, it seems that the "natural" viewpoint has certain validity in explaining or characterizing the process of place formation in the ceded Karelia, although new inhabitants encountered a lot of cultural products upon their arrival, and in this way elements of places, from Finns. Thus, the Russians did not encounter just a physical or natural space but an environment organized by human culture in many ways. My actual problem is to determine how much of the totality of culturally constructed Finnish places could the Russians experience and how did all this fit into the Soviet system of cultural and social institutions and practices.

Initially, old Finnish place-names were used by Russians everywhere in the ceded Karelia. According to the peace treaty, Finns were required to give maps of the ceded territory to the Soviet Union and in this way the new administration obtained a very detailed picture of the territory it ruled. Naturally, officially documented toponyms did not cover everything and the creation of local place names was left to the inhabitants.

The memory of the Finnish past carried by the old toponyms on the Karelian Isthmus was ideologically unpleasant for the Soviet leaders, because that area was annexed to the Leningrad oblast in 1945 and was no longer included in the Karelian-Finnish Soviet Republic, as was the case after the war in 1940. A decision was made to totally change toponyms into Russian on the Karelian isthmus and this was carried out as a campaign in 1947–1948. (Balashov 1996: 55–57.) The monotonous result of this is still seen today in the place names of the Isthmus. The town of Vyborg and the river Vuoksi are the sole remnants of the pre-Soviet past of the area. In addition, several railway stations have preserved their old, Finnish names until today. The reason was simply bureaucratic practice: the railway administration refused to accept new names for the railway stations as there were already stations with their suggested names and many stations with a similar name would have led to confusion. (Stepakov & Balashov 2001: 77.) The village soviets were asked to invent new names suitable for a narrow scale of possible themes and their proposals were examined at higher levels in the administration. Changes were sometimes made before final names were adopted.

One of the topics of this article is the mental construction of the milieu by the naming of places and the gradual creation of the places as an accumulation of lived experiences. This kind of mental occupation of a territory is one of the ways people begin to interact with their surroundings, as has been studied from ecological viewpoints. Place names and the stories connected with them are one form of local tradition that attaches people and places to each other. It is typical that places are created and named as a consequence of pragmatic action: in order to be able to orientate and communicate, people have to name points in the environment important for them for various reasons. Lauri Honko has, in his theory on ecology of tradition, pointed to milieu dominance: certain points in the milieu are tended to attract attention and become subject to tradition formation like stories and beliefs. Traditionally, distinct points in the surrounding draw the attention of the inhabitants and become milieu dominants around which various traditions are generated. Elementary forms of the local tradition might be stories that explain the origin of the place, the origin of its name or transmit some historical event that took place there. (Honko 1985.)

Human geographers have also had interest in places as subjective, experienced entities. Yi-Fu Tuan states that a profound attachment to one's homeland is a universal phenomenon and not limited to any particular culture. Place is, therefore, an archive of fond memories and splendid achievements that inspire the present. The "feel" of a place gradually develops during a period of time as experiences accumulate in the minds. (Tuan 2001: 154–156.) Other authors in human geography and, conversely, in geographically oriented cultural anthropology underline, in a similar way, deep meaning, traditions and local knowledge as the essence of a place. In this way, places are a part of local history and tradition, not just coordinates or names on the map or road signs. Sometimes a place name can refer to a totality of stories from the past and the values expressed in them (Basso 1996).

From this viewpoint, we can argue that places were totally lost by the evacuation of the Finnish population. Just the empty names formally fixed on maps and signs were left when the new inhabitants arrived in the territory, but these names did not have any meaning for the newcomers, particularly as they were written in Finnish. The new inhabitants had, in turn, to create their own places based on their findings and the beginnings of life in their new milieu.

Peter Gow has characterized the lived, subjective place as a result of a combination of one's own moving around, seeing traces left by other people's movement amongst the surroundings and hearing narratives about the place (Gow 1995: 59). Gow's characterization relates to the native people of Bajo Urubamba in Amazonia but, apparently, one's own movements and experiences, traces of others' activities, and narratives told by others offer, in general, the basis for any place knowledge. In the former Finnish Karelia, the most important element for the new inhabitants were initially their own experiences. Of course, anything left by the former Finnish inhabitants was also important, but narration about the places could be formed only by the accumulation of experiences among the Russians as they became acquainted with their new environment.

In both regions where our group has conducted its field work – Melnikovo (former Räisälä) on the Karelian isthmus and Lahdenpohja and Kurkijoki on the West coast of Ladoga – the settlers acquired the most important place names as ready-made by the newly formed Soviet administration. Initially, the purely geographic names were the old Finnish ones that still served the new system. That name system, apparently, served as a general structure or topographic skeleton for the spontaneous naming of minor and personal places.

– How did you know these names?
– I don't know. When we arrived they already existed. I think there were road signs. And roads were arranged so that they all had signs.
– In what language were the signs?
– In this language, in Finnish.
– Was somebody able to read it?
– Yes, probably.
(PF 27, 2001; Melnikovo.)

The first inhabitant or inhabitants have often given their name for the place where they live. In Melnikovo, former Räisälä, this general rule was confirmed. Single houses and their surroundings, especially khutors[2], were named by their inhabitants, for instance *Mayorov house* or *Mayorov island*. Another example is *Ryabinkin khutor*. The situation was similar in Ladoga Karelia: close to Kortala one lake became known as *Garamovskoye ozero* because of a Garamov, one of the first inhabitants, and the lake still has this name (MD 4, 2002). According to the memory of informants, the naming of places and formation of toponyms was a spontaneous process based on practical activities of local inhabitants:

Who invents. That and that field, someone lived close, so according to him it was called. Lahdenpohja.
(PF 14, 2002.)

Sometimes a place has no fixed name but it is just pointed out by using the family name of the inhabitants: "Now let's go further, when you drive to the direction of Studyonoye, so on the left, there live *Voikovs*." (PF 12, 2001 Melnikovo.) Exceptionally, the national background can have served as grounds for a place name. In Melnikovo, one khutor was known as *Mordvinian khutor* because the first inhabitants were Mordvinians. They do not live there any more but the house still carries that name. Of course, no house was named *Russian* because the vast majority of the people were Russians and "Russian" could not specify any place or house. As a default, everyone was Russian.

Another source for local place names have been the ideas of the Russians about the Finnish past of the place. In this way, they formed the toponyms *Bolnichnoye Pole, Popovka, Stadion, Melnitsa* and *Vetryak* in Melnikovo and *Popovskiye doma* or *Sanatorii* in Lahdenpohja. This is a very interesting group because it reflects some interest by the Russian inhabitants in the Finnish history that was almost unattainable for them until the beginning of the 1990s, when former inhabitants and their children began nostalgic tourism back into the former Finnish Karelia. The place names are also a sign of a mediated Finnish influence in the practice of how places are created and maintained among the Russian inhabitants.

Interestingly enough, Russians claim that some place names that are still in use are Finnish, although they are not found on old Finnish maps, like *Putoriia* close to Melnikovo village (there is *Puttonen*), and, conversely, sometimes Finnish place names are taken as Russian ones. One informant in Melnikovo argued that the name of the local railway station *Myllypelto*, which has actually retained its old Finnish name, had a Russian name and she tried but could not remember its "Finnish name". (PF 11, 2001.) In Lahdenpohja, some informants thought that the place name *Ihala* was Russian. It was also interesting to note that the Finnish name *Kurkijoki* as well as other Finnish toponyms ending with *i* was inflected by the Russians as a Russian word in plural form, "v Kurkijokah" – another example of adaptation of Finnish elements into the Russian culture.

A third source of place names that we seldom met in the interviews have been the characteristics of the nature: in the village of Vasilevo, former Tiuri, a lake was called *Lopata* because it looked like a spade (PF 23, 2001). Some buildings in Lahdenpohja received the name *Spruce house* because of the spruce trees growing as a fence around it. In Lahdenpohja we also got information about the formation of place names according to the compass directions:

> – For instance, there was to the North, we called "North".
> "Northern fields". There it was possible to plough and make hay.
> (PF 14, 2002 Lahdenpohja.)

The renaming of the places in Russian caused great change in Räisälä. Many informants told us that although they were much easier to learn and pronounce people were not eager to adopt the new names. So, the old Finnish names were used later alongside the new, official Russian ones, and even nowadays people can say that they are going to *Räisälä* when they go to the old centre of the village where some old Finnish houses are still preserved. The renaming and the existence of two parallel toponymic systems must have been an irritating factor in the formation of places.

> – Why is this called *Melnikovo*?
> – Later, it was renamed. Higher organs decided, that the Finnish names have to be erased and named it in honour of, somebody *Melnikov*.
> – Did you like the new name?
> – Oh no, for a long time we could not adjust. It was just so nice to write "*Räisälä* school"
> (PF 27, 2001 Melnikovo.)

Occasionally, old Finnish place names can appear in the description of the territory alongside the official Russian names:

> – On the second farm live Maksimova Raja, still Maksimova on the *Irjapskaya* road to that direction. They live.
> – On what road?
> – *Irjapskaya* road. You just pass the garage there...
> – How is the road called?
> – *Irjapskaya*[3].
> – And why does it have such a name?
> – Well, I don't know. It's *Balakhanovskaya* nowadays.
> (PF 12 2001, Melnikovo.)

It was interesting to note that the origin of the Russian name Melnikovo was not clear to all local inhabitants. Some of them associated it with the old Finnish mill and miller (*melnik* in Russian); many did know that the name was given in honour of a fallen soldier in the Great Patriotic War but when and where this Melnikov was killed they did not know.

The situation was different in Ladoga Karelia, in the territory of the Karelian Republic, where the old, Finnish place names were not changed. The reason for this must have been the fact that the Republic was, until 1956, the Karelian-Finnish Soviet Republic which called for something Finnish, unlike on the Isthmus which belonged to the Leningrad region. Nevertheless, the Russian-speaking population began to use Russian surrogates for the Finnish names. Usually, in each village a kolkhoz was formed and it received a Russian, typically Soviet-like name, and people began to use the name of the kolkhoz instead of the purely topographic Finnish place name. "We lived in *Mayak*... It means, in *Lasanen* we lived" (MD 10, 2002 Kurkijoki). In some cases, the new inhabitants brought the name of their kolkhoz, and in practice their village, with them from the place of origin; this is also a well-known practice for researchers of toponyms, by which people create their own places in a new territory:

> – What name did your kolkhoz have in Vologda?
> – It was *Novyi Put* ("New Way"). *New Way* there too.
> – And there is a place, they say, where kolkhoz was *Oborona* ("Defence")?
> – Yes, I know *Oborona*. We lived in Vologda at a distance of half a kilometre. Our *Novyi Put* was, and *Oborona* was half a kilometre from ours, their village was *Pomestovo*. And our village was *Sokolniki*.
> – This was in Vologda?
> – So you knew already in Vologda those people who lived in *Oborona*?
> – Yes, we knew them in Vologda too.
> – And did they arrive here together with you?
> – With us together. Only they with their kolkhoz *Oborona* and we with our kolkhoz *Novyi Put*. They went to one place and we to our place. But in Vologda our villages were located at half a kilometre from each other, and we walked and had fun together.
> (PF 9, Lahdenpohja 2002.)

We expected to encounter several Russian transformations of the Finnish place names because of the differences in the structures and basic characteristics of the languages, due to the fact that Finnish words are difficult to pronounce for Russians, but this kind of Russification seems to have been exceptional. The reason might be the administratively produced Russian alternatives for the Finnish place names. Additionally, administrative toponyms have been created by various Soviet institutions: close to Lahdenpohja have been *Voyennyi gorodok* ("Military town")1 and 2, *Gortop* (abbreviation: "Town heating") and several suburbs called *posyolok* with a numeral, for instance *pyatyi posiylok* ("fifth village").

However, there were also unintended transformations like Putoriia in Melnikovo, and the Finnish name of the village, like many Finnish toponyms, is also usually given in a slightly altered form *Räiselä*. Close to Lahdenpohja we heard the Finnish place name Huhtervu in a more Russian-like form *Huhtorovo*, although the latter was considered to be Finnish and people used the kolkhoz name Trud instead of it and the place was commonly known as "Trud" ("Work"; MD-8, 2002). The sole example of a conscious adaptation or transformation of a Finnish name is *Verholahti* in Melnikovo that was called *Verkholapka* by the local inhabitants (PF 23). Most of our informants argued that the name "Lahdenpohja" was not difficult to learn and pronounce at all, but in some interviews we heard a Russian transformation of the name: *Landokha*. For instance, northwards from the town Sortavala there are *Korennoye (Koirinoja)* and *Semeika (Shemeikka)* (information from Alexandra Stepanova, Petrozavodsk).

When comparing the toponymic practices found on the Karelian isthmus and in Ladoga Karelia, it seems somewhat contradictory that some inhabitants of Melnikovo explained that they liked, even preferred the old, Finnish toponyms rather than the new, Soviet names of places and sometimes still used the old name of the village centre "Räisälä". In Lahdenpohja and Kurkijoki, where the old Finnish place names remained unchanged, people began to use Soviet surrogates, mainly names of kolkhozes instead of the Finnish names, apparently, because the Soviet style Russian names were easier to remember and they referred to actual, lived places formed by the new inhabitants and were, thus, meaningful to the people.

In towns and centres like Lahdenpohja, there has been less room for the spontaneous production of toponyms as the territory has been named by the administration in a more detailed way. Some of our informants had arrived in Lahdenpohja in the middle of 1945 but, according to their memory, the streets already had Soviet style names at that time, but, as we were told, both in Russian and in Finnish.

In general, it was surprising how little spontaneous toponymic material we recorded in Melnikovo and especially in Lahdenpohja. There must have been a real need for inhabitants to name points in the surrounding terrain that were important for them in daily life, like places where it is good to pick berries or mushrooms or to fish. Clifford Geertz has noted that it is not possible to visit a place and in a short time collect data concerning the place. One has to stay longer and "hang around" with the local people and gain knowledge which the locals are unwilling or unable to give instantly. (Geertz 1996: 260.) In this sense, one reason for the scanty result may be due to the purely folkloristic fieldwork method we applied: more or less structured interviews of a lot of people in a short span of time. But the alternative, an anthropological field trip and a lengthy period of "hanging around" was not a viable alternative.

Nevertheless, it might be that 50 years or two generations is not enough for the creation of a stable system of local toponyms in the situation in which Russians have lived in the former Finnish Karelia. In a similar way, a former inhabitant of the countryside close to Lahdenpohja pointed to the lengthy period of time needed for the formation of local oral tradition and explained, when the interviewer asked him why there was a lot of magic in the old Vologda village but nothing in Lahdenpohja:

> – There the places have been inhabited a long time, since time immemorial, and it has been transmitted, this kind of crazy things.
> (PF 14, 2002 Lahdenpohja.)

The only milieu dominant discernible in the stories both in Melnikovo and Lahdenpohja was the Finnish church. In both places, and also in Kurkijoki, we were told that there was a subterranean passage from the church to somewhere in the surrounding. In Melnikovo, the heating system of the church with its wide tubes for warm air below the floor can have served as a reason for the stories. Probably more importantly, has been the theme of the secret passage that is common in Russian folk tradition which has provoked stories related to the prominent buildings in the new territory. There have been an abundant number of stories about subterranean passages between palaces in St.Petersburg and also between the old fortifications of the so-called "Mannerheim line" at the Karelian isthmus and the present day Finnish territory. An additional motif in Melnikovo was the "rubber priest" that was told to stay in the subterranean passage or elsewhere in the church:

> – Well, I remember, that there ... when our friends went inside, classmates. They spoke that there are steep stairs and there stays a rubber priest. So they said – rubber priest. I don't know ... they saw at the top. So they spoke, classmates. I don't know anything more.
> – Rubber priest?
> – Yes. So what? Some kind of figure, supposedly, was made. Why they thought from rubber? Perhaps it was not rubber.
> (PF 7, 2001 Melnikovo.)

The formation and preservation of places and place names by the Russian inhabitants has been severely hindered by the sharp administrative turns in the development of the Soviet countryside. Initially, people were settled in Finnish khutors and small villages. When a decision to enlarge kolkhozes and later to transform the kolkhozes to even larger soviet farms, sovkhozes, was put into action, a lot of places were left uninhabited and so the places created until that by the local Russian people were gradually lost again as people did not reproduce them any more in their everyday life. The final stroke for the disappearance of places in villages has been the decline of Russian agriculture and rural life because of the collapse of the Soviet Union.

Image of Finns

Until the nostalgia tourism from Finland to the former Finnish Karelia began, practically none of the new inhabitants had seen any Finns except those living in the Soviet Union before the 1990s . The Russian inhabitants had to construct their image of Finns on the basis of their observations and experience and cultural models based on their life in Soviet society. Charlotte Linde has defined the *explanatory system* as a system in which one statement may or may not be taken as a cause for another statement. The system offers a means for understanding, evaluating and interpreting experience but also guides future behaviour. Linde argues that Marxism is one example of explanatory systems. (Linde 1995: 343, 351.) Accordingly, the settlers of former Finnish Karelia had a Soviet Russian explanatory system from the point of which they made everything understandable in the new territory.

Analogies seem to have been a strong mental tool for comprehending everything the settlers encountered on the new territory and, therefore, an important means of the explanatory system. In general, analogies are powerful ways for understanding how things work in a new domain. They offer generative mental models and new inferences. A major way in which people reason about unfamiliar domains is through analogical mappings, which are transition rules from a known domain into the new domain, that help to construct a mental model that can generate inferences in the target domain. (Collins & Gentner 1995: 243-247.)

Russians could construct analogical models based on their own past experiences and cultural competence in the Russian culture and Soviet society which included many peculiarities of the Soviet administrative practices of that period.

One example of an analogical model is the explanation of the departure of the Finns. In many cases it was apparent that the Finns did not have very much time to prepare their departure and to collect and send away all their property. Many Russians applied here the model of deportation known to them, that people were given 24 hours to disappear. This explanation was often mentioned in relation to the way the Finns departed, and sometimes the informant even emphasized that "Stalin gave the Finns 24 hours to go" (PF 12, 2001 Melnikovo; MD 8, 2002 Lahdenpohja).

A common opinion seemed to be that Finns were clever and rational in agriculture and, in general, in their economy which was well adapted to local conditions. However, the Finnish methods of agriculture were not easy for the Soviet system to adopt because they were based on individual, not collective work.

> – (We kept hay) in stacks outdoors. But Finns did not have stacks. They had all hay in barns. Barns were more civilized, they were good."
> – And when Finnish hay barns broke, did you make your own ones?"
> – No, it was already, the kolkhozes were liquidated and people went to sovhoses. So the state organized this. And we couldn't do anything.
> (PF 14, 2002 Lahdenpohja.)

A common theme in the stories concerning the fields were the ditches dug by Finns. Usually Russians neglected their maintenance and this resulted in wet fields that did not give a good crop. Many informants explained that the meaning of the ditches was understood only afterwards when the damage was already done.

> – There were open ditches ... in order to prevent the fields from becoming peaty. All right. But our people later, it can be said, spoiled. They began to plough these fields in every direction and make covered ditches. But

later those pipes became blocked and again fields became peaty. And all, all were speaking later – Finn, he knew how to do this. As it was so, it meant that it must be so.
(PF 7, 2001, Melnikovo.)

In general, the Soviet society did not favour individual initiative and adjustment to local conditions. However, there were certain attempts to imitate Finns or to benefit from their experience. In Lahdenpohja and Kurkijoki, the good quality of the gravel roads was a topic of admiration. According to one informant, Soviet specialists tried to find out the composition of the surface material of the road pavement and sent material several times for analysis to Petrozavodsk but without success, and gradually the roads were spoiled under heavy trucks used by the Soviet transport system. (MD 12, 2002 Lahdenpohja.) In agriculture, Finnish species of grain and other economic plants were used for some time, usually for as long as the inhabitants lived on old Finnish khutors, before the reformation of the kolkhoz system. (PF 30, 2001 Melnikovo.)

An important feature of the impression the surrounding made on the settlers was the beauty and cleanliness to be found everywhere. A general opinion among our informants was that everything was beautiful and clean, initially, even the forest. A quite common statement by the Russians was: "It was a fairytale". The forests were so well maintained that, according to a particular metaphor, it was possible to find a needle there. In addition, the amount of flowers, bushes and apple trees was surprising and a topic of admiration for the Russians, except those who came from the southern regions of USSR.

Sometimes the informants mentioned that the further development was, in fact, a gradual decay and sometimes blamed the "Russian Ivan" for his inability to maintain all in its previous state. One informant commented upon this complaint about the general decline stating that people were just unable to maintain the Finnish standard - they were mainly mothers with children but without men, and they had to work hard in kolkhozes (PF 18, 2001 Melnikovo). Another reason was probably the structure of the local administration: the houses were not the property of their inhabitants but of the kolkhoz instead or another unit of local administration. If a repair was needed, people had to ask for it to be done by administration (MD 10, 2002 Lahdenpohja). This bureaucratic way of maintenance naturally weakened the result.

The post-war period was a hard time of hunger and poverty for the Soviet people. Many of the settlers had very little property when they arrived, and the supply system, including the food supply, did not work well in the initial phase. Therefore, anything Finns had left was significant for the new inhabitants. This fact is one reason why there are many stories about food having been found somewhere and used by the local people. A common theme in the stories was the suspicion that the food could have been spoiled or even poisoned. Usually, one of the family tried it first and when there was no adverse consequences from eating the stored food it was exploited by all. (Cf. MD 10, 2002 Kurkijoki.)

Another constant theme in the narration was the bowl of warm soup, usually cabbage soup, that the new inhabitants found in the oven (PF 2, 2001,

Melnikovo). This theme, apparently, reflects the idea that Finns had to leave their homes in such a hurry that they did not even have time to eat. But it also emphasizes the importance of food in the post war-period.

> ....They were there accommodated, in that home. And she (told), so, we came in, and in the oven there was hot cabbage soup. So this babushka. She told personally ... when they went to the house, it was open, and the padlock with keys was hanging in side.
> (MD 8, 2002 Lahdenpohja.)

Stories about Finns returning to their old homes were told mainly in the Ladoga Karelia, in Kurkijoki and Lahdenpohja, perhaps because the border was closer than in Melnikovo and not so carefully guarded, particularly in the initial phase. So it was easier for Finns to penetrate the Soviet territory and local inhabitants also found it more probable to see a Finn.

> There were rumours, supposedly, a Finn crossed the border, took a look how people lived in his house, and went back. Again it was told that the border guard arrested them.
> (PF 14, 2002 Lahdenpohja)

Both in Melnikovo and Kurkijoki and Lahdenpohja people feared, in the initial phase, the Finns penetrating the border. There were stories about Finns eager to kill new inhabitants. Some real incidents caused by local people would have been explained as the deeds of Finns if the real killer were not found immediately (PF 21, 2001 Melnikovo; field diary MD 1-2, 2002 Lahdenpohja).

This fear of violent Finns may have been grounded in the assumption that Finns must have suffered a lot when leaving their nice homes, and this feeling of a loss had led to a hate against the new inhabitants. It was supposed that Finns knew secret paths cross the border and were able to avoid the Soviet border guard. In the initial phase, there was a certain general feeling of guilt, that the soil did not belong to the new inhabitants: "we do not live on our soil". Perhaps this sub-conscious or half-conscious feeling initiated their fear of "avenging Finns".

> – We were afraid in the night. Go to sleep - and fear comes, certainly, Finns are coming... There were stories about Finns who came and killed, because people lived in their house.
> (PF 14. 2002. Lahdenpohja)

> – Did you dread Finns?
> – I did not. But my mother feared a lot when we arrived.
> – Why did she fear?
> – Yes, I don't. But I knew that we lived on an alien territory.
> (PF 21, 2001 Melnikovo)

> – We settled in the Räisälä main village, because we feared Finns. Our mothers arrived here. We were sixteen families – mainly widows only... So we feared. We settled – there was a Finnish house, big, so we were two

> families who packed in the house, although it would have been possible to have an individual house and "live like the gentry". People feared. They did not settle on the khutors. And significantly many khutors burned in the initial period, for some reason, and there was a common rumour that it was Finns who set their former manors on fire. They come along secret paths and put fire.
> (PF 13, 2001 Melnikovo)

One informant suspected that the security service (NKVD) actively supported and spread this kind of attitude in order to have the people be more cautious and vigilant (PF 30, 2001 Melnikovo).

This kind of fear and rumors apparently already emerged in the spring of 1940. One narrator, in the book of Stepakov and Balashov, relates a story about when he and some other fellows arrived at Vyborg in 1940 after the peace treaty, when the Soviet administration was under construction. A local official received them, gave them accommodation and the advice: "Comrades, don't go out during night". When they asked the reason for this, he explained: "Finns cross the border and kill our people behind the corner". (Stepakov & Balashov 2001: 45.)

The general impression of hastily leaving Finns and various items left by them, together with the apparent prosperity of Finns in comparison with Russians evoked the idea by many that Finns may also have hidden something in the earth or in the buildings. Sometimes people even found something hidden by Finns. For this reason, some Russians think that the Finns who nowadays come to visit their former houses or native places are, in fact, seeking valuables left by themselves or their parents.

> – Did someone speak that the Finns when leaving could hide something somewhere?
> – Yes, they said. They say, the Finns wanted to clean the river, and they proposed some time ago that they will clean the river, it is going to be blocked, but they want to keep everything they will find at the bottom. But our people did not allow that.
> (PF 12, 2001 Melnikovo)

> – Last year or the year before, there is a village ten kilometres away from here, they arrived – nowadays it's permitted. ...They arrive and go to look, there is a mark, apparently, where there is something hidden. They visited the hosts and gave gifts, coffee and some other presents. They stayed at the hosts a while. But then during the night they came and dug this ... their treasure. The hosts woke up, and there was just a hole behind the yard and all taken away.
> (PF 3, 2002 Lahdenpohja)

If something was found it was usually dishes, clothes or some other everyday items, but the fact that it was possible to find useful things caused hopes for something extraordinary too.

> – There were discussions that when the Finns were leaving they dug their valuables in the pits, and someone found those pits. I don't know. ...There

were rumours that Finns did dig.
(PF 13, 2001 Melnikovo)

There are many stories told by the Russians about Finnish food being found somewhere, and sometimes the former Finnish host of the house uncovers the food storage for the Russian inhabitants. The stories of the latter case can be interpreted as an imagined ritual where the former host is handing over his house to the new settlers, his successors. In some cases, these stories seem to have acquired a truly folkloric character:

> – I was lying in a hospital in an operation. ...And there was a woman from Ihala village. She told that she worked in the past in the village soviet. And she heard this kind of story:
> Once, in a khutor lived a woman, it was a red army family. Her husband was in the army. And they had three kids. A Finn crossed the border. He arrived at her and said: – I came here to die. – How, to die? – Yes, I came to die. He sat down on the bench in the kitchen. She was really afraid. The evening was at hand. She had her kids around her. And no adult person was available. He went and opened a latch in the floor of the kitchen and went to the cellar and bustled there a while. Then he said to the woman: – Come here, come down here! – She was afraid. So, she went down too and thought: – May it come what is coming. The Finn was tall and brisk but pretty old. So, she went down too. And there he opened one more latch, and there was a storage of food. There was meal, grits, butter, canned food. And he said: – This all will be yours. Her eyes went wide open. How much food! –It was really a time of hunger.
> – And he said: – This will be all yours. Only you have to bury me where I say you. So, they took something for evening meal. Then he said: – I go now to the woodshed. You don't go out from the house before morning. When you go out in the morning, look – I will be dead. Bury me – there is a birch alley. Bury me on that alley.
> So she did not go out before the morning. She could not close her eyes. How to sleep! In the morning she looked at the man – he was sitting. When she touched his hands, they were cold. She went to the chairman of the village soviet. – To the woman with whom I was in the hospital. – Lida, I have a dead Finn. What shall we do? – What to do. Let's bury him together. So the buried him.
> – Did they bury him in the place he wanted?
> – Yes. Where he wanted, on the birch alley. There they buried him. Apparently, he had passed his years of youth. Perhaps, in Finland, who could know it, he did not say what he had there. Perhaps his wife was dead and no one from the family was left. And he was longing and went along paths he knew well. Border guard could not catch him, because he only did know those places not far from the border.
> (MD 7, 2002 Lahdenpohja)

This story reflects many traits of the image of Finns the Russians have had: they knew the local territory better than Russians and could avoid the border guard, they longed for their former homes and they could have food stored in hidden places. The common evening meal and the suicide of the former host can be interpreted as of the symbolic handing over of the house, in the imagination of the Russians, to the Russian successor. In some other stories, Finns are represented as resembling tutelary spirits, appearing from nowhere at a former Finnish house to warn the hostess to not pour water onto the wooden floor in order to prevent it from decay (MD 10, 2002 Kurkijoki).

Details of Finnish culture that were difficult for Russians to understand or accept

Usually our informants have said that they had no difficulties in understanding the meaning of or how to use of any of the items they encountered. But in the structure of the community, single houses, khutors, at a distance from others, were anomalous for Russians, and they were difficult to engage into the collective agriculture. Therefore, several houses were moved during the interwar period of 1940–1941 to the main village. When Russians returned in 1945 they discovered, to their surprise, that Finns had moved the houses back to their original place. (PF 24, 2001 Melnikovo: MD 10, 2002 Kurkijoki.) In addition, the small fields around the khutors were strange and impractical for Russians working on collective farms.

Many Russians disliked the khutor type dwelling (MD 1, 2002 Lahdenpohja; MD 3, 2002 Lahdenpohja; PF 9, 2002 Lahdenpohja). It did not suit Soviet collective agriculture but also it was culturally alien for the new inhabitants, who were accustomed to living in tight villages and to have neighbours quite close to their home. This, together with the fear of Finns in the initial phase, made dwelling in khutors unpleasant for some Russians.

A Finnish owner rebuilds his house on its original place, Kurkijoki 1941–1944. It was a real surprise for the Soviet settlers in 1945 that houses moved during the Soviet period were brought back to their original place by the Finns. (Photo: Kurkijoki-säätiö)

Finnish houses moved by Soviet settlers are being dismantled to be moved back to their original place in Kurkijoki, 1941–1944. (Photo: Kurkijoki-säätiö)

The Finnish way of haymaking is a very illustrative case of initial confusion for the Russians. In Finland, including the Isthmus and Ladoga Karelia, hay poles were already used in the pre-war years – they were an innovation of the beginning of the 20th century – while the Russians used to put hay into hayricks. In Melnikovo, we were told how the meaning of a huge number of sharp, polished poles was unclear until the leader of the soviet farm finally solved the problem by discovering that one was meant to erect the poles on a hayfield and then to put hay on the poles. (PF 1, 2001.) In another interview, the fate of the hay poles and barns and the limited ability of the Russians to benefit from the Finnish infrastructure is well illustrated:

> – In the beginning, when we arrived here, the Finns had a barn on every hayfield. A whole barn full of poles - they were racks on which they formerly dried hay. Do you know what it is?
> – No, please, tell us.
> – Well, a pole has wooden pegs, and hay is put on the rack and a peg put on its place, and hay becomes dry and good in every weather. ... So, our mothers first took these poles as firewood, then barns... Later when barns were finished they began to travel to the khutors. Big khutors they could not dismantle. But when there was a small lonely hut like this mine in the forest, they broke it down together and brought home by horse.
> – Was it not a pity – whole houses?
> – It was a question of life for them, to heat.
> – Could you say, why these poles were burned and not used as racks?
> – I don't know. Probably they did not know for what purpose they were.

> – And how do you know?
> – I became to know only recently. But in those years I didn't either. Only when I became adult and began to work.
> – And barns why. Were they not needed?
> – Apparently yes. Our people put hay in hayricks, Russians who arrived here. Finns did put hay in the barns and keep there. But for some reason, we put in hayricks and stacks. It has been usual in that way in Russia (на Руси).

There is an interesting detail at the end of this quotation: our informant used the expression *na Rusi* which usually refers to the traditional, even archaic Russian countryside when referring to the cultural tradition of Russians. Apparently, she wanted to emphasize the progressive character of the Finnish way of working, by referring to the backwardness and inertia of Russians in this sense and their inability to adopt the new technique.

In Lahdenpohja, one informant gave us an explanation he had invented, just by using his own reason and experience, to explain the meaning of these poles lying around a hay barn: they were meant to be erected in the field close to the barn and then hay was to be put on the poles for drying. Usually the Russians did not adopt this way of haymaking, although the method was considered to be effective and well adapted to local conditions, so the hay poles were often used as firewood. (MD 8, 2003.)

Settlers can have various expectations and "ways of reading the landscape" as Tom Selwyn writes. According to him, Jews moving to Israel have had certain attitudes and ideas about what they would see in the landscape and what this landscape symbolises (Selwyn 1995: 128–132). Russians arriving in the new Karelian regions seem to have been without preconceived ideas and attitudes. They knew very little about the history of the region and the only information given was by the state recruiters or individual villagers who were sent in advance to clear the conditions in the target area of the settlement. It is indeed surprising that there was apparently no ideological control for channelling the general opinion formed on the basis of the relatively wealthy houses and other findings not in line with the image of bourgeois Finland and its suffering small peasants and workers spread by Soviet propaganda. We have practically no information about the ideological work done among the new inhabitants. However, this must have been some kind of problem, according to recollections of Red Army soldiers of the 1939–1940 war who often made comparisons between the Soviet propaganda and their own observations on the occupied territory, this was unpleasant for the politruks who had to explain everything in an ideologically suitable way (Stepakov 1996: 322–325).

The image of past Finnish life was formed spontaneously among the new inhabitants and some of its aspects have been presented in this article. Ironically, a certain preconceived ideology and, conversely, ways of reading the landscape can sooner be found among the former Finnish inhabitants and their children who, from the beginning of the 1990s onwards, came to see the lost homeland and the for them the miserable fate of their former places under the new rule and social order.

A Finnish house in Melnikovo, former Räisälä, in 1959. Photo taken by a Finnish tourist who illegally visited his old home during a tourist trip to Leningrad. (Photo: Räisäläisten-säätiö)

A Finnish house partially dismantled and the timber numbered for transportation purposes. Kurkijoki 2002. (Photo: Pekka Hakamies)

Vanishing traces of the past

Certain structural factors hindered the preservation of the places initially created by the settlers in the countryside, not to mention the development of deeper ties and meanings and real local tradition. Similar factors, a hierarchical administration with very little place for individual initiative and abrupt changes in the development of the village, seem to be the reasons for the gradual decay of the physical environment and the traces left by Finns, their buildings, fields and other infrastructural aspects mentioned by the majority of the narrators.

Under Soviet rule the land and even the houses did not belong to any single person or household, which may be one reason for the weak ties with the land and places. This has also weakened the motivation and possibilities for people to take care of the houses and their surroundings. The Soviet society and administration did not serve as a collective landowner, like, for instance, nomadic societies or other societies without private land ownership. The Soviet economic and social system emphasized the conquering of nature, including the environment. The system called for rapid achievements and ignored the price paid for them. Therefore, the cultural environment was not given much attention. The housing problem was neglected and the minimal resources were allocated to the maintenance of the existing building mass.

In some interviews, local people openly presented their opinion that during the Finnish period each house had its master who maintained it and skilfully cultivated the land, but the situation changed after the war when the territory became part of the Soviet society. Similarly, some informants spontaneously spoke about "korennye zhiteli", inhabitants with roots, who were missing during the Soviet period and which caused indifference towards places and environment.

Nowadays, the attitude of the people towards the places and the history, including the Finnish past, depends to a considerable extent on the ties the local Russians have with Finns and Finland. People living in former Finnish houses often have contacts with the previous owners of the house and are thus motivated to know the history and maintain the house. They are usually supported in this by the Finns. Some local people have become amateur historians and try to trace archaeological and historical details of the district and are also supported by the Finns. Not all people are interested in this. In Kurkijoki, for instance, the old wooden church burned down in the beginning of the 1990s after the Finns had began its repair, and the old wooden hotel building of Kurkijoki, which was a Russian-Finnish joint enterprise, burned in the beginning of 2003. Some places, like the town of Sortavala, can be characterized as an open-air museum of past Finnish architecture, but, in general, in the rural areas traces of the Finnish past are gradually disappearing.

NOTES

1. Although there were other nationalities as well I call all settlers simply "Russians". Russians is the shortest term which suitably characterizes well the settlers in general. When needed, I define more precisely the nationality of the inhabitants.
2. "Khutor" is a Russian word which means a lonely farmstead located at a distance from the other houses, opposed to the tight village. Khutors were the prevailing type of dwelling in the former Finnish Karelia but anomalous for the Russians.
3. The Finnish name has been *Äyräpää* which is very difficult to pronounce for Russians.

REFERENCES

Balashov, Ye. A. 1996: *Karel'skii peresheek. Zemlya neizvedannaia. Chast' 1. Yugo-Zapadnyi sektor.* Sankt-Peterburg, Izdatel'stvo V. V. Valdina "Novoye Vremya".

Basso, Keith H. 1996: Wisdom Sits in Places: Notes on a Western Apache Landscape. In: *Senses of Place.* Ed. by Steven Feld & Keith H. Basso. Santa Fe: School of American Research Press.

Casey, Edward S. 1996: How to Get from Space to Place in a Fairly Short Stretch of Time. Phenomenological Prolegomena. In: *Senses of Place.* Ed. by Steven Feld & Keith H. Basso. Santa Fe: School of American Research Press.

Collins, Allan & Gentner, Dedre 1995: How people construct mental models. In: *Cultural Models in Language & Thought.* Ed. by Dorothy Holland and Naomi Quinn. Cambridge: Cambridge University Press.

Geertz, Clifford 1996: Afterword. In: *Senses of Place.* Ed. by Steven Feld & Keith H. Basso. Santa Fe: School of American Research Press.

Gow, Peter 1995: Land, People, and Paper in Western Amazonia. In: *The Anthropology of Landscape. Perspectives on Place and Space.* Ed. by Eric Hirsch and Michael O'Hanlon. Oxford: Oxford University Press.

Honko, Lauri 1985: Rethinking tradition ecology. In: *Temenos* 1985.

Linde, Charlotte 1995: Explanatory systems in ora life stories. In: *Cultural Models in Language & Thought.* Ed. by Dorothy Holland and Naomi Quinn. Cambridge: Cambridge University Press.

Selwyn, Tom 1995: Landscapes of Liberation and Imprisonment: Towards an Anthropology of the Israeli Landscape. In: *The Anthropology of Landscape. Perspectives on Place and Space.* Ed. by Eric Hirsch and Michael O'Hanlon. Oxford: Oxford University Press.

Senses of Place. Ed. by Steven Feld & Keith H. Basso. Santa Fe: School of American Research Press 1996.

Stepakov, V. N. 1995: *Sodalla on hintansa.* Helsinki: Otava.

Stepakov, V. N. & Balashov, Ye. A. 2001: *V "Novih raiionah". Iz istorii osvoyeniia Karel'skogo peresheyka 1940–1941, 1944–1950 gg.* Sankt-Peterburg: "Nordmedizdat".

Tuan, Yi-Fu 2001: *Space and Place. The Perspective of Experience.* Minneapolis, The University of Minnesota Press (8. printing, originally printed 1977).

Fieldwork materials (PF and MD) from Melnikovo, Karelian isthmus, Leningrad region, in 2001, from Lahdenpohja and Kurkijoki, Republic of Karelia, in 2002 and 2003.

IRINA RAZUMOVA

On the problems of local identity and contemporary Russian "migratory texts" (with reference to the Northwestern region of Russia)

The problem

The study of ethnolocal identity and the factors which influence it must promote a deeper understanding of civil or national self-consciousness. Now it is one of the most topical tasks of ethnology studies, especially, at the post-Soviet stage of development in Russia. In this paper, some questions regarding the interaction of proper ethnic, local and family stereotypes and their influence upon the perception of place and the effect of migrational strategies are considered. In connection with this, of real interest are the processes of interaction of proper ethnic and local components in the construction of the ethnocultural identity, that is the degree of influence migrations have upon the dynamics of these processes. On the one hand, local symbolism plays a significant part in the formation of ethnic self-consciousness. On the other hand, ethnic stereotypes influence perception of place, its "appropriation" or its being torn away, and affect migrational strategies. Therefore, there is undoubtedly a correlation between the local symbolism and the migratory behaviour of people in contemporary Russia, as there is anywhere else.

The northwestern region of Russia, multiethnic and heterogeneous from an economic perspective, is characterized by highly intensive of migratory processes, generated by different social and economic causes. Today, views on migration are relevant due to the catastrophic situation in the economy, ecology and socio-cultural climates in some areas of the region. Judging by daily discourse and freely circulating rumours, these feelings sometimes become critical (panic-like) and destabilize the emotional-psychological microclimate, and this, in turn, threatens the stability of the development of northern territories.

Migratory processes in contemporary Russia have become much more intense. Apart from the processes already well-studied by modern sociology – such as the emigration and migration of local ethnic groups caused by geopolitical change (Russkiie 1992; Migratsii 1996), there are very intensive processes of internal migration: a general craving to live in big cities, the mass movements of migrant workers, the quests for "a better place" etc. To a great extent these processes shape the mental climate of modern Russia.

The analysis of migratory process is impossible without studying the migratory expectations of people and their basis – specific perceptions of space. The widespread observation that Russians are prone to moving and regard resettlement as a panacea for all earthly problems was long ago trivialised. In relation to this opinion, both in Ancient and in Modern Russia, escapism, tramping (*"brodiazhnitchestvo"*) and wandering (*"strannitchestvo"*) "were the single form of an individual's protest against various inconvenient circumstances" (Yadrintsev 1882: 351; Maksimov 1877). In fact, the territorial scale of Russia makes it possible to resettle massive population groups. These claims enjoy the status of a "national myth", but on the whole they are to a degree verified by statistical data. Taking into account the stability of "Social Utopia" myths and plots in the national culture, which, in their turn, stimulate the "Quest for the Land of Happiness" (Chistov 1967), we assume that the migratory behavior patterns of Russians will remain more or less stable. Thus, migratory expectations are actualized in categories of "world outlook", which we could hypothetically regard as "specific for Russia" as they are able to become explicit only within the system of national language.

It seems obvious to us that in the Post-Soviet period both the migratory behavior and migratory expectations connected to it have changed a lot. In the era of Soviet Russia important migratory processes were caused by 1) forcible resettlement of certain population groups – those ethnically discriminated against or those considered "of dangerous social origins", 2) industrialization or the building of large plants and factories, determined by the geopolitical goals of the Soviet government, 3) urbanization, which took the form of a more or less unwilling "emigration" of country people into towns and cities. Thus, these emigrations were largely forced (Bugay 1989, 1992; Donnikov 1992; Zemskov 1990, 1991, 1994; Maksudov 1991; Parsadanova 1989; Polian 2001; Shashkov 1996).

The phenomenon of emigration occupied a special place within the migratory processes of the Soviet era (Shkarenkov 1987; Kostikov 1990; Rossiia v izgnanii 1999; Russkiie bez Otechestva 2000; Iontsev et al. 2001 etc.). It did not envelope all the groups of the Soviet society but principally the intellectual elite – predominantly, in the cases of the so-called "first wave of emigration" – the post October Revolution expatriation of the culturally and socially privileged – and the "third wave" – a mass exodus of intelligentsia to the USA, Germany, Israel and other countries. Apart from them there was the so-called "second wave" – emigrants who left Russia after the Second World War (they have the lowest status in emigrant society). In some instances, the emigration took the form of forcible deportation of dissidents.

"Migratory text"

Migratory processes are the constant subject of historical, ethnological and sociological interest (Glaesser 1993). It is our belief that the study of local and ethno-local consciousness as well as migrations happening in real life is inseparable from the study of the migratory feelings and the cognitive stereotypes that shape them. In my opinion, it is necessary to study migratory strategies in relation to migratory text – or the sum of texts circulating within the given society that expresses migratory feelings and to assess real migrations of individuals and groups. Every type of migration whether internal or external, is accompanied by the creation and circulation of texts in everyday discourse that accumulate and conceptualize real experiences and behaviour strategies involving migratory processes. These include stories about moving house, of resettlements – forcible or voluntary, meditations on the negative and positive results from changing one`s "place of living", the assessment-oriented descriptions of those people who went away or refused to quit their homeland etc. All these texts express the authors' own experience along with the others'; these can also be a reaction to both real cases of moving away and to information obtained from official sources. We call the sum of these stories, meditations or observations "migratory text".

We introduce this superconcept by analogy to the designations "local text", "provincial text", "family text" etc. (see, for instance: Abashev 2000; Razumova 2001; Russian province 2001). It is worth noting that in the framework of a semiotic approach definitions like the ones above are thought to belong to a totality of discursive practices that deal with a definite reviewer and are connected with him through circumstances of actualization.

The migratory text seems to us a subject of utmost importance. Primarily, it is the evidence of forces that provoke these or other migratory processes, which in their turn shape migratory "flows". In other words, if a person declares his or her intent to move away (for example, to the capital or abroad), he/she would not necessarily do it in real life – but these declarations are a signal of a certain mentality that exists in the corresponding socio-cultural, local or family environment and generate some emotional context. For example, in the modern life of Apatity town, situated in the Far North region, within the Polar Circle, the assurance of its population's majority that they live in this town only temporarily plays a large role, because in the modern economic situation people are not needed in the North anymore and, besides, "it's difficult to live when the night lasts half a year" (this is a typical sentence). Thus, migratory text accompanies real migratory processes and, in its turn, influences them, formulating behavior expectations and motivations accepted by a specific microsocium, and a specific person, taking these into account, makes migration-involved decisions.

The main goals of my research were as follows: 1) to collect so-called "local" and migratory texts, both modern and "retrospective" examples (on the subject of past resettlements), in some areas of the Russian Northwest; 2) to identify the cultural patterns that shape local and migratory texts, along with the specifics of their accumulation and translation; 3) to identify possible correlations between ethno-local symbolism and migratory dispositions, especially among the youth; 4) to define the power of family influence over individual strategies; 5) to identify, if possible, the dynamics which shape migratory text in Soviet and post-Soviet times.

The goals of this research are attainable only by an interdisciplinary approach, which synthesizes the methods of cultural anthropology, sociology and practical folklore studies. A special place in our methodological "tool kit" is occupied by the methods of microsociology (among them the "biographical method"), based on ethnomethodology.

The chosen region and the materials

The research process involves the creation of an empirical basis by interviewing the inhabitants of different loci of North-West Russia. The resultant audio recordings were processed, archived and analyzed. The practical fieldwork involved interviewing the inhabitants of several cities, towns and villages in the Russian northwest, particularly young people at an age of 17–25. We partly worked with people born between 1920 and 1975, which provided us with an empirical base that reflects migratory processes of the post Second World War period – from the 1950s till the 1990s. The northwest region was chosen due to several important facts:

1. Northwest Russia is one of the border regions of Russia. Its population is multiethnic. As a result of ancient and modern migrations a lot of big and small ethnic groups have settled there: Russians and other Slavs (Belorussians, Ukrainians), Karelians, Finns, Vepsians, Ingrian Finns, Izhora, Saami, Komi etc. Throughout the 20th century, the official borders of Russia were repeatedly moved; and there were periods when they became more or less penetrable. In the geopolitical mentality of a common Russia, this area is associated with the notion of "west" – namely, with a space that is both Russian and foreign at the same time. Today, the perception of this area is influenced by intense attention from both government and society regarding all the northern regions of Russia; issues surrounding the economic vitality of the North are widely discussed. The northern dwellers' self-consciousness could not escape the impact of widely repeated claims that the North is an "ecological disaster" zone and extremely unfavourable for economic development conditions.

Due to the above-mentioned factors, the northwestern region, peaceful enough from an ethnic perspective (it's well known that this multiethnic region, in fact, has no instance of interethnic conflicts), is a zone of intense migratory processes, which makes the analysis of their causes and forms of explication an important scholarly task. For example, the Kola region (Murmansk region) suffered from 1993 to 1997, the most powerful wave of migration in the Barents region. It has lost 80900 inhabitants (Lausala 1999: 69).

2. In the past, the North-West was also the site of important migratory processes, which included: a) mass exodus of the Finns and North Karelians from Karelia, caused by 1) the 1917 Revolution, Civil War and Soviet power establishment; 2) the "Winter Campaign" or the Soviet-Finnish war of 1939 and 3) post perestroika liberalization; b) the forcible deportation of Baltic-Finnish people, specifically the Ingermanland-Finns and Izhora, from the Leningrad region in the 1930s and 1940s (new materials: Polyan 2001: 84–87, 115–116); c) massive inflow of people, including workers and members of scientific and technical intelligentsia, into the Murmansk

region and other areas of the Far North in the 1920–1930s due to industrial reclamation of these lands; d) colonization by Russians of Ladoga Karelia and the Karelian isthmus – the territories annexed by the Soviet Union after the "Winter campaign" and Second World War; e) the resettlement of a great number of Belorussians in Karelia after Second World War; f) massive migrations due to the creation of industrial centres (Apatity, Tikhvin, Slantsy) in the 1950–1960s; g) the continuing exodus of people from villages and small towns towards big cities (Saint-Petersburg, Petrozavodsk, Murmansk) etc. (Spetspereselentsy 1997; Shashkov 2000; Targiainen 2001 etc.).

Our field experience bears evidence that all mentioned migratory processes – both those of the past and those, which are happening now – are accompanied by active circulation of migratory texts, which represent and determine behaviour strategies and display the mechanisms of adaptation. Such texts have become a part of historical memory and oral tradition for many families in this region. They are reproduced in relative groups and form definite behavioural and mental stereotypes among younger generations.

The materials were chiefly recorded in the cities of the Murmansk region (Apatity, Kirovsk, Monchegorsk), and also in Petrozavodsk and Saint Petersburg amongst the native and newly arrived young people and the members of their families. Our interest in the Kola region particularly centres around the demographic structure of the cities. The absolute majority of the population of this region consists of first – third generation migrants: the families of workers, engineers and technical personnel and intelligentsia. The population of the city of Apatity is slightly different, the social structure of which is, to a considerable degree, represented by the scientific intelligentsia and students in conjunction with a relatively high percentage of workers in the field of education and cultural spheres.

3. The region of Northwest Russia is extremely variegated in relation to socio-cultural and economic aspects. This fact provides us with a chance to compare future migratory texts and migratory feelings in cities, towns and settlements with different standards of living, thus identifying specific features that may belong to each locus.

Local migratory text

We are sure that the migratory processes of Russia can not be seen as something unique, as something exclusive from the context of Pan European and world processes of globalization (Segal 1993). However, at the same time, it is necessary to identify dominant patterns that through further comparative, cross-cultural study may demonstrate their specific nature. These dominant patterns are shaped by historical, cultural and geopolitical circumstances (Russkiie 1992: 10–89).

One of our theses argues that the specific features of the migratory processes in Russia are caused by specific social, economic and value oriented stratification of the space, its hierarchy. The organization of space follows the "centre-periphery" ("capital-provinces") model, or concentrically (in an arbitrary sense of that term) (Kaganskii 2001). In quite different historical contexts, there is evidence of a predominantly stable centripetal migration flow in the direction "village-town- city-capital". By developing this model further, we can see that the goal of all aspirations is the "Abroad" model (the "west": *zapad*). In this regard, it is interesting to analyze notions relevant to the Russian mentality, such as "provinces" vs. "capital" and "periphery" vs. "centre of the world".

The results of our interviews among the youth, that is the analysis of their opinions show, that the orientation to move "abroad" (*zagranitsu*) yields considerably towards efforts to move to a larger or capital city. The given migrational sentiments the words of the informant express generalizingly: "Yes, I'd like to go abroad, but for a while, not for a lifetime (*ne navsegda*). Although, I'd like to live forever in my city, I need new possibilities, which just cannot be fulfilled in my city" (Tatiana, a student, 18 y., Apatity, 2002).

Research into the juxtaposition of the province and the capital, the "large" (*bolshoi*) and the "small" (*malyi*) city has been carried out in recent years intensively enough (by literary critics, linguists, folklorists) (Russkaia provintsiia 2000; Provintsiia 2001). In connection with our subject, I would like to define more exactly how the notions of "large" and "capital" (*stolichnyi*) cities are differentiated. None of the informants (there are hundreds of them) mentioned Moscow as a city where he or she would like to live. This is connected 1) with the orientation of the north-western areas of Russia to Saint Petersburg and with the reputation of this city being the "cultural capital" (*kulturnaia stolitsa*), as opposed to the administrative center; 2) with the clearly expressed "anti-Moscow" feelings, intensified during recent years. Therefore, in Karelia the very popular text is about the anti-cultural behavior of the Muscovites, who "come with their cars, trample down everything, tear out the mushrooms with mycelium, and spoil all of nature" (E. N., 40 y., a teacher, Petrozavodsk, 2001). It is the Muscovites, who are referred to, even though inhabitants of Murmansk, Saint Petersburg, and Petrozavodsk also come. According to some Muscovite informants, they are "afraid" or "ashamed" to admit where they come from, when they are in provincial cities, because they do not wish to arouse open hostility. This article does not deal with the historical, cultural and socio-economical backgrounds of this phenomenon, because they are not within the scope of this paper.

The mutual perceptions of the ethnolocal groups about each other regarding the Russian space and behavioral stereotypes are also created in accordance within the wider spectrum of the geopolitical, ethnic, characterological and other meanings, which are related to the oppositional notions of "north" and "south", "east" and "west". An important role in the formation of local identity is played out by natural and cultural objects, including specific objects of urban and rural environments.

I will illustrate this point by exemplifying of the city of Apatity, because the materials gathered there were especially impressive. The migrational statements of the inhabitants of this city correspond, on the one hand, to well-known strategies, yet on the other hand, they demonstrate local peculiarities.

The city of Apatity was established in connection with exploitation of the

Khibini deposits, and it was given the official status of a city in 1966 and bears the name, which comes from the denomination of the mineral. The folklore interpretation of the name and urban etiologic legends show that this area is ethnically associated with the Saami population: "In general, it is a Lapp name, which means "fertility". That's why the apatite is often called "the stone of fertility" (Natalia, aged 17, a student, Apatity, 2002). "Something strange about the city is the fact that before its foundation the reindeer, who grazed in these parts, were afraid to come into the circle, which coincides with the limits of the present-day city. They bypassed this place every time. Probably for this reason our place is called "a black hole" (*chornaia dyra*)" (Katarina, aged 18, a student, Apatity, 2002). Like any other city, Apatity receives a number of stereotypical characteristics: "In relation to the fame of this city I can say that it is a city which is ecologically relatively clean; it is a city of youth, it is a city where life was started by the hands of prisoners from the time of Stalin's rule" (Elena, aged 19, a student, Apatity, 2002).

The main symbolism of the city and the topics of the urban informants are typical for the image of the provincial city: "We can breathe better here than in the big cities. It is not so dirty as, for example, in Moscow. Not so noisy... For some reason, we imagine it as a toy. With short streets and little houses" (Natalia, aged 20, a student, Apatity, 2002). "You often meet familiar faces, you greet them and smile at them" (Aleksandr, aged 18, a student, Apatity, 2002). The natural geographical and meteorological symbols are accentuated: "Our peculiarity is the winter with its polar night and abundance of snow" (Natalia, aged 19, a student, Apatity, 2002). The answer to the question: "What is your city especially famous for?" – "Khibini, of course. Crowds of people come especially to see Khibini, not the city" (Aleksei, aged 19, a student, Apatity, 2002). The second natural symbol of Apatity is Imandra Lake. An indubitable speciality of the polar city is the northern lights. Another typical characteristic connected with the north is also specified: "compared to southern regions and large cities it is more or less calm in Apatity" (N., aged 23, a worker, Apatity, 2002).

The obscurity of a small city is compensated for by definite advantages, which are also locally determined. Such is one of them – an idea about high earnings of the northerners. This idea is based on the fact that in the northern parts of Russia state wages are higher, since a so-called "northern coefficient" is added to them, while in areas of the Far North, in particular in the Murmansk region it is called a "polar rise" (*poliarnaia nadbavka*). In Soviet times, it was generally thought that people came to the North with the exclusive purpose to "earn money". This idea is still intact today. The following joke (anecdote) is based, on this fact, which can be associated with every northern city: A taxi driver in Los Angeles refuses to take the client to Apatity, but, having seen a batch of dollars with him, asks him immediately to which district of the city he must drive. At the same time he reveals his knowledge of unofficial toponyms.

One of the symbolic objects of the city is the Kola science center of the Academy of Sciences. For the absolute majority of the townsfolk, the favorite place of the city is the Academic campus (*Akademgorodok*), which is a park with some cottages. This scientific centre provides a special quality to the image of the town: it "makes people feel situated at the proper level" (Tatiana, aged 18, a student, Apatity, 2002); "in principle, our city is a city, we may say, of science" (Liudmila, aged 51, a citizen of Apatity, 2002); "it is an intellectual city – we have a scientific institute and many scientists" (Nadezhda, aged 18, a student, Apatity, 2002) etc. It should also be noted that there are many institutes of higher education in the city, which is why it is presented as a place for the young and students. The image of a typical inhabitant of Apatity entails the image of a northerner, supplemented by social characteristics: "The northerners, in particular, the inhabitants of Apatity, are corrupted less than the others. Here you can not bribe anybody, not everything can be bought, and communication is also much more good-natured, they still believe in friendship" (Katarina, aged 19, a student, Apatity, 2002). "When defining the character of a northerner let's remember that their roots come from exiles and scientists. That's why they are soft and calm, and not oppressed and hostile" (Mariia, aged 27, a student, Apatity, 2002). Apatity represents the centre of a certain area. Whilst admitting to the provinciality of the city an informant answers: "Our city is far away from the large centres. And the city is almost the hearth, the middle of the Kola Peninsula" (Natalia, aged 20, a student, Apatity, 2002).

An important role in the formation of local identity is played by the perception of the city or of its name only from without. For the inhabitants of other regions of Russia, the main distinctive feature of Apatity is its geographical position, supplemented by its ethnographical details (signs). "Some people ask about reindeer and Polar bears, when they learn, that it is in the north. They think that here there is no civilization, that we live in yourtas" (Olga, aged 21, a student, Apatity, 2002). As a reaction to this, a text that meets these expectations is born, being either direct or a parody: "Apatity – it is a town, where reindeers are walking round the yourtas". According to the words of an informant, "sometimes it is so easy to convince a man that you live in the primitive society of Saami in the middle of the icy and snowy desert, by the sea, where the seals swim" (Katarina, aged 19, a student, Apatity, 2002). The northerners themselves indubitably play a role in the creation of the exaggerated "image of themselves" through the eyes of "others". An uninitiated "southerner" (an extremely wide notion from the point of view of the inhabitant of Kola Peninsula) becomes a fantastic (anecdotic) personage in stories about the inhabitants of the north. He (she) believes, for example, that "the school is a large tent of skins (*chum*), with the teacher sitting in the middle, and reindeer walking around" (Natalia, aged 18, a student, Apatity, 2002). Such images are a considerable part of a northerner's local identity.

While composing a text, characterizing the city, the locality, or the typical inhabitant, the key words are of great importance because they mark the place or objects. As a rule, they create formula statements, which are often ironic: "People here are frozen" (*zamorozhennyie*), "There are no villains, all of them have been destroyed by frost" (*vymerzli*); "In the cold people are longer preserved"; "Even the representatives of the south (Caucasus) behave relatively calmly – they are probably just frozen" etc.

A comparison of "local texts" representing different cities and localities offers us an opportunity to reveal not only the parameters of their likeness and specific character, but also to show how they are included into a special system of relations with other cities and localities, for example, within the limits of the region or a wider space (state). So, in the Kola Peninsula, Apatity and Kirovsk are territorially near-by cities, partly rivaling, partly being perceived as something common; Murmansk is more of a "capital" city (the regional centre) and contrasts partly with Apatity, which is the "scientific centre" of the territory; Monchegorsk is "more provincial", "more uncultured" and more unhappy (*neblagopoluchnyi*) than Apatity etc.

The majority of the inhabitants of the city answered, when asked where they would like to live, that they dreamt "of the warm coast of one of the southern seas" (Katarina, aged 19, a student, Apatity, 2002) or a city in the mid-zone of Russia. As an ideal, a similar city is imagined, but in southern (opposed) latitudes: "I want to live in Sochi, in the mountains" (Mariia, aged 27, a student, Apatity, 2002); "If I have an opportunity, I will leave Apatity, but it will be for rather a small town, but only in the south" (Natalia, aged 17, a student, Apatity, 2002). Some statements of a similar kind are significant in that the preferable city to live in should be – "the real double" of Apatity, "but where there would be no problems either in the economic sphere, or in the political, or in the cultural one" (Tatiana, aged 17, a student, Apatity, 2002). A distinct orientation towards Scandinavian (more often - the "Swedish" ones) cities as ideal cities is also expressed.

If we summarize all our materials, including those gathered in Karelia and Saint Petersburg, no more than 2–3% of young people have a migrational attitude aimed towards the "west". If we were to name at the same time the desired country of destination, then it would be the USA or France, and to a lesser extent Germany (as a rule, if one has friends or relatives there). Eastern and southern countries are completely ignored. At the same time, the majority of informants expressed a wish to travel or to live abroad. The maximal period of stay was determined as a few years. Many people would like to increase their professional standard and to earn some money. But we must not forget the importance of the cognitive motive, among other motives, for visiting foreign countries. In different formulations, informants also express the necessity to widen their own social and ethno-cultural space. This wish is especially typical for the inhabitants of provincial towns. The majority of the informants would like to live in a small town ("their own"), to study in a large center, and to go to various countries of the world "in search of impressions". It is quite possible that we deal with the definite transformation of the migrational feelings and the actualization of what we can call the feeling of local identity in modern young people. At the same time, these conclusions are still of a preliminary nature.

Family migratory text

Yet, relatively not long ago any travel, business trip "abroad", seamen's traveling "overseas" etc. were regarded as a high status sign. On the other hand, persons who were not allowed to go "abroad" (*refuseniks*) had all the grounds to be proud of the fact that the state openly recognized them as being in opposition. At present, the basic reason for "going abroad" is to earn money, which intensifies the contrast between the "material" and "spiritual" in a corresponding discourse and conditions are created for the actualization of a patriotic text. Discursive practices, explaining the concept of "Homeland" (*rodina*), are clearly analyzed in a recent interesting study by I. Sandomirskaya (Sandomirskaya 2001). We will dwell on just one function of this rhetoric.

I. Sandomirskaya justly emphasizes the conceptual difference between "Homeland" as a fetish of the State system on the one hand and as an "ideal state of the local" on the other (Sandomirskaya 2001: 17–18). On the basis of the first meaning, the concept of homeland-state is formed, while the concept of "one's minor homeland" is formed on the basis of the second one. From the perspective that interests us (the point of view of migration strategies), the idea of "perpetual return" is connected with the minor homeland (*malaia rodina*), while ideas of exile (ibid. 69–70) or escape are associated with the homeland-state. In certain contexts, equally important for Soviet Russia (which I. Sandomirskaya writes about) as well as for post-Soviet Russia, the "minor (little) homeland" is seen as an alternative to the "great homeland" (ibid. 54–55). In fact, we deal with two cultural concepts, which start a complicated dialogue. They both may serve as a form of rationalization of real migrations and migrational attitudes, moods etc. In our opinion, both notions can correlate with categories of Love and Duty, which create different migrational texts. At the same time, only the concept of "minor homeland" is associated with the concept of "native background"(*rodnyye korni*), in which meanings of local and family genealogical closeness are joined.

The state idea having been discredited, as a result the family space, which had previously expanded to include the whole country, now as a result includes the space of the "motherland" (including one's "homeland", the place where one grew up). We would like to present here two fragments of a discussion - between a grandmother and her granddaughter, – they were obtained as an answer to the question of whether they wished to go abroad:

> 1) "...I've always been a patriot of this country, whoever might be in power... How could I leave this place, if my mom is buried here and my dad died, while defending our land from Nazis. It looks as though I would have betrayed them and would turn my children into traitors. I would have become an enemy of my people, my country and myself. If you are a citizen of your country, if you are a patriot, nothing can be more valuable to you than your homeland and it is beyond anybody's power to make you abandon it" (Irina Stepanovna, aged 74, St.Petersburg, 2001. Recorded by E.Sheiko;

2) "Family and homeland: for me these two notions are closely related... I love very much my hometown St.-Petersburg... I spent my child years here, it is with this town that my best recollections and the best moments of my life are associated. It is here that my grandmas and my grandpas got acquainted, my dad and mom were born. Just for this reason alone I would not change my homeland for the world. However, there is one more reason. St.-Petersburg in a way became a member of my family, the wisest of my friends... I greatly hope that in the future neither me nor my family would leave this beautiful country, that my children, grandchildren and great-grandchildren will love their homeland as much as I do and will remember that once their grandmas and grandpas walked on stony pavements and admired the gardens and palaces of the city on the Neva river" (Elizaveta, aged 18, student, St.-Petersburg, 2001. Self-recorded).

The maintenance of kinship unity is the basic idea and a strategic project of family existence. At the same time, the conception of the family identity is, in many ways, based on the identification of a group with its localization located in a specialized narrow sense ("home" for a family) and in a broader sense ("homeland" for relatives). Studies on modern family folklore, biographic accounts and spontaneous texts about family allow one to define the character of the mass idea, in relation to concepts of "kinship", "family", "home", "homeland" etc. (Sandomirskaya 2001).

The semantics of connection and disconnection of relatives is the most significant for the "family text". Disintegration in any form causes "family stress" (Hill 1949; Boss 1988). The disconnection of related people in the form of spatial distancing acquires the largest number of forms and ways of interpretation. In situations solved by mutual agreement, it is thought of as a forced, inconclusive one, which is overcome using various means of communication, including extrasensory ones. The extents of the dividing space and the border, strictly speaking from home limits to the state ones, are experienced differently depending on familiar and personal attitudes. In situations of spatial disconnection (parting, departure etc.), the moment of farewell is always ritualised, and it symbolizes temporariness or uncertainty with regard to time, or loss of a relative. This concerns the traditional ceremony of seeing young men off to the army, stable family forms of farewell with children, who leave to start studies, with family members, whose occupation involves traveling, at the moment of relatives' separation after a traditional "get-together" and in a number of other cases. In many families, the daily departure is also ritualised. The ritual of saying farewell, meant to maintain group balance, is oriented towards the subsequent safe return of the near one even under the most unclear of future outlooks. At the same time, the elderly relatives are often inclined towards considering similar farewell situations as the "last" ones, which may be expressed in oral texts of "instruction" and "will" types.

Depending on the family value attitudes and on social and biographical circumstances, a relative who went abroad still remains a member of the family or else he (she) is considered lost, "dead". In reality, a relative who stayed abroad often 'slips' the family memory. It is worth mentioning that the word combinations themselves "to go far away", "to go abroad" (less often) and – the one that became the most traditional – "to leave for America" are, along with the typical "he left us", a metaphoric substitute of an indication of human death, since they combine the meanings of an extreme remoteness and separation.

Staying in some other country may be regarded as "high treason' and a betrayal of one's family at the same time: "One of my grandpa's brothers was taken prisoner of war and so he stayed in Sweden for good. My grandpa and my dad both renounced him. They believed him to be a traitor. It was just shortly before he died that my grandpa forgave him and went to meet him in Leningrad" (Elena, aged 17, student, Petrozavodsk, 2000) etc.

The antagonism of family and state constitutes one of the most important structural fundamentals of a family biography, which in the overwhelming majority of cases appears in a story of "survival", overcoming a series of crises with more or less numerous losses. In this opposition of strong and weak, the family group does not only play a passive and suffering part. Escapism is a widespread form of counteraction for a family against the "main antagonist". Among the motives for migration there are flight from "taxes", "persecutions of old-believers", "conscription", "oppression of landowners", "dispossession of kulacks" etc.

Besides "escaping" within the limits of national space (a way of getting rid of something, which is generally assumed to be a "traditionally Russian one") there is emigration. Under well-known circumstances, in the period of the Soviet State's repressions, the separation of relatives and the flight of one or some of them abroad was considered a means of self-preservation for a family. So, according to one legend of a Karelian family, the decision for two elder brothers of an informant's grandfather to emigrate to Finland, with their families in 1917 was made at a family council and, ever since, the family considered itself as two separated clans, the relations between which were entirely dependent on the political situation at various periods of time (Emiliia, aged 17, student, Petrozavodsk, 1999).

It is worth noting that for the majority of the native inhabitants of Karelia (Olonets district) the Revolution of 1917 was not a turning point, which had changed their kindred relations, however the border line between Karelia and Finland established after it was undoubtedly such a point. This fact affected the division of the family history into periods and is recorded in family memories: After the revolution <...> a border was established between Karelia and Finland, villages were divided along with families, relatives, kinsmen" (Julia, aged 18, student, Petrozavodsk, 1999); "Once, Ivan's father was told to take a wounded officer to Finland (during the Civil war, 1918–1920, – I.R.). <...> Ivan took the officer as far as Salmi (a borderline village – I.R.), and then the war was over and the border was closed. A 15-year old boy remained in Finland. So, the family lost their son" (Tatyana, aged 16, schoolgirl, Petrozavodsk, 1999); "In the '30s, grandma's uncles often traveled there for earnings. Once, when they went to Finland again, the border was closed and they remained there. However, one of them swam across the river separating Finland from Karelia, but the other could not swim and was afraid of jumping into water, so he stayed in the foreign country" (Anna, aged 17, student, Petrozavodsk, 1999).

Both, the establishment of the border in 1918 and its "fortification", due to the beginning of hostilities in 1939 were conceived of in the same way: "they closed the border", which means: relatives were separated by force. This theme re-emerged again in the early 1990s, because of the establishment of borders between the former Soviet Union republics. A popular subject, connected with events of the near past, is presented in stories about relatives' separation and about difficulties in contacting them. Not only the new borders, but also the higher tariffs for all kinds of communications are conceived of, at first, as a separation of relatives and friends by a force with some perfidious goals. At the same time, there were some stories about the establishment of contacts with relatives who lived abroad and had previously been considered "lost".

In the Soviet time, if people wanted to know something about their relatives living abroad, they more often did not respond to their letters, for fear of being disloyal to authorities. Nowadays, on the contrary, the search for foreign relative is both materially and morally grounded. In recent years, the reunification of related groups has become somewhat popular as a) renewal of contacts, interrupted because of historic cataclysms, b) finding "new" relatives, i.e. previously unknown. A story of how they managed to find relatives, who turned up in Finland (Sweden, Germany), is built upon a detailed description of the process and stages of the search (the initiators are, most of the time, the representatives of the foreign branch of the family), while obligatorily mentioning "the first letter", accentuating the first meeting and the concluding assertion for the need for a stable established contact. The motive for the search may be initiated by an unexpected recognition, for example, like having a surname spotted in a newspaper.

It is natural that texts concerning migrations depend on the age and kindred status of the informants, and on the communication situation (the rhetoric may be either non-reflexing or intentional). The concepts "homeland"/ "abroad", "our people"/ "foreigners", "native"/ "alien" are included in a semantic kernel of the examined narratives. In the rhetoric of the discourse "on homeland and foreign land" the word "homeland" (*rodina*) is associated differently (homeland = state vs. homeland = family).

The motives of Russian texts about foreign countries are typical enough and do not require any detailed comments in this respect. They are related to traditional socio-utopian ideas and that escapist strategy which is oriented towards the search for a "land of happiness" (independently of the real migrational behavior and the life project in a specific case). One of the typical positions is based on a stereotype statement, that "one can not live in Russia". Let us note, that the statement itself is usually neither defined concretely nor verbalized very often, since it is considered general knowledge. As to "abroad", foreign countries, as such, may be perceived in the generalized sense to limit the meaning of "foreign" to "better". At the same time, there is, undoubtedly, a differentiation and value stratification of "foreign" spaces. Namely, this is what I. Sandomirskaya meant as she wrote about "imaginary geography" with respect to the symbols of "East" and "West" in Russian culture. (Sandomirskaya 2001: 71).

First of all, "foreign countries", "the west", are utopian lands of fabulous wealth. This motive is repeatedly found in stories of those who had succeeded in another country as well as in texts of informants for whom moving abroad is a long-range strategy:

> I'm bored with working every day for next to nothing, and over there, a man's work is valued justly. All in all, people are treated with more respect in Europe than here. I am fond of Russia and if it would be possible to live a decent life here I would stay… (Ekaterina V., aged 46, accountant, St.-Petersburg, 2001, recorded by O. S. Sapegina).

Texts are absolutely formula-like and, therefore, do not need to be cited abundantly.

Those that are noteworthy are accounts about one's returning home after staying abroad: they deal with contrastive negative impressions, depressions during the first days and the need for adaptation ("Had to stay in for a few days"). They, as a rule, illustrate the statement: "One has to get accustomed gradually to our life (analogous to "their" abundance)."

This idea also affects marital behavior and plots of stories about marriage contracts. With regards to the latter, the narration develops according to a fabulous screenplay. A foreigner is one of the preferred marital partners. Such a marriage equates with the opportunity to be rid of problems typical for Russia and with comfort and prosperity. For example, preaching parental text:

> Take your second cousin Lena, she's your junior, right? She got married last year and she lives now in Los Angeles, that's something."(Lyubov, aged 21, reproducing a recurrent remark of her father, Petrozavodsk, 2001, recorded by I. V. Ruppieva). Alevtina N., 52, continuously says to her god-daughter: "You're so stupid, you let go a guy like that, he's handsome, lives in St.-Petersburg, studies at the University, his mother lives in Canada. Sooner or later, in a year or two you would have been with him over there too. You'd be in clover. (Petrozavodsk, 2001, Recorded by I. V.Ruppieva).

At the same time, comical stories concerning marriages with foreigners also circulate. Just like verbal and literary funny stories, dealing with Russian citizens' travels to the west, these jokes use, with good effect, the collision between behavioral strategies of characters, their temperaments, the divergence of etiquette standards etc.

As an alternative to the fairy tale type marriage subjects, there are terrifying stories which speak about a sorrowful fate, losses and even the death of women who married foreign citizens and found themselves deceived. As a rule, such stories are related to eastern and southern countries (Muslim ones, but not exclusively). It can be noticed with regard to this subject matter, that the contrast between the "west" and the "east" is more pronounced (by and large, concerning gender problems). Another country always means alien space, however, it is, undoubtedly, differentiated.

The alien nature of another country is best of all felt in nostalgic emigrants' texts, which concentrate on motives of tragic guilt, emotional dissatisfaction etc. The unsuccessfulness of an emigrant in a new place is usually regarded as a punishment for "breaking off with one's roots (homeland)". (We do not consider texts of this series, since it is a special subject matter).

A fearful attitude towards one's relatives' departure abroad is usually motivated by dangers of various kinds, which make up a part of everyday life. Here are some parting words of a mother: "... and you should lead a healthy way of life, not eat whatever comes your way and not drink those "chemical" things..." (Irina M., aged 61, engineer, St.-Petersburg, 2001, recorded by O. S. Sapegina). "Luxuries" injurious to health, and artificial food are included into the number of distinctive marks of foreign (western) life and they coexist with some more important phobias.

Fear, as a rule that of parents, is equally the fear for those leaving and for oneself. The most undesirable consequence of the moving away is the impossibility of coming back, to be unable to reunite with one's relatives. In the opinion of the overwhelming majority of informants, the absence of relatives' support in a new place is the main reason that prevents people from moving (including within their own country):

> In no way would I let my children go abroad. In this country one can earn money too, and there, you never know, whether you'll come back or not. They have the same kind of problems over there, but we're used to ours. There may as well be some ill-disposed people, coming their way, who might use them for their interests so they won't be able to come back home. The more so they won't have any support there. If they get into trouble, where'd they go? Yes, some people leave, but it's their personal business and those who can stay there without problem, they're just lucky. (Ekaterina I., aged 50, St.-Petersburg, 2001, recorded by O. S. Sapegina).

With some isolated exceptions, all are convinced of the idea that relatives should, if not live together, "stay nearby" (physically, territorially):

> I believe that, in principle, a family, separated by a few thousands kilometers, loses in itself the sense by which it had been initially attributed to the notion of "family". Certainly, modern communication technologies enable one to keep in contact with one's relatives even at distances like that, but they can not replace the real feeling of family, which develops only through direct permanent contact. Having let one member of the family go away, the others will never be able to restore the atmosphere of a family dinner in the kitchen, the one which had been there, before he left. Although it often becomes impossible to prevent the departure, then there is nothing else left, than to leave, first for one member of the family and later on very often for the others. (Larissa M., aged 56, St. Petersburg, 2001, recorded by O. Yu. Kharitonova).

Thus, in the situation of a positive migration attitude, the strategy of group movement and the idea of overcoming fears and difficulties by joint effort prove to be prevalent:

> Well, what should one go there for? I can't see what's so bad here... Well, actually, if my husband would have to leave somewhere, then I'd follow him. You're not afraid, when you're two. (Maria Vassilyevna, aged 73, retired schoolteacher, St. Petersburg, 2001. Recorded by O. S. Sapegina).

Attention is drawn to the motive of "parental victim", typical as a whole for the family text. It is intensified by the difference in attitudes between different generations. We managed to record a story of a woman whose daughter had emigrated from St.-Petersburg to Estonia. In spite of the vicinity of this territory, the presence of the state border and traditional perception of Estonia as "west" (alien space) are psychologically traumatizing factors for the informant:

> ...Just think, how awful it is for me. Now, the moment I look at her cheerful face on a picture my heart bleeds. How terrible, she is not just in another town, she's in another country. We call each other on the phone every day, but it's not the same... I, actually, didn't oppose her moving too much. Here in Russia, wages aren't paid, you sometimes can't afford even, sorry, to have something to eat and Olenka had to get kids. How can we have kids over here?! I, for one, have been toiling all my life. I worked really hard and saved enough to buy me a room in a communal flat and still count every kopek. Let my daughter have a decent life. Estonia is west, actually. Our family still remains a family, as it used to be. We celebrate the New Year night together; they come around, she and her husband. I am really looking forward to having grandchildren. They wanted to take me down there, but I wouldn't go. I love Russia and its stinky communal flats. Recently, I've been having a strange kind of dream: as if Olenka is running away from me, but my feet wouldn't move and I cry and look at her going away from me. Well, all those dreams are just rubbish though. (Nadezhda I., aged 45, nurse, St.-Petersburg, 2001, recorded by E. A. Tsareva).

We should note that images of the dream correspond to oniromantic symbols of death. The following statement: "The main thing is that they (the ones who left) are OK, never mind us..." is one of the most typical. It is supported by arguments in favor of the continuation of the family: the young, in order to survive and have children, should have more favorable conditions. Stories, dealing with how pregnant women, resorting to various tricks, go abroad to give birth to their child, offer one of the most popular subjects (for example, stories about a woman who takes a rowboat to Finland or, hiding her condition, takes a plane to America, to bear a citizen of another country). The situation is considered as an act of saving one's family. Similar motives are: saving a child, a young woman at the cost of the health, well-being and sometimes even life of other relatives, often appear in family stories about war.

According to a family myth, relatives are a unified organism in space and time. The land is sacred where one's relatives are born and buried ("you can't leave the graves"). One should recall the custom of taking some soil from the graves of relatives, buried far from the place, which is considered "homeland". The rhetoric of texts on family and homeland demonstrates a formulaic expression of this set of notions. In an apologetic text, telling about the homeland of informants of a different age, one has to recognize the basic arguments, connected with the unity of related people, to be primary, even if they are supplemented with other reasons:

> Going abroad to make studies? No! I believe education is better in Russia. Well, abroad the available education is highly specialized. Besides, what's good there after all? I don't understand why somebody should leave. Here are our homeland, relatives, friends, and native tongue. And there everything is alien. Who waits for us down there? The grass is always greener on the other side of the fence. And as to here, no matter how bad you live, it is your homeland. Here, my mom, dad and grandmom live. (Inna, aged 21, teacher, Kolpino, Leningrad region, 2001, recorded by O. A. Palchikova).

Belonging to one's "homeland" is an ontological property of a human ('homeland – in oneself") associated with his/her fate. Well, whereas, a Soviet man identified "people" = "homeland" = state; the man of today (the post-Soviet one) accentuates the idea of related identity and his need for family protection is increased. At the same time, notions of state and homeland are differentiated, which has a double consequence. First, the stereotype of a "suffering motherland" is actualized and the moral imperative calls for suffering together. Second, a strategy is formed, which aims at the preservation of family through movement elsewhere ("to bear children abroad", "to go away all together") and at possible return.

A well-balanced position suggests the combination of a positive migration attitude and affection for one's homeland. This attitude is manifested, in particular, in discussions of parents:

> Well, this is surely not for life. Just spent some time there and then came back home. (Irina M., aged 61, engineer, St. Petersburg, 2001. Recorded by O. S. Sapegina).

> I would very much like myself or my relatives to go abroad. If my son would go abroad to study or to work, I wouldn't mind. Well, however, marriage with a foreigner, this I wouldn't really like as my son could then stay there for good. Well. I believe if your children live abroad, then somehow their relationship with their parents is lost" (Alla M., aged 36, librarian, St.-Petersburg, 2001, recorded by O. A. Palchikova). The possibility of expanding one's cultural space is included in the circle of positive values: "In my opinion, it is only normal. One must not live one's whole life in one place. They'll work there, they'll come back here again to spend their money... One should liberalize. One should get interested in everything while abroad like going to theaters and museums during one's spare time. (Irina M., aged 61, engineer, St.-Petersburg, 2001, recorded by O. S. Sapegina).

In this connection, there are some culturally distinguished countries: France, Italy.

Thus, we can identify the basic types of texts about the subject matter of interest to us: 1) apologetic, 2) balanced ("on the one hand ... on the other hand"), and 3) compensatory (using the formula "but in return"). For all the traditional nature of culturally determined rhetoric (the tradition of the dichotomous relationship between Russia and "foreign countries", the stability of Soviet and anti Soviet stock phrases like "iron curtain" etc.), an adaptation of texts (change of meanings and associative relationships), stipulated by a change in the geopolitical situation in Russia has been observed.

An important task seems to be the further verification of the thesis that behavior strategies, including migratory ones, are primarily influenced by the family's (generational) historical and cultural experience. We believe that there is a "family" migratory text, which through vertical translation (from generation to generation) programs the behavior of the individual.

In this regard, according to our observations, the most stable and the most emotionally felt notions are Motherland, ancestors, "old country" or one's own home place and parental home. The possibility for free choice makes them especially relevant, and they prove to be one of the major stabilizing factors.

Conclusion

Thus, there is a correlation between the local symbolics, local identity and migratory behavior of individuals and social groups. From our point of view, the operational term "migratory text" promotes one to model and to predict the migratory situation. It is concerned with the representation of migratory feelings and the real migratory practice conceptualization in a given culture. Migratory text is an objective factor influenced by migratory process and life strategies.

We determined the local and the family migratory texts to be the main components of a whole one. Undoubtedly, there are some other modifications in accordance with different social parameters. Regional materials represent the specific mental stratification of Russian space and local symbols as factors formed the identity of individuals and groups, that is their orientations, values, life projects. Family migratory text, in accordance with kin identity, family history and locality, occupies a important place in this process.

In our opinion, the migratory processes and strategies of post-Soviet Russia are undergoing a whole score of changes. These concern external factors, as well as (and, obviously, in the first order) internal motivations for movement in the case of individuals and families. In the past (in the Soviet geopolitical space), the State fully controlled not only emigration or any visit abroad, but also where people lived. With the disintegration of the totalitarian state, the role of personal choice definitely grows – this is a consistent pattern. At the same time, Russian tradition is characterized by the individual's orientation towards family and microsocial (subcultural) experience, which constrains and corrects the process of individualization. We believe that in the context of post-perestroika Russia the function of controlling migratory behavior is assumed by the immediate family, by other relatives and – to a lesser extent – by social orientation groups.

There are traditional narrative and cognitive patterns of Russian migratory text. At the same time, contemporary text data demonstrates definite behavioral transformations in relation to the motivations which underlie migratory activity and some cultural mechanisms of stabilization. The study of these is a task of great importance.

REFERENCES

Abashev, V. V. 2000: *Perm kak tekst: Perm v russkoi kulture i literature XX veka*. Perm.
Boss, Pauline 1988: *Family Stress Management*. Family Studies text series 8. California: Sage Publications.
Bugay, N. F. 1989: K voprosu o deportatsii narodov SSSR v 1930–1940-ie gg. In: *Istoriya SSSR* 6/1989.
Bugay, N. F. 1990: Pravda o deportatsii chechenskogo i ingushskogo narodov. In: *Voprosy istorii* 7/1990.
Bugay, N. F. 1992: 1940-1950-ie gody: posledstviia deportatsii narodov (svidetelstvuiut arkhivy NKVD-MVD SSSR). Ed. by N. F. Bugay. In: *Istoriia SSSR* 1/1992.
Chistov, K. V. 1967: *Russkiie sotsialno-utopicheskiie legendy XVII–XIX vv*. Leningrad.
Donnikov, V. P. 1992: *Spetsposelentsy Zapadnoi Sibiri. Vesna 1931 – nachalo 1933 gg*. Ed. by V. P. Donnikov. Novosibirsk.
Glaesser, Hans-Georg 1993: *Bibliography on migration: German and English language literature*. Ed. by Hans-Georg Glaesser & Frauke Siefkes. Kiel: Bibliothek des Instituts für Weltwirtschaft.
Hill, R. 1949: *Families under stress*. Westport, CT: Greenwood.
Iontsev, V. A. & Lebedeva, N. M. & Nazarov, M. V. & Okorkov, A. V. 2001: *Emigratsiia i repatriatsiia v Rossii*. Moskva.
Kaganskii, V. 2001: *Kulturnyi landshaft i sovetskoie obitaemoie prostranstvo*. Moskva.
Kostikov, V. V. 1990: *Ne budem proklinat izgnanie... Puti i sudby russkoi emigratsii*. Moskva.
Lausala, T. 1999: *Economic Geography and Structure of the Russian Territories of the Barents Region*. Ed. by Tero Lausala & Leila Valkonen. Rovaniemi: Arctic Centre.
Maksimov, S. V. 1877: *Brodiachaia Rus Khrista radi. Moskva*. Ibidem: Brodiachaia Rus. – *Otechestvennyie zapiski* 227–230.
Maksudov, S. 1991: Nekotoryie dokumenty smolenskogo arkhiva o raskulachivanii i vysylke kulakov. In: *Minuvsheie*, Vyp. 4. Moskva.
Migratsii i novyie diaspory v postsovetskikh gosudarstvakh. Ed. by V. A. Tishkov. Moskva.
Parsadanova, V. S. 1989: Deportatsiia naseleniia iz Zapadnoi Ukrainy i Zapadnoi Belorussii v 1939–1941 gg. In: *Novaia i noveishaia istoriia* 2/1989.
Polyan, P. 2001: *Ne po svoiei vole... Istoriia i geografiia vynuzhdennykh migratsii v SSSR*. Moskva.
Provintsiia kak realnost i obiekt osmysleniia. Materialy konferentsii 29.8.–1.9.2001. Tver. Tver.
Razumova, I. A. 2001: *Potaiennoie znaniie sovremennoi russkoi semi. Byt. Folklor. Istoriia*. Moskva.
Rossiia v izgnanii: Sudby rossiiskikh emigrantov za rubezhom. Moskva 1999.
Russkaia provintsiia: mif – tekst – realnost. Moskva – Sankt-Peterburg 2000.
Russkiie: Etnosotsiologicheskiie ocherki. Moskva 1992.
Russkiie bez Otechestva: Ocherki antibolshevistskoi emigratsii 1920–1940-kh godov. Moskva 2000.
Sandomirskaya, I. 2001: *Kniga o Rodine. Opyt analiza diskursivnykh praktit*. Vena.
Segal, A. 1993. *An Atlas of international migration*. London Melbourne: Hans Zell.
Shashkov, V. Ya. 1996. *Raskulachivaniie v SSSR i sudby spetspereselentsev (1930–1954)*.

Murmansk.
Shashkov, V. Ya. 2000: *Repressii v SSSR protiv krestian i sudby spetspereselentsev Karelo-Murmanskogo kraia.* Murmansk.
Skarenkov, A. K.1987: *Agoniia beloi emigratsii.* Moskva 1987.
Spetspereselentsy v Khibinakh. Apatity 1997.
Targiainen, M. A. 2001: *Ingermanlandskii izlom. Borba ingermanlandskikh finnov v grazhdanskoi voine na Severo-Zapade Rossii (1918–1920 gg).* Sankt-Peterburg.
Yardintsev, N. M. 1882: *Sibir kak koloniia.* Sankt-Peterburg.
Zemskov, V. N. 1990: *K voprosu repatriatsii sovetskikh grazhdan.* In: Istorija SSSR 4/1990.
Zemskov, V. N. 1991: "Kulatskaia ssylka" v 30-ie gody. In: *Sotsiologicheskiie issledovaniia* 10/1991.
Zemskov, V. N. 1994: Spetsposelentsy. 1930–1950 gg. In: *Naseleniie v Rossii v 1920 – 1950-ie gody: chislennost, poteri, migratsii.* Moskva.

Fieldwork materials in Apatity, Monchegorsk and Kirov in the Kola Peninsula and in Petrozavodsk and Saint-Petersburg in 2001–2002.

ALLA SOKOLOVA

Contemporary images of the shtetl amongst the Ukrainian population of urban-type settlements and villages of Podolia[1]

A visit to a small town located nearby, on market and fair days, or to a parish church on religious holidays prompted a merging, in the consciousness of village dwellers, of town images and architectural environment, which led to the formation of ideas about the structure of town space. The market square or street is the major functionally and semantically significant element of the structural arrangement of the commercial centre in a town.[2] Its architectural environment, coloured by the holiday revelry of fairs, allowed the city to appear, in the eyes of peasants, as a land of abundance, archetypically related to the "other world" (Propp 1986: 290). Cult buildings are important dominants of the spatial and structural arrangement of a town, they determine its silhouette, so that in some contexts the image of a town, the parish centre of an area, and that of a temple, were, basically, indistinguishable.[3]

Although for the inhabitants of town suburbs and neighbouring villages the image of the town was not exclusively limited to town fortifications, the latter remained the key element for the semantic designation of a city as an "alien" space. At the same time, city fortifications and landscape borders that provided the isolation of the town space raised an "ideal town-dweller" for whom the opposition inside/outside was understood not so much as inside/outside of one's own house, but as "in the city/outside of the city".[4]

Resettlement from a village into a town (even if this city was only a local commercial centre) may be seen as a transitional situation, which propels the mechanism of "accumulation, by the space, of the (new) content" (Baiburin 1983: 19). A "new town-dweller", even if he regularly visited a given city while living in its suburbs or in the nearest village, re-considered the semantic marking of the town's spatial structure. A "new town-dweller" needs to comprehend the town previously mastered by him as an "alien" space, in relation to the quality of his own world.

It is clear that the deeper the socio-cultural differences were between the population of a town and the town area, the more acutely the countrymen felt the "alien" character of the town habitat.[5] The more unusual the look of the town streets and squares were for them, the stronger the "new town-dwellers" became interested in dialogue with the carriers of the tradition of town life, or, in case these "new town-dwellers" considered this tradition devalued, in the fundamental reconstruction of the material and spatial environment that they were mastering, in its interpretation according to their current sociocultural assumptions.

The subject of this research is the process of mental adaptation by the Ukrainian, mostly rural, population of the living environment of urban-type settlements – former small towns or townships in Podolia, and the style of life, the image of which was, till the beginning of the XX century, determined by the basic principles of the patriarchal life of the Jewish commune.

Participation of Jews in the urbanization of the region

The urbanization of Podolia in the second half of the XVI through to the beginning of the XVII c. had been organized under a script tested in Poland: the leading role was allocated to immigrants who were invited to the region, who possessed trade skills and conducted craft activity. A new period of construction of castles and fortified towns started after the influential Polish and Lithuanian clans managed to take hold of extensive grounds in this territory.

Owners of the cities that had been established on important commercial routes aspired to receive income from custom charges and the sale of local agricultural and cattle-breeding production on international markets. Implementation in Podolia of the legal norms already adopted in the towns of Western and Central principalities of Poland and Lithuania made resettlement much more attractive for the merchants and craftsmen who had been well acquainted with these norms. Jews were among the first re-settlers to be invited to the towns of Podolia from *Chervonnaya Rus*[6] and *Volyn*[7].

The formation and growth of Jewish communes in Podolia were directly connected with the intensive urbanization of the territory. In Podolia, the same way as in *Chervonnaya Rus* and *Volyn*, the economic life of Jews in the XVI–XVII c. "was developing with more diversity compared to Poland Minor and Grand Poland, were the major occupation of the Jewish population (at that time) was the loaning of money" (Vishnitser & Shipper 1914: 248). Jews were leaseholders of townships and villages, of estates, mills, ponds and apiaries that belonged to mighty Polish landowners.[8] In Podolia, Jewish communes participated in all forms of economic life: they obtained permission from authorities to "participate in any enterprise, whether in trade or in handicraft, together with the town"[9] (RYA Ch. 1.¹ 62). They combined trade and intermediary activity.

The reason for the successful competition of Jews with the towns' petty bourgeoisie, especially in privately owned towns, was economic cooperation between landowners and Jews, which allowed the Jewish religious commune to turn into a "legally acknowledged corporation" (Antonovich 1869: 88).

Leasing activities made relations between Jews and peasants more complex. The feeling of dependence upon a Jew, a leaseholder, acquired hypertrophied forms in Ukrainian folklore: Jews "plundered the whole world, seized the light of the sun, and the keys to paradise".[10] Social, ethno-cultural and confessional distinctions prompted sharp recurrent conflicts between the Ukrainians living in villages and town suburbs, and the Jews.[11] The cost for their intermediary role in the system of feudal exploitation was the destruction of the majority of Jewish communes in Podolia during the Cossacks-and-peasant wars. This was accompanied by the demolition and devastation of towns.[12]

Systematic restoration of small town trade centres in Podolia began in the XVIII c.[13] At this time, Jews composed the majority of re-settlers from the town of Chervonnaya Rus and Volyn. Landowners, interested in the restoration of the trade centres' system, concluded various leasing agreements with the new settlers,[14] granted them the rights of propination (production and sale of alcoholic drinks), and of trade, including their own artisan products[15]. Newly established Jewish communes became the legal successors of the communes which had perished during the Cossack-and-peasant wars.

In a description of the Vinnytsya district of the Podolia province, written in 1799 shortly after Podolia, following the divisions of Poland, became a part of the Russian Empire, it is said that "generally settlers are land-tillers, and the Jews are merchants, handicraftsmen, but the richest of all are tavern owners and distillers" (RSHA, Fund 1350, Inventory 312, File 216 (1), Sheet 3). Ukrainians lived on the margins of the city centre, in suburbs and villages.[16] Until nowadays, it is a custom to call some of these villages Polish[17].

Several Jewish families, or at least one Jewish family (of a Jew who leased the tavern, the property of a landowner[18]) lived in every village virtually. As a rule, they were engaged in the purchase of peasant production surpluses and the delivery of goods produced in townships to villages. All Jews living in villages were ascribed to the commune of the closest township. It should be little wonder that the Russian authorities regarded Jews as a separate estate, urban by nature (Klier 2000: 119).

Already by the beginning of the XVIII c. the compact residence of Jews in town centres contributed to the rise and spread of the notion that the Jewish population predominates in small towns of Podolia.[19] This notion influenced the formation of the residence pattern. In small towns and townships the desire of the Jews engaged in trade and crafts to live in the districts close to the market did not contradict the need of the Jewish commune for the organization of a separate place of living that could provide for the possibility of cultural self-isolation. The fact that the borders of a shtetl coincided with those of the commerce-and-crafts centre contributed to the isolation of the former from Ukrainian suburbs. At the end of XIX c., it was possible to say that in each small town in Podolia its commercial centre "was inhabited primarily by Jews who enlivened its inner life and invigorated trade and industry…", whereas "remote streets, or, to put it better, localities … inhabited by the Ukrainian population, … looked rather like villages" (Afanasiev (Chuzhbinskyi) 1893: 255).

A dense network of commercial townships was a landmark of the Western provinces, formed on the territories annexed to Russia as a result of the divisions of Poland; the presence of this network differed in these territories from the Russian provinces with their dispersed structure of residence with a predominance of rural residential organization. Linked to terminology based on Polish administrative division, the term *township* was preserved as a designation of small commercial settlements in the Western territories. From a socio-cultural perspective, townships differed dramatically from urban settlements in the central provinces where small cities were not so much centres of trade, but rather administrative centres.

Already by the beginning of the XIX c., the term *mestechko* (township) in the Russian language had acquired the meaning of "Jewish township" (*evreiskoe mestechko*).[20] The term *shtetl* ("a small town" in Yiddish), suggested by the American ethnologist M. Zborovskyi, contains the meaning of the socio-cultural space within the limits of the commercial centre of a small town or a township in the territory of Eastern Europe. The life of the majority of Jewish communes up until the Second World War evolved precisely in shtetls.

Impoverishment of Podolian townships, as well as the whole Western territory of the Russian Empire, was caused by the destruction of the system of regulated economic connections. This happened as a result of shortsighted decisions taken by the Russian administration that poorly understood the structure of economic relations in the annexed lands (Klier 2000: 233).[21] Because the estimation of the role of Jews in the economy of the annexed regions was erroneous, no attempts by the Russian authorities to integrate Jews into the existing city estates could be consistent and successful. Overpopulation of shtetls, as well as unemployment of their population, increased after the introduction in 1882 of the so-called "Temporary rules" that existed till 1917. According to these rules, Jews were prohibited to live not only in villages, but also in the suburbs of towns and townships; the lease and purchase of real estate in the countryside were also forbidden.

The numerous pogroms of 1905 caused mass emigration of Jews from Russia. The pogroms during the civil war would have been seen as the reason for the final crash of prosperity in shtetls,[22] if only they had not been followed by the destruction of the market economy, which doomed shtetls to economic catastrophe. After the establishment of Soviet rule (1920), trade and domestic crafts remained the basic source of income for many Jewish families, so the prohibition of private trade and nationalization not only of large enterprises, but also small artisan workshops during military communism deprived the majority of the Jewish population living in townships of a source of income and their civil rights in the new society. Trying to rescue themselves from poverty and unemployment, the Jewish population of former townships fled to big cities, especially those lying beyond the pale.[23] Another solution to the problems of the declassed Jewish population in small townships was their transition to agriculture.[24]

During the years of the New Economic Policy (NEP), many craftsmen returned to their old trades although they could hardly endure the load of ever growing taxes. The NEP partly returned to the shtetl its pre-Revolutionary function based on the mechanism of economic self-organization of local commercial centres. Yet, by this time the traditional world of the shtetl, with all its values and foundations based on the patriarchal life, had been destroyed from within.

With the Bolsheviks in power, Jews found themselves a part of the national policy of the new state. In 1918, simultaneously with the creation of national sections in the Workers and Peasants Party of Bolsheviks, the Jewish section of the party and its local branches were created, and the Jewish Commissariat, also with its local departments, was established. Jewish political establishments and bodies with Yiddish as the language of office work conformed to the leading ideology and played their role in the implementation of revolutionary principles and the construction of a "new life" in former townships. Numerous Jewish communal establishments connected with social security were placed under their control. At schools where teaching was performed in Yiddish, anti-religious propaganda was conducted. During the anti-religious campaign of 1925, many synagogues and prayer houses were closed. Possibly, discussions between Zionists and communists, or the internal struggle in the Bolshevik party, and even the opposition of successful party functionaries and the traditionalists, "private owners", were perceived by the majority of the Ukrainian population of former townships as events of internal Jewish life. Childhood memoirs of this time preserved by many hereditary Ukrainian petty bourgeois, reflect upon their aspiration to join the Jews as the majority who dictated the style of life in an urban-type settlement (the majority of townships received this status in Soviet times), and through this perceive themselves as townspeople in the full sense of the word.

> I had friends among Jews..., because ours <Ukrainians> would think up something <would somehow deceive>, both now, and in earlier times: so I did not like to be friends <with them> and only <had friends> among Jews (A. A. Skibinskaya, b. 1915, Sataniv).[25]

For the majority of the Ukrainian population living in Soviet settlements, the image of a shtetl and the image of their settlement turned out to be links in the same chain.

Upon the curtailment of the NEP the shtetl ultimately lost its characteristics of a local trade and craft centre. At the turn of the 1920s, a transformation took place from a self-regulating urban body into a "residential annex" of an industrial enterprise (Senyavskiy 1999: 158–162). The Soviet urban-type settlement had to be an alternative to a township – "the town of the past". Soviet school manuals of the 1930s represented this town as "capitalistic slavery", in the image of Western cities.[26] Romantically coloured theoretical constructions by architects about the ideal socialist "city-garden" of the 1920s were scattered after they came into contact with the strategy of "extensive socialist construction". Enforced industrialization of the region demanded the mobilization of the major bulk of its population, that is its peasantry. Characteristic features of the organization of the city-type settlements were, to a large extent, determined by the nature of industrialization and its submission to the rigid centralized state regulation. In practice, urbanization was a by-product of industrialization, and urban-type settlements were halls of residence for industrial enterprises.

The social infrastructure that determined the quality of living space in urban-type settlements was formed in accordance with the "principles of leftovers". Minimization of expenses for social needs and low standards of living utilities, combined with the idea of "collectivization" of life (a separate house was seen as a representation of "petty bourgeois way of life"), left a corresponding stamp on the look of urban-type settlements.

The Second World War became the boundary by which the style of life appropriated to the new social pattern started to be perceived as the only possible one. Traditions of shtetl life, and thus the cultural codes of its historical architectural environment with its strongly pronounced ethno-cultural specificity, were ultimately depreciated both in the eyes of the hereditary Ukrainian petty bourgeoisie and of post-war migrants from villages.

The ordinary layout of a shtetl differed drastically from that of Ukrainian streets in the suburbs (Sokolova 2000: 48–49). Till the beginning of the XX century, the house-building practice of small cities in the Russian Empire was determined not so much by the officially recognized norms and standards, but by the cultural concepts of the proper house construction found within popular culture.[27] Construction of a house, even if it was conducted by a small cooperative association (*artel*), was fully supervised by the house owner. The artisan character of construction provided for a continuity of house-building traditions.

Contrary to a Ukrainian petty-bourgeois house, a Jewish house representative for the ordinary layout of a shtetl experienced virtually no influence on the part of house-building traditions from the rural suburbs. Shtetl culture "canonized" the basic architectural features of the Renaissance burgher house intended, first and formost, for trade-and-craft activities and only secondarily for residence; these features were seen to correspond to the appropriate organization of a Jewish house.

The fact that the traditional culture of Polish-Lithuanian Jewry belonged to the European urban civilization determined the choice of a medieval fortified city as the paradigm for a shtetl. Isolation of the shtetl planning structure, a high density of ordinary building, and the "interior" character of street spaces performed the role of morphological attributes that determined the specificity of a shtetl's architectural environment.

Notwithstanding the long period of de-urbanization in Podolia, a conservatism of popular culture allowed the shtetl to reproduce the morphology of an urban architectural environment even in proto-urban formations to which, according to the level of their economic development and the quality of construction, the majority of shtetls belonged. In this connection, the opinion of the author of the ethnographical-statistical review of Podolia province (1849) seems to be quite justified: "a Jew preserves the character of a town-dweller even there where there are no towns" (ARGS Category 53, Inventory 1, File 3, P. 12).

Re-settlers from the neighbouring villages, who in post-war years rushed into urban-type settlements and district centres in search of work, received state apartments in the nationalized houses that before the war belonged to Jews. New owners did not consider these houses a constant dwelling place, and did not properly maintain them. Nowadays, the majority of these houses are in a dilapidated condition, dumps often form on the place of fallen houses.

Till very recently, a small-sized apartment in a four- or five-storied apartment house constructed in the 1950–1970s was the embodiment of the dream of an ideal dwelling for the majority of the population in urban-type settlements and regional centres. With regular turn-offs of water and electricity that became very common in the 1990s it is clear for everyone that an apartment in such a house is a considerably inferior standard of living compared to a one-storey house on a personal plot of land.

Substantial fragments of the traditional ordinary buildings of the former shtetls are preserved on the territory of Podolia that was a part of the Romanian occupation zone where no actions of mass extermination of Jews were conducted (According to present-day administrative division this includes a number of districts in the Vinnytska and the Odeska regions). Here the replacement of the Jewish by the Ukrainian population acquired a precipitous character only in the 1990s, with the beginning of mass immigration to Israel, USA and Germany.

Nowadays, when the model of the urban-type settlement of the "socialist construction" epoch is destroyed and partly discredited, the process of formation of an acceptable model of life for a small city prompts the revival of interest in shtetl traditions, both among hereditary Ukrainian petty bourgeoisie and among the "new town-dwellers", natives of neighboring villages.

Imagining a shtetl as an "alien" space – image of a town as "another world" in contemporary representations of a shtetl

Typological similarity allows most different urban settlements, irrespective of their size and architectural-topographical organization (i. e. both a capital and a "market township"[28]), to act in folklore texts as a ritual "king of cities" situated "in between villages" (Yerofeeva 1996: 274–275). Obviously enough, a town appears in the image of "another world" due to its isolation, its de-territorialization.

The idea that urban settlements possess a past of their own, a past that is only partly connected to the past of the region, is widely spread among the inhabitants of urban-type settlements and district centres that prior to the establishment of the Soviet rule had the status of a town or a township. The origin of such cities is usually attributed to some extraordinary, outstanding event that happened in "ancient times", e.g. the Turkish invasion. (As a result of the assault of the Ottoman Empire upon Poland, Podolia was under Turkish rule from 1672 till 1699).

In traditional consciousness, urbanization is not seen as a natural process caused by the requirements of civilizational development of the territory.[29] The role of demiurges, the giants of the epic "time immemorial" are played by the "Turks". It is generally believed that the "Turks" not only dug underground tunnels, but erected all ancient "monumental" buildings and constructions: castles, churches, Roman cathedrals and synagogues.

> Once Turks lived here. The Turks were building huge cellars here in Sharhorod, such passages that <they could> speak over the river …

There are full <of them> under the houses..., the Turks lived, but it was before I can remember (N. A. Loyanich, b. 1931, Sharhorod. Rec. by A. Sokolova, 2001).

[The fortress] was built by the Turks. Starting from the river over there – this way – there is an underground tunnel, yes <...> This is a Turkish fortress and the banks. [It is called] "Turkish fortress", that's it (N. A., b. 1926, Sataniv).

There were Turks here... They built churches, very strong houses they were building... They built the church and the synagogue. So many shells struck (there was war) – there are holes, <they> but couldn't destroy <them> (A. A. Skibinskaya, b. 1915, Sataniv).

The origin of the name of the Podolian town Sataniv is customarily related to a phrase from the ""Turkish" language: "*sat aut non?*" (shall we stop or not)"[30]. The ancient nature of the town is the only fact of historical significance for the local rural population: Sataniv is a historical place. Hundred times it was ruined, and hundred times rebuilt... They say, it is older than Moscow in history. (N. A., b. 1926, Sataniv.)

In a certain sense Jews are seen as the successors of the Turks.

Grandmother said: Minkivtsi is a Turkish town. Since that time <there is> an underground tunnel: from the Orthodox cemetery through all of Minkivtsi... When the Turks left for the village of Gorodiska, Jews settled in Minkivtsi. (L. Yakshina, b. 1959, Minkivtsi. Rec. by A. Sokolova, 2001.)

It is widely believed that Jews always lived in the towns of Podolia – from the beginning of "historical" times, separated from epic times by the "Turkish

Panorama of Sataniv. A view of the synagogue from the Jewish cemetery. (Photo: A. Sokolova 2001)

Cellar of the Jewish house located near the synagogue in Sataniv. (Photo: A. Sokolova, 2001)

invasion". However, the "ancient" character of shtetls[31] is not seen by Ukrainians as sufficient grounds to consider Jews "aboriginal inhabitants".

> It seems to me that the first ones <who were> here were the Poles ... Because we have a lot of Poles. In Sataniv – very few, but in all surrounding villages – only the Poles. They are like aboriginal inhabitants... In the town there are few of them, probably because Jews lived here... So they settled nearby. (L. I. Leibina, b. 1946, Sataniv. Rec. by A. Sokolova, 2001.)

It would seem that the necessary condition for an ethnic group to acquire such a status was its engagement in agricultural production.[32] Therefore, the Poles are considered to be aboriginals.[33] The "Poles" are only nominally "others", the real aliens are Jews and Gypsies.

The hereditary Ukrainian petty bourgeoisie preserve a respectful attitude towards agricultural activity even though they realize that they themselves do not belong to the social group for which it was the basic occupation. They recognize that a somewhat ironic attitude towards them on the part of rural inhabitants is fair.

> Till nowadays <they> tease <us> – hey, you were petty bourgeoisie... Well, they distribute land – take as much as you want. This one takes, that one takes, but somebody does not <take>. <The majority disapproves> – you, petty bourgeoisie. (L. I. Leibina, b. 1946, Sataniv. Rec. by A. Sokolova, 2001.)

"Cat-eaters from Minkivtsi. We bought everything. Since we buy, we are cat-eaters ..." (V. F. Maisryuk, b. 1924, Minkivtsi. Rec. by A. Sokolova, 2001).

The majority of the inhabitants of small towns and district centres do not feel themselves to be successors of the tradition of the urban style of life. It is indicative that memorial stone steles erected by Polish magnates in their towns (e.g. in Medzhibozh and Tulchi), called in local history sources "pillars of Magdeburg Law"[34], are called "Turkish". The XVIII c. building of the town hall in Horodivka is generally called the "Turkish jail". All constructions symbolizing independence of the town's self-government, as well as all other constructions where the purpose of which is either unknown or unclear are considered to be "Turkish". The notion "closeness to the land" is highly valued in the Russian, and later in the Soviet "literary" culture and contributed to a strengthening of the corresponding criterion in the evaluation of "us or them".

The senior generation of hereditary Ukrainian petty bourgeoisie identified Jews as an ethnic group whose adherence to the urban way of life was a specific cultural feature. "Where there are three Jews, there is a township" says one Ukrainian proverb.[35] It is thought that without Jews there would have been no urban life at all.

> When they appeared ... they had always been here. Verbovets was considered to be a town. Here Jews had always been around... Q.: Is it so that in every town there were Jews? A.: Yes, in Kurylivtsy, in Ushitsa..., but in villages there were none of them... Nobody lived. (S. I. Hladyi, b. 1927, Verbovets.)

The same picture of residence patterns is drawn by Jews:

> Jews in Pischanka – nobody lived on the outskirts ... <they> lived only in the centre... When you move outside of Pischanka, there in the villages... Jews never lived <there>... That direction, to the Jewish cemetery, around there no Jews ever lived. (A. I. Kushnir, b. 1936, Pischanka. Rec. by A. Sokolova, 1998.)

Their individual memoirs stated that till the XIX c. there were at least several Jewish families living in every village virtually and, even more so, in the suburbs, both Jews and Ukrainians, present exceptions that prove the rule: Jews are town-dwellers.[36]

The idea of the absolute de-territorialization of a shtetl, the successor of the "Turkish town" lies at the core of this notion and allows a shtetl to perform the role of the "other world". This image required that the place occupied by a shtetl be clearly defined, which probably explains the characteristic way of "rounding off" the shtetl borders, used both by the Jews and the Ukrainians. Shtetl boundaries are expanded till they reach the most prominent landscape borders, such as a river or a pond.

> Where we were at Dodic, there was a Jewish street there, here there was a Jewish street, the Jewish centre was <here>... A Jewish family lives down there ... close, to the church. This is the end, Jews never lived further down... Already there, where there is the pond, no Jews ever lived there. (A. I. Kushnir, b. 1936, Pischanka. Rec. by A. Sokolova, 1998.)

> On the other side of the river – everything was Jewish there... They <lived> in a heap <over there>. (B. I. Ridvjansky, b. 1919, Verbovets.)

When discussing past life in a small town or a township, Ukrainians usually use the term *misto* (town) to designate the commercial centre built-up by Jewish houses, and when they speak Russian, they say "township".[37] "That's how it was said: let's go to the misto. Centre, that's what is called misto" (L. T. Kuzevitch, b. 1929, Sataniv. Rec. by O. Belova, V. Petrukhin, 2001). "And in the centre of everything – Jews lived there all the time" (N. A., b. 1926, Sataniv).

> I was small. When I wanted to buy something, mother wouldn't let me go to the *misto*: <she> says, Jews will grab you, throw into a barrel, twist you, take your blood. That's how she frightened me. I would never go to the misto, for I was afraid. (S. I., b. 1927, Verbovets. Rec. by A. Sokolova, 2001.)

Basically all stories about the past contain a plot centring around "Jewish gold":

> Our church was rich, gilded. So that everything was gilded, utensils and icons. Jews had a lot of gold. Our people didn't understand that it was gold. "Catherine's coins" – these were pennies, big and new. Jews had gold, and we bought <it> from Jews and gilded <things>. (A. A. Skibinskaya, b. 1915, Sataniv.)

In folklore, a city is quite often "stamped" with the mark of "the other world" (Propp1986: 285). The assumption that the whole spectrum of corresponding symbolic meanings is being projected upon the town (Khrenov 1996: 30–32) seems to be true in respect to a shtetl as well.

The presence of various stores is an important mark of abundance for a big town. Everybody agrees that a shtetl was a world of abundance owing to the fact that all stores in it belonged to Jews. "If Jews would be <here> now, our stores would be full" (I. A. Kruplyak, b. 1916, Murafa). To order a suit at a Jewish tailor's, to shoe a horse at a Jewish smithy, or to receive medical treatment from a Jewish doctor – this all seems to have been typical of life in the past, yet to buy goods on credit in a Jewish shop, or to borrow money from a Jew were wonderful things that disappeared together with the Jews.

> It was very difficult to live. Had it not been for Jews, we would have been lost. They gave <money> for a year, for a month, or two months, so <we> paid back little by little and so we lived. (A. A. Skibinskaya, b. 1915, Sataniv.)

It is widely believed that in contrast to Ukrainians, Jews lived easily, and easily parted with their goods and money.

> They were, by what I know from my grandmother, they were... If you come to them in a difficult moment and ask <for something>, they will never refuse..." (L. P. Kolonchuk, b. 1963, Sataniv. Rec. by A. Sokolova, 2001).

Jewish wealth, acquired through cunning rather then real work, seemed to be inexhaustible. This stands in full correspondence with the notions of abundance to be found in the "other world".

> They were sly people, <the Jews> – working – no... Ivan works, and they... <don't>. Where there were Jews, life was rich. (V. S. Hladiy, b. 1917, Verbovets).

Not only in the rural environment, but also among the hereditary petty bourgeoisie only work on the land is considered to be "real" work. During Soviet times, craftsmen and tradesmen were declared "parasites". The same people who speak about Jewish "specialists", shoemakers and smiths, specify that "they did not like to work. Just allow them to sell and <deal with> money..." (A. T. Logvinchuk, b. 1910, Sataniv. Rec. by A. Sokolova, 2001).

It is widely believed that "commerce ... may be natural with them <the Jews>, it was probably handed down <to them> through generations..." (I. A. Kruplyak, b. 1916, Murafa). Commerce is considered a traditional Jewish way of live. That is why motifs of Jewish adherence to commerce, as well as of their responsibility for the crucifixion of Christ, intertwine in Ukrainian stories about the everyday life of a shtetl.

> ...he was Jewish, yes. And he was baptized at 32, he was circumcised, and then baptized, for he thought to himself that Orthodox faith was better ... and <he was> a hard worker... Jews ... they only know how to buy, to resell – that's what they did. They didn't understand what it means to work on land. So, they started to torture him. (A. A. Skibinskaya, b. 1915, Sataniv.)

Sometimes informants directly connected Jewish cunning, which allows them to become rich, with their knowledge of "all languages" (B. I. Ridvyansky, b. 1919, Verbovets). It is only an illiterate person whom they can outwit or deceive: "– So you lived among them and learned the language? – I understand everything, Jews will not deceive me... I can read..." (Yu. S. Reznik, b. 1929, Murafa). For our informants, commercial activity may seem to represent ritual Jewish practices, it provides for the transmittance of special "knowledge" necessary for the accumulation of gold. "Jewish gold" performs the role of an object received from ancestors (i. e. brought from the world of the dead) and possesses the wonderful quality of being able to provide eternal abundance (Propp 1986: 284).

> Somehow they all had gold. I do not know how, either it was transferred from the forefathers <or...> It was not without reason that <in olden times> Sharhorod was called Little Istanbul – it was a commercial centre.[38] All Jews were engaged in commerce at that time. (A. I. Boyarskaya, b. 1941, Sharhorod. Rec. by A. Sokolova, 2001.)

Therefore, awareness as to where one should keep "gold" constitutes an important part of "knowledge".

> I asked Genya Aronovna about gold. (At our place <it was hidden> in the foundation of the house. Well, but how does one get there afterwards?) She says, us, Jews, didn't hide gold too far... <In there houses they> had such niches, so that one wouldn't see it ... but they always knew and could take it any time. (L. I. Leibina, b. 1946, Sataniv. Rec. by A. Sokolova, 2001.)

A campaign for the confiscation of gold and silver coins from the Jewish population (1930), called by the people the "gold rush", could have partly been provoked by the idea that the accumulation and storage of gold is inherent to all Jews without exception, irrespective of the level of their well-being. In the course of this campaign, almost the whole Jewish adult male population was subjected to the torture-chamber of the Chief Political Administration. In the majority of Jewish houses still preserved but left without supervision the hearths are broken (both ovens and heating furnaces, built into partitions between rooms). People used to search for hidden treasures – hiding places for gold. This can be explained by a notion, widely spread both among the Ukrainians and the Jews, that the hearth is the most appropriate place in the house for hiding treasures. Everybody believes that the destruction of the hearth portends trouble for those living in the house.

Both in Jewish houses and in the houses of the Ukrainian petty-bourgeoisie a manhole would be made under the mouth of the oven. Cellars and underground courses is an important motif both in Jewish and in Ukrainian folklore:

> ...they used to dig here, under Kopaihorod, when the Turks were here. See, they built a store here, and all of a sudden there was a hole beneath, and the store could tumble down there... Scary, isn't it. It is scary to walk in Kopaihorod because of those ... those Turkish underground <tunnels>. (D. I. Yatskova-Kreymer, b. 1924, Kopaigorod.)

Ukrainians believe that cellars, constructed by the Turks, were appropriated by Jews for their trade activity: "Each of their <Jewish> houses had a cellar. There they <kept> all kinds of wines and beers" (A. T. Logvinchuk, b. 1910, Sataniv. Rec. by A. Sokolova, 2001). "Continuous underground cellars. <They stretch> under my house downwards and also to the side. Jews used to know some kind of passages there." (husband of L. I. Leibina, b. 1948, Sataniv. Rec. by A. Sokolova, 2001). It is believed that Jews knew how the system of underground passages was structured. After having built a house on the place where a Jewish house used to be, Ukrainians could not feel totally confident. "There is a cellar beneath our house, it stretches far over there. We closed it up, for it was scary to go there." (L. I. Leibina, b. 1946, Sataniv. Rec. by A. Sokolova, 2001).

Evaluation of a shtetl layout and the architecture of Jewish houses based on traditional Ukrainian notions of Jews and their customs

At the present moment there are not many people who would wish to live in Jewish houses. The main reason for this is the absence of kitchen gardens on the territories of former shtetls.

> Here on the Jewish <plot> ... there is no garden, no nothing... <There is enough space> only to built a house <on the place of the old Jewish house>, that's all. When one builds <a house>, one wants to have a piece of garden. (N. A. Loyanich, b. 1931, Sharhorod. Rec. by A. Sokolova, 2001.)

A kitchen garden close to the house, even if it's a small garden plot, is necessary for a rural person to develop the feeling of "inner freedom", of a comfortably organized living space. "I need a household, I need more freedom... We can't <live> without a kitchen garden. Me not having a vegetable bed?" (G. Kalko, b. 1951, Kopaihorod). A dense layout on the territory of the old commercial centre, once compactly populated by Jews, is one of the most prominent marks of life in the past, known even in those places where no pre-war construction is preserved.

> – Here, this was a Jewish street – and the houses here were very close to each other...
> – Have you been told about this?

Empty Jewish house in Sharhorod. The building is in an emergency condition. (Photo: A. Sokolova 1993)

> – They say so. My parents, my grandmother – they all were local dwellers.
> (L. P. Kolonchuk, b. 1963, Sataniv. Rec. by A. Sokolova, 2001.)

"All houses starting from the sugar factory till here <were Jewish> ... One could walk on the roofs, <so densely they stood>, one house to another." (N. A., b. 1926, Sataniv.) Descriptions of the compact dwellings of Jews are quite often accompanied by attempts to explain this phenomenon. A "rational" explanation about "Each one wishing to have an exit to the street for the sake of merchandise" (A. I. Boyarskaya, b. 1941, Sharhorod. Rec. by A. Sokolova, 2001) is given very seldom.

It is generally believed that close kin relations allowed Jews not to think about the arrangement of private space around their houses:

> As soon as I finished to build <a house> – all this belongs only to me. They <the Jews> would gather together, four to six people approximately, <and this was> something like an assembly, probably, <they were> relatives. (M. A. Kovalsky, b. 1951, Verbovets.)

> When they were choosing a place <to built a house>, they wanted all their relatives, all their nation to be around (I. A. Kruplyak, b. 1916, Murafa).

According to the common notion, Jews treasured their kinship relations, which allowed them to count upon the help of their neighbours-relatives in a difficult situation. The compact manner of construction, traditional for shtetls, made it possible to help neighbours out in the case of danger, and hence was highly treasured by Jews. "– Did Jewish houses differ from the Ukrainian ones? – They did, because they were placed one house next to another" (V. S. Hlady, b. 1917, Verbovets).

Many informants particularly stress the fact that Jews living close to one another could easily turn to each other because of narrow lanes that stretched between side facades of their houses: <There were> doors on the one side and on the other, just in case. <They would> share <something> to each other, tell secretly..." (M. V. Buryachenko, b. 1939, Sharhorod. Rec. by A. Sokolova, 2001). Close kinship ties, strengthened as a result of such a dense layout, allowed Jews to preserve "traditions", or, in other words, to transmit knowledge necessary for merchant activity.

> – Under one roof, like swallows, ... never abused each other, never had quarrels.
> – Why did they live so closely? Were they very poor?
> – Not poor, but <they had> such a big love... That how they learned <to live> from the patriarchs. (Yu. S. Reznik, b. 1929, Murafa.)

> Jews had, so to speak, such a tradition: houses should touch to each other, the same way as people should be, so to speak, devoted to each other the same way as their houses. This house, for example, and that one, and another one <were> close <to each other>. (M. V. Buryachenko, b. 1939, Sharhorod. Rec. by A. Sokolova, 2001.)

The attitude of Ukrainians to the dense layout of shtetls, so distinct from the sparse farmstead-like layout of the suburbs, is not unambiguous. Dense arrangement of houses is a sign of good neighborly relations inside the Jewish community, relations that "one can only envy", yet at the same time refusal to have garden plots testifies that Jews "didn't want land", which was unconditionally disapproved of both among people living in urban townships and in the villages.

> – They "heaped up" together <while building>.
> – Why so?
> – Our peasants – they worked, and they <Jews> <were engaged> in commerce.
> (B. I. Ridvyansky, b. 1919, Verbovets.)

> Here Jews lived one close to another. They say, one would empty garbage upon each other's head, ...so little space there was.
> (Leibin, b. 1946, Sataniv. Rec. by A. Sokolova, 2001).

Many Ukrainian informants, representatives of the senior generation, realize that "ancient" Jewish houses essentially differed from Ukrainian huts in their internal arrangement.[39] The fact that, except for the main entrance situated on the street façade, Jewish houses also had auxiliary entries leading from the kitchen through service rooms into side streets, is usually explained by the desire of cowardly Jewish dealers to provide for the possibility of flight to escape creditors or pogrom-instigator: – "These doors <led> here, and those <led> there. – Why so many doors? – I don't know why they made it so... They could run away through these doors." (S. D., b. 1923, Verbovets.) "Jewish houses always had two exits... The doors should be small, so as to make them unnoticeable". (A. A. Skibinskaya, b. 1915, Sataniv.) Jewish cowardice is mentioned in the descriptions of their everyday life. For instance, one informant, speaking about how he would come to his Jewish neighbors on Saturdays to turn on and off an oil lamp, observed that Jews spent too much lighting their rooms because of their inborn cowardice.

> You would come, turn on the lamp, and she would give you a candy. They burnt <lamps> every hour, for they were afraid..."
> (V. S. Hlady, b. 1917, Verbovets).

One cause of fear among Jews was a bell pealing. A Jewish funeral procession could and should not have moved to a cemetery when bells were ringing. Children and teenagers, upon noticing such a procession, would start to ring the bells in order to get "pay-off" candies from Jews.[40]

> They immediately throw down <a stretcher with the dead body>... let there be cars here ... throw on the road and scatter ... this direction and that one... They were very much afraid when the bell starts to ring. Our chimes are so loud. (A. A. Skibinskaya, b. 1915, Sataniv.)

The idea that a peal of bells causes panic among Jews finds correspondence with a widely spread belief that evil powers react in a similar way to a bell chiming (Vadeisha 1999: 202). For Ukrainians, Jews as ethnic neighbors were the most suitable candidates for the role of devils (Belova 2002: 198). This image of Jews was conducive for attempts to benefit from relationships with the Jewish community.[41] One can draw a conclusion that the way Jewish houses were placed in respect to each other, as well as the peculiar feature of their arrangement, strengthened traditional Ukrainian concepts of Jews being born tradesmen, sly and cowardly people.

A Jewish house did not correspond to the image of a "proper" house for Ukrainians, not only because of a large number of entries and exits,[42] but also because this house, due to the main entrance being on the street façade, was, in their opinion, too closely connected to the street.[43]

> The first room opens up straight out <to the street> ... so that if it snows or rains – everything falls <into the room> (M. V. Buryachenko, b. 1939, Sharhorod. Rec. by A. Sokolova, 2001).

> – I even <said> once: one could add a small verandah here… <And they say> Let it be so, that's how we build… We were ordered <to build> in such a way – you enter and you find yourself right in the room.
> – What does it mean "they were ordered"?
> – Well, that's how they liked it, it was good for them this way … (A. A. Skibinskaya, b. 1915, Sataniv.)

In contrast to a Jewish dwelling, the houses of the Ukrainian petty bourgeoisie were always built behind a fence, in such a way that there was some distance between the house and the street. The structure of this house ascends to the model of a rural house – a hut "divided into two parts": the entrance, constructed on the longitudinal façade of the house, leads to the inner vestibule, and only from there into the rooms.

Peculiarities in the arrangement of traditional Jewish houses are quite often explained by the fact that Jews had to follow a specific building canon:

> – Did the Jews have such big hearths in their homes?
> – There was one hearth… Such a big love it was, that <they had> only one hearth, and here is one fire-place, and there – another one (Yu. S. Reznik, b. 1929, Murafa).

In our informants' opinion, obedient observance of a traditional house arrangement gave Jews the possibility to lead the very way of life they needed and which they "liked". Reconstruction of a Jewish house by its new owner usually means that the main entrance constructed on the street façade is blocked up.[44] As a result, the *auxiliary* exit leading from the service rooms into the side street becomes the main and only entrance into the house. Consequently, a thorough change in the whole ideology of the spatial structure of the house occurs. For the Jews, the old design was justified by the high status of the "Jewish street" space. "Actually, they <former owners, the Jews> had the front <street façade of the house> over there <to the street>,

House in Shargorod (late 19th century). Since 1922 till 1942 this building was owned by Moshe Shaevich Reifman. Photo of 1930s. Personal archive of A. Sokolova. In this photo one can see the front door entrance which led from the gallery to the hall. (Photo: A. Sokolova)

The Reifman's house reconstructed at the end of 1970 by its new Ukrainian owners. The front door entrance was blocked up (Photo: A. Sokolova 1998)

and I needed it here <to the garden plot>." (G. Kalko, b. 1951, Kopaihorod. Rec. by A. Sokolova, 2001.) A feeling of discomfort experienced by the new owners of Jewish houses was at times so strong that they would decide to destroy the house altogether in order to build the new one. "Such a big house, and such a wrong one... It was impossible to live <in it>. We started to build everything our own way." (M. V. Buryachenko, b. 1939, Sharhorod. Rec. by A. Sokolova, 2001.)

The repair of a house is often described in words that better correspond to the process of its destruction: "I came here, took an axe in my hands and <did> everything my own way ... The first thing I did, I just broke off all these." (A. A. Boyarskaya, b. 1941, Sharhorod. Rec. by A. Sokolova, 2001.) "Before I threw out and cleaned out <everything> there was this very heavy smell... even the stones were saturated with it" (G. Kal'ko, b. 1951, Kopaihorod). The "horrible smell" mentioned in some interviews, the smell issued by the walls of Jewish houses, is, according to Medieval European legends, a characteristic sign of devil's presence.[45] It is considered necessary for the new house owners to consecrate the former Jewish house. Some of the new owners, when the reconstruction is completed, perform the same type of ritual as is performed when people move into a newly built house. Others think this unnecessary.

> They took away everything ... there are only a table and a mirror left ... she left <the mirror> and asked <me> not to take it down for a year... They have such a sign... When I was moving in, I called the priest. He sprinkled the holy water, and that was it... and <now> I am living <here>. (V. N., Minkivtsi. Rec. by A. Sokolova, 2001.)

This motif of the "horrible" smell does not seem to contradict the belief that "Jews lived cleanly, hygienically" (A. A. Skibinskaya, b. 1915, Sataniv).

> What was good in them <the Jews>, <and> what I liked, <was that although> they were poor, <worked as> water-carriers, <they were> so unfortunate, so poor – <they were one> big family. <During> dinnertime – a separate place for everybody. With us people eat... <even> the rich ones ate all out of one big bowl. (A. T. Logvinchuk, b. 1910, Sataniv. Rec. by A. Sokolova, 2001.)

According to general opinion, Jewish houses were "nicer" inside than the Ukrainian ones, not only because Jews were richer, but because the level of their daily culture was higher. In their houses, new owners keep the furniture and other things that used to belong to the old proprietors, the Jews. Many of these things were unusual for the natives of neighboring villages and hence were regarded as objects of luxury. "They lived better: it <was> nice in the room – carpets... <they> had two, even three rooms, feather beds, pillows, all this they had <what other people> didn't know here" (A. A. Skibinskaya, b. 1915, Sataniv).

Judged by the conclusion above, in order to organize the house the way Jews did it, one had to possess special knowledge. It was probably considered possible to obtain this knowledge by means of establishing a dialogue with Jews. The majority of Ukrainian informants talk about how their Jewish neighbors treated them to matzah (ritual bread), and how they, in turn, invited the Jews to holiday meals, in order to point out close neighbourly relations. (We never heard such stories from Jews). This treating obviously had a symbolic significance; probably, the "new town-dwellers" saw it as a way to justify their intrusion into somebody else's semantically meaningful space.[46]

It seems that those things left in the house by its former owners after the house was sold were regarded by the new proprietors as the "share" allotted to them, they were a means of appropriation of the new place/space and way of life. To some extent these things performed the function of junk, left by the former owners for the new ones as a token, to wish them a rich life in the new place (M. V. Buryachenko, b. 1939, Sharhorod. Rec. by A. Sokolova, 2001). Probably, the things left, in the same way as junk, allowed the house to continue its life cycle (Kushkova 1999: 253): the new owners were given the possibility not to regard the purchased house as a new construction. A connection would be established between the old and the new owners of the house (sometimes it was postal correspondence); both sides were interested in this connection. Quite often, the former Jewish house owners, upon immigration abroad, hoped that from time to time they would be able to visit the gravestones of their relatives.

Mental designs of the territory of a former shtetl by re-settlers as a way of adaptation in an "alien" space – names and toponymics

Within the precincts of the small town or a township the names of the biggest localities are usually connected with their positioning in the landscape in respect to a shtetl, or *misto*: *Dolinishniy Kut* (Valley Quarter) – the lowest part of Sataniv, *Horishniy Kut* (Hill Quarter) – its upper part. Because this system coincides with the division of Sataniv into two parishes, it is still in effect today.

Another system of designation singled out various ethno-cultural enclaves of Sataniv: "Volokhi, Gypsy: Gypsy – that further over there. Here it is Gypsy, that's how <it was> called. Now that they say Gypsy, now they don't say <it this way>." (L. T. Kuzevich, b. 1929, Sataniv. Rec. by O. Belova, V. Petrukhin.) The second system is basically forgotten, possibly because the borders of the localities it refers to are completely effaced. In addition, whereas the system connected with the characteristic features of the landscape is more convenient for approximate designation of directions. In Verbovets, there is a mixed system of designation: *Vitranka, Meshany, Pidsi, Horyany* (M. A. Kovalsky, b. 1951, Verbovets). It is almost exclusively used for indication of the most significant direction from the *"misto"*: to the church, to the Catholic Church and to the cemetery (up the steep slope of the hill).

The fact that among other names of big settlement localities one comes across the name *Meshany* (lit. petty bourgeoisie) proves the assumption that the Ukrainian petty bourgeoisie were an ethnic enclave excluded from the limits of the *misto*, or shtetl.[47] In spite of the fact that the houses of the Ukrainian petty bourgeoisie differed from rural huts, informants do not include the street containing the houses of the petty-bourgeoisie to be within the limits of the "town centre".

The street where the Ukrainian petty bourgeoisie dwelt often has a special name connected with the trade they were engaged in, e.g. *Shevchikov* (Shoemakers') street in Sharhorod. It is indicative that the Jewish population also called this street a *Goishe Gas* (Non-Jewish street in Yiddish), which shows that Jews considered all other streets within the limits of the commercial centre to be Jewish.

The space of a shtetl had many more functionally significant directions and poles, than the suburbs, therefore a shtetl was divided into small localities – places. Such places were frequently named after an event of Jewish life, connected to it by a particular territory. For example, a small square in the centre of Sharhorod, where Jewish merchants would gather to discuss news and would bargain, was called the Stock Exchange.

The borders of many places were defined by streets that are still present nowadays, so that by the quality of the street names the names of such places are known to the majority of the population. The street that led to the place of Jewish ritual cattle butchery was called Slaughter. Hereditary petty bourgeoisie of the senior generation recall that the slaughterer was an important person for Jews, for he possessed special knowledge: "...and he could do it so: he hits a hen somewhere with such a sharp knife, and all its feathers fall down" (M. V. Buryachenko, b. 1939, Sharhorod. Rec. by A. Sokolova, 2001). The name of a well situated on the territory of the former market in Min'kivtsi – Jewish well, is well known, probably because it is still used today.

The hereditary petty bourgeoisie called the river flowing at the foot of the hill near the Jewish cemetery in Sataniv, *Shmaivka* – possibly, by the first word of the biblical verse "Hear, O Israel..." (Deut. 6: 4), i.e. "Hear, O Israel: The Lord our God, the Lord is one", which, as a symbol of faith, is a part of all prayers. The hereditary petty bourgeoisie remember that Jews would come to this small river on the holiday of Rosh-Hashanah (New year) and performed the custom called "Tashlikh" which symbolizes purification from sins. When they did this they would shake out bread crumbs from their pockets into the river "...there is such a holiday in the fall: they all go for prayer and whatever they have in their pockets, they throw this away" (A. A. Skibinskaya, b. 1915, Sataniv). The name of this river becomes known to those native of villages who have children of school age: due to communication with children of the same age, they master the new territory quicker, and learn the names of different places and stories connected with them.

A preserved synagogue building (or its ruins), as well as other monuments, serve for the orientation as a designation of a certain locus. With all this, the synagogue in Sharhorod, with a beverage plant in it, depending on the context, is called either a juice plant or a Jewish school/synagogue. The synagogue is looked upon as a cult building which is being incorrectly used. In one interview, the disapproval of such improper use was illustrated by stories about a church where a bakery had been constructed and about a synagogue which had been turned into a club. It is considered that in such cases "there is no way", in other words, the cause will not progress.

For the hereditary petty bourgeoisie, the major reference points for routes designation are long destroyed or rebuilt buildings that formerly presented functionally significant poles of spatial and planning structures of the centre, which defined the most important routes within the precincts of the settlement in the past.

this is already called *Old misto*, and previously the centre was here, …approximately where there <was> the old court building, over there, … now there is nothing but ruins there (N. A. Loyanich, b. 1931, Sharhorod. Rec. by A. Sokolova, 2001).

Toponymic designation of the micro-location of the shtetl was set by the names of Jews – proprietors of various trade and craft enterprises. "This was over there, near Yudki…, where Pesia's oil manufacture was situated. The name was Pesia, Pesia <was> Jewish." (M. V. Buryachenko, b. 1939, Sharhorod. Rec. by A. Sokolova, 2001.) The importance of such toponymic designation for the population of suburbs and neighboring villages was so big that it formed the basis for including the space and time of "misto" into the sacred biblical spatial-temporal continuum.

> Murafa … because there were two Jewish families: Mur – Shlema Mur and Moisha Mur, brothers. Old Shlema Mur lived there … in his honor Murafa was named, and on the mountain <lived> his brother Moisha Mur… Twelve generations of Israel lived here: Vaiman lived, and Reuben, <and> Isakhar … all names of the old generation… Benjamin, Dan, Gad…, Isakhar the dyer lived over there, and Reuben (from the generation of Reuben) was sewing on a sewing machine. (Yu. S. Reznik, b. 1929, Murafa.)

Presently, the network of territorial designation in the former shtetl is considerably larger. Some of its units were kept from the past, having acquired a different semantic coloring. For example, the place of a destroyed Jewish coaching-inn, a key element from the point of view of the planning structure, is occupied by a church. In Sataniv in the 1970s, the old storehouses were replaced by a department store, in Bershadi – by a hotel. Stories about deep underground caves that suddenly opened up during the construction of modern buildings are also common.

Contemporary deurbanization

According to the observation of Ukrainian neighbors, both during the period of 1920–1940 and in the post-war years Jews neither built themselves new houses nor repaired the old ones.

> – These houses are probably two hundred years old… I don't remember a single house to be under construction. All were already built.
> – And were they altered, reconstructed?
> – Jews did not <reconstruct>. They were getting ready to leave to their own land … all their intentions were there. Old Shlema, he left, lived up <to the departure> (Yu. S. Reznik, b. 1929, Murafa.)

These observations are quite precise. Renovation of the ordinary shtetl building after 1910 and up until the beginning of the Second World War was reduced to repair and reconstruction of dilapidated houses.[48] Not only did the pogroms of 1905 and 1919 cause mass Jewish emigration from Russia; the very idea of emigration, first as a way out from a desperate situation, and then as the only possible life perspective, determined for a very long period the character of everyday life for the majority of Jewish families.

Today, the majority of houses left without supervision by their owners who emigrated in the 1980s have turned into ruins or are almost completely destroyed. This is used as grounds when accusing the last generation of Jews for the impoverishment of the majority of settlements, former shtetls, and their transformation into villages.

> There was such an opinion: that they, the Jews would live in God knows what house... <The house> falls down over his head, but he <a Jew> would not repair it. Once the old Jewish owners had built it, and the generation that lived under the Soviet regime... <they> did not build. So they live – the house falls down over their head, and they constantly have a rest – sit on a bench, do not hurry anywhere. (A. I. Boyarskaya, b. 1941, Sharhorod. Rec. by A. Sokolova, 2001.)

According to general opinion, Jews always avoided house repair work and construction, as well as any other physical labor: "<They> did not build, the paid money. Jews were smart. They did not like to work and lived easily." (A. T. Logvinchuk, b. 1910, Sataniv. Rec. by A. Sokolova, 2001.) "... to whitewash the house himself – God forbid! Jews never did this, ...even the poor ones. For this purpose there were Ukrainian women. It was them who whitewashed <houses>." (A. I. Boyarskaya, b. 1941, Sharhorod. Rec. by A. Sokolova, 2001.)

The process of degradation that started in the 1920–1930s and continued in post-war times of small town settlements which had become district centres or urban-type settlements was caused by a complex set of socio-economical reasons. The majority of the Ukrainian population saw Jewish emigration as the reason for this process. At the same time the hereditary petty bourgeoisie of the older generation discuss the return of Jews, which for them would be connected with the restoration of the lost dynamism of town life.

The unpredictability of the post-perestroika decade, especially in contrast with the stagnation of the 1950–1970s, produces the most fantastic ideas to emanate from the economic dead impasse of the majority of urban-type settlements in Ukraine. Leaders of a historical-ethnographical expedition of St.Petersburg's Jewish University have often received suggestions from local leaders to establish business. The belief shared by the local level authorities about Jews being capable of attracting foreign investment to towns and settlements enforced and simplified the process of return of synagogues to Jewish communes (Beiser 2002: 51).

In those settlements where Jews live no more, or do not claim the preserved synagogue building, there is a widely spread conviction that one should turn these synagogues into museums with the financial support of Jews who emigrated abroad, first of all to the USA.[49] There is a belief that the appearance of a museum can act as bait for Jewish tourists. In the village of Minkivitsi, a former shtetl, a private house repaired several years ago by a Jewish person who is remembered there as a child and who now lives in the USA is called a "museum". Neighbours keep the keys of this completely empty "museum". The majority of the population in urban settlements recognizes the necessity to preserve the Jewish cemetery and to turn it into a memorial. The story about car accidents happening especially frequently on the road paved by Jewish tombstones "in Nazi times" is quite demonstrative at this respect. When local inhabitants mention that they started to graze cattle in the Jewish cemetery only "under German occupation" and "have been doing this ever since", this sounds like some form of an apology.

Conclusion

The estimation given by Ukrainians of the role Jews played in the life of the region in the past is contradictory. The traditional Ukrainian image of Jews, filled with horror of the demonized Jew counting his dishonestly accumulated gold in an underground cellar, are intertwined with idealized reminiscences of good neighborly relations with Jews. The destruction of Jews during Nazi occupation caused the appearance of folklore texts in which this destruction is inscribed into a biblical context.

> The Jews – why did Germans shoot them down? Because when they were crucifying Christ, <they> said that the sin is on us and on our children. When was it! <This> was a thousand years ago. And they said that the blood is on us and on our children. And that's what happened, and that's why they were shot down. (B. I. Ridvjansky, b. 1919, Verbovets.)

In the occupied territories, the destruction of Jews occured under the eyes of their nearest neighbors Ukrainians. The majority of the Ukrainian population that had survived the occupation felt a necessity to judge those reasons that led to the mass murder of Jews, arranged by German fascists. This has assisted in the creation of folklore texts in which the destruction of Jews is presented in a biblical context.

Such forms of memorization of the most important, from a common perspective, events is claimed for the provision of an indisputable generally accepted version of its comprehension. Not only does it provide integrity for a picture of the past, it also forms a strong basis for representations about predestination for the present. Comprehension of the presence and disappearance of the Jews is an initial point in designing the present for the overwhelming majority of inhabitants of former shtetls in Podolia. It is a way to gain some profit from the unclaimed Jewish inheritance.

Until nowadays, the ability to produce a couple of phrases in Yiddish is often seen as some form of "genteel manners"; knowledge of Jewish rituals is presented as proof of belonging to an urban estate. With all this, folklore narratives accentuate unattractive, from our informants' viewpoint, features of these rituals: instead of organizing a solemn funeral ceremony Jews carry the deceased person to the cemetery at a run; the canopy under which the bride and the groom stand during the wedding ceremony is raised "where there is ... a pile of dust <rubbish>, ...not on a clean <place>" (N. A. Loyanich, b. 1931, Sharhorod. Rec. by A. Sokolova, 2001).

> <They> would necessarily go to a place where <there was> a pile of rubbish...That's where they would perform the marriage... According to the tradition. There was no such a big pile there, but for some reason, to be rich, these bride and groom <one had to fulfill the wedding ceremony like this>, where there is a lot of rubbish. (M. V. Buryachenko, b. 1939, Sharhorod. Rec. by A. Sokolova, 2001.)

By pointing out the unattractive character of such a choice, informants stress their approval of the fact that Jews strictly followed ancient traditions, however strange they might be.[50] The preserved ordinary buildings of a shtetl are evaluated by the hereditary Ukrainian petty bourgeoisie and natives of nearby villages in a similar way.

According to the words of Sh. Ettinger, Jews in Russia constituted an "urban estate of "Western" orientation", yet with an extraordinary traditional culture that turned to the past and protected its separate existence (Ettinger 1993: 23). Preservation of the methods of compact ordinary construction in shtetls until the beginning of the XX c., of methods designed in the Medieval European town, proved to be an effective means of providing for the unique character of the shtetl, and thus presented a certain "defense" against borrowings.

As a result of considerable differences between Western and Russian urbanization,[51] in which Podolia found itself after the third division of Poland, the process of the introduction of urban culture of the Western type into small towns and townships was interrupted. Even if certain features of the way of life, seen first of all as Jewish from the outside and only then as urban by its nature, were borrowed by the Ukrainian petty bourgeoisie by the end of the XIX c. their trace was effaced by the beginning of the XX c. when the shtetl was turned into a Soviet settlement.

The result of the essential change of social reference points was that until nowadays it has been easier for the "new town-dwellers" to fundamentally reconstruct their historical object-and-space environment than to accordingly transform their socio-cultural views. The negative estimation of houses of the ordinary shtetl building, which prevails in their present-day descriptions, allows one to draw the conclusion that these houses have not been recognized as a valuable resource, neither by the Ukrainian population of former shtetls, or by authorities. The same conclusion can be made on the basis of the fact that traditional shtetl houses have been preserved until now only in those settlements of Podolia in which a proportion of the Jewish population managed to survive the war. Thus, investigation of preserved houses allows one to express a rather high opinion concerning the quality of the ordinary shtetl building at the end of XIX – the beginning XX c. This actually allows us to compensate for "a deviation from the facts" in the oral source which "gives us much more for understanding the past, than actually authentic stories" (Portelli 2003: 42).

The idea of the futility of any constructive activity, widely spread among the population of de-urbanized settlements, found expression in the choice of strategy for the mental appropriation of the space of the former shtetl. The destruction of a historical architectural environment that accompanied this process allows us to compare it with the "conquering of another world".

NOTES

1. Podolia is a historical and geographical name of the region, which, according to the present-day administrative division, covers the eastern part of the Khmelnytska, Vinnytska and the western part of Odeska regions of Ukraine. This research was conducted in settlements in the Vinnytska and Khmelnytska regions.
2. S. Kravtsov published a song recorded in the 1830s in the village of Kalnytsa: "There stands a pine tree in the middle of a market: / in the roots of a pine tree there are quails, / and the stump of the pine tree there are fierce bees. / And on the top of the pine tree there are black martens" as an example of "sacralization of a market place", its incorporation into the system of popular cosmological beliefs (Kravstov 1999: 57).
3. In his research on the symbolism of a town in Galicia S. Kravtsov cites the text of the song "Full of glory was our Lvov built. / Oi, Lado, Lado, Lado! / On three pillars established, / And the forth pillar is golden, / And a golden cupola on the golden one..." as an example of "re-considering the town in terms of a temple" (Kravtsov 1999: 57).
4. The ambivalent character of the architectural space of town streets and squares (both open and inner) seems to be conditioned by the absence of any barrier in the downward direction, contrary to a house with its space which is usually seen as internal (Tsyvian 1978: 74).
5. In many Eastern European regions, the urbanization, which in the XI–XIII c. was heavily influenced by German urban colonization, the "dichotomy of a town and a village" was complicated by ethnic and confessional confrontation (Melnikov 1999: 151).
6. "Galicia in foreign sources of the XVI–XIX c." (Bolshaya Sovetskaya Entsiklopedia 1991: 630).
7. It was precisely at this time that Jews were being ousted from this town of Great Poland, where upon the formation of urban estates their representatives were aiming at diminishing competition in trade and urban crafts of Jews – by limiting of their rights.
8. The legal status of Jews in Poland was established under the influence of the traditional relationship between the rulers and the Jewish communes in Western Europe, where Jews were the "subjects of the treasury" (*servi camerae*). In Rech Pospolita, Jews constituted a specific estate: inviolability of person and property, rights for various types of occupation and benefits were granted to them through privileges from the king or the landowners whose territory they inhabited. It was the Jewish religious commune that usually received such a charter of privileges. In accordance with these endowments, Jewish communes possessed legal autonomy and had an opportunity to create living conditions that would accord with religious norms. The autonomous character of a self-governed Jewish commune conformed not only with its own needs, but also with the interests of the state in the creation of an effective fiscal organization of its subjects – Jews (Balaban 1910–1911).
9. With the exception of Kamyanetsk-Podilsk, the ancient capital of the area, that had the privilege "de non tolerandis Judaeis", officially cancelled only in 1762.
10. Songs tell about how Jews were holding Orthodox churches on lease (Zelenin 1916: 1091). Some scholars doubt the fact that Catholic landowners transferred to Jews

the right to collect taxes for religious rites (e. g. marriages, baptisms, funerals) in the churches situated on their estates.
11. According to V. Lukin's estimation, on the eve of the Cossack-and-peasant wars (1648–1667) there were about 22, 000 Jews living in Podolia (including 20% in the rural area) (Lukin 2000: 462).
12. V. Lukin in his article quotes the report of the Cossack hetman A. Mohyla that in 1684 the majority of town in the area turned into villages, "got overgrown with weeds they are only called towns, yet there are even no house foundations there" (Lukin 2000: 40).
13. Jews already started to return to the towns of Podolia when the region was under Turkish rule (1672–1699).
14. According to the estimation of specialists, before the first division of Poland over a third of the Jewish population was engaged in leasing activity. In spite of the fact that Jews could not own land, they were in charge of vast agricultural lands in the capacity of managers. The right to lease was often given by the right of succession.
15. Owners of small townships in Podolia were, as a rule, not inclined towards developing crafts at their places, while satisfying themselves, as in the preceding epoch, with profits from agricultural trade in the form of payment for the place in the market and the use of scales (Kompan & Markina 1966: 351).
16. The local Ukrainian population, even assigned to petty bourgeoisie, hardly had any opportunity to quit agricultural activity. Quite often town owners declared suburbs "settlements" in order to make their population perform land service (Kompan & Markina 1966: 352–353). The Ukrainian petty bourgeoisie combined home crafts with agriculture and market gardening. Not only in privately owned, but even in royal towns and townships of Podolia scanty Polish and Ukrainian petty bourgeoisie had practically no chance to win when in economic competition with Jews.
17. In "Polish villages", ethnic Poles compose the minority. The term "Poliaki" (Poles) in Podolia possesses not so much an ethnic, but rather a confessional flavor: the word "Poliaki" is applied to Catholic Ukrainians. Upon elimination of Uniate churches in Podolia (1830–1839) a portion of the parishioners converted to Catholicism. The distance between the Orthodox and the Catholics, determined by ethno-confessional differences, was gradually diminishing, owing, among other things, to mixed "Ukrainian-Polish" marriages. Presently this distance is minimal.
18. Polish noblemen possessed the right of "propination", i. e. could produce and sell alcoholic drinks made of grain on their estates. Peasants were obliged to buy these drinks in the landowner's tavern. Yet, accusations of "turning peasants into drunkards" were made almost exclusively against Jews (Klier 2000: 154).
19. Following the return of this territory to Poland, the Polish petty bourgeoisie again emerged in towns, yet proved to be incapable of sustaining competition with Jews in small towns. The Danish envoy at court of Peter I, participant of the Prussian campaign of the Russian army in 1711, Just Jul, stressed in his report that the town of Bar is populated "predominantly by Jews" (Jul 1899: 355), the town of Dunaevtsi "is populated only by Jews…" and, in general, "on these territories Jewish population prevails over the Polish one" (Ibid. 357).
20. In the Soviet time the term *mestechko* was removed from the dictionary of administrative statuses of places of residence, yet preserved its meaning as a socio-cultural phenomenon, e. g. the combination "*evreiskoe mestechko*" was often used in the discussion of issues related to urban-type settlements in the Ukraine.
21. One should stress that by the end of the XIX c. the level of economic development in small towns and commercial townships on the territories that after the divisions of Poland occurred within the pale of the Russian Empire were hopelessly lagging behind those situated in the regions annexed by Austria.
22. Altogether in 1918–1921 there were 2000 pogroms, mostly in Ukraine. 150,000 Jews died, half a million remained homeless. The Jews of Podolia became victims of mass extermination in 1919.
23. In 1917, all restrictions based on ethnic and religious differences were banned.

Migration to big cities increased after the possibility to immigrate to America was limited (1924).
24. The majority of Jewish cooperative associations (*artel*), Soviet and collective farms were relatively prosperous, yet in some cases their well-being was undermined by high taxation. Others were stifled in 1933, when all grain, including that for sowing, was taken away from agricultural cooperatives.
25. Citations of field materials include: informants' names or initials, their date of birth, place of recording, name of the researcher, date of recording. Interviews cited with no year of recording or the name of the interviewer were taken in 2001 by the author together with O. Belova and V. Petrukhin.
26. As stated in the foreword to one such school manuals "…for the reader to perceive capitalist slavery, it would be sufficient to grant him the possibility to travel, together with literary artists, to modern cities like Berlin, Paris, New York and London" (Vladislavlev 1925: 3).
27. Nowadays, it is also easy to see the essential difference in the character of construction of small towns situated on different sides of the former Austro-Hungarian border. In the look of small towns in the territories annexed by Austria after the divisions of Poland the influence of popular house-building traditions were leveled owing to the unified standards of urban building maintained here in the XIX c.
28. According to M. Weber's classification (Weber 1994: 315).
29. Reflection upon the town-building activity of Polish magnates, to whom the region owes its urbanization in the second half of the XVI – beginning of the XVII c., is virtually absent in Podolia.
30. Putting aside the genesis of this phrase, it should be mentioned that the legendary plot of the Turkish army that was asked "shall we stop or shall we go further on?" is known to all people living in Sataniv thanks to the popular article on local lore (Sokha 1991: 18).
31. In the XIX c. the authors of local history descriptions used to mention the fact that the establishment of this or that town is customarily dated by the time Jews were recorded to have settled in it. For example, A. Dyminskyi in his work "Everyday Life of Peasants in Kamenestky and Proskurovsky Districts" (1864) mentions that the laying of the foundations of Zhvanets township is dated back "to the XV c. according to the tombstones on the Jewish cemetery" (ARGS, Category 30, Inventory 1, File 23, P. 48).
32. Having analyzed interethnic relations in Polish Carpathians, Ya. Mukha arrived at a similar conclusion: Germans in Boiki villages were considered to be "aliens" because they had a "non-agricultural way of life" (Mukha 1994).
33. Nowadays, the term "Poles" features not so much an ethnic, but rather a confessional coloring. Partial recognition of ethnic Poles as "us", an "aboriginal population", allows one to extend this definition to Catholic Ukrainians.
34. The system of urban self-government based on the pattern of Magdeburg law and adopted in the towns of Western and central principalities of Poland and Lithuania was an example of legal norms both for royal and privately owned towns of Podolia.
35. The proverb is cited by A. Dyminskyi in the manuscript *Everyday Life of Peasants in Kamenestky and Proskurovsky Districts* (1864) (ARGS, Category 30, Inventory 1, File 23, P. 95).
36. Jews who lived in villages were ascribed to the commune of the nearest shtetl.
37. In contrast to relatively large multiethnic towns and cities, where only a part of the central quarters are commonly called "Jewish" (usually this is the part where the "old" synagogue was located), in small towns and townships the whole commercial centre was considered to be Jewish.
38. Accounts of Sharhorod being called Little Istanbul during the time of the Turkish rule in Podolia (1672–1699) may be found in a number of local history essays. The image of Istanbul as an exemplary trade centre must have been formed in post-Soviet times after the beginning of mass "shuttle" trips to Turkey for cheap goods of mass consumption.

39. My studies on the architecture of Jewish houses allows one to come to the conclusion that the house pattern, traditional for the ordinary construction of Podolian shtetls in XVIII–XIX c., preserved archaic features of a one-storey Renaissance burgher house with a Gothic type of planning. Such a burgher house was representative for the construction of small urban settlements in Central and Eastern Europe where German colonization served the foundation for urbanization. By the beginning of the XIX c., the house-building practice of a shtetl modified the arrangement of the burgher house: it had become a rule to construct the main entrance door on the street façade of the house (Sokolova 2002:19).
40. Such a prank was well known not only in Podolia, but also in the region of Bukovina. "Our people would ring the bell – they <Jews> would put the body down. We stop ringing – they run again <to the body>. Youths were engaged in this. <And> old men used to scold" (S. K. Prodontsev, b. 1939, Vashkivtsy. Rec. by A. Sokolova, 2001). This tradition has its own historical roots, the reconstruction of which presents a separate scholarly problem.
41. Informants' stories about their own good neighborly relations with this or that Jewish person is almost always accompanied by generalizations in respect to the Jewish community as a whole.
42. "The right entrance and exit are performed through one door only" (Tsyvian 1978: 76).
43. Traditionally, for Russian Jews, the image of a street populated exclusively by Jews, as a sacred inner space, is clearly expressed in Yiddish: a *Yiddishe gas*, which is the synonym for the "Jewish commune". To some extent, this is equivalent to the Russian word *mir* and its meaning of "peasant commune". Spatial and social aspects of the notion a "Yiddishe gas" are inseparably tied together.
44. Reconstruction of traditional Jewish houses by Ukrainians usually starts with the tearing off of the shutters and the painting of doors and window frames with a new color. As a rule, brown is changed for blue, the traditional color for Ukrainian architecture.
45. A priest from the village of Yapolot', Rovenskiy district, wrote in 1854 that "Jewish houses, high and full of light, with big windows, are full of junk, stench and negligence" (ARGS, Category 8, Inventory 1, [1] 5, Sheet).
46. For more about treating as a plausible excuse to intrude into somebody else's space without permission see Utekhin 2001.
47. The emergence of names such as *Erusalimka* in town topography (in Vinnytsya) testifies that the structure of the town space has become more complex: a new commercial centre appeared that "deprived" the old one, densely populated with Jews, of its right to be called a "*misto*". In some sense, this is one of the signs that a shtetl has turned into a town. *Erusalimka*, in the same way as *Volokhi* or *Gypsy*, is a name for an ethnic enclave of the town.
48. In the work by I. G. Isics "Examination of the Sanitary Conditions of a Jewish Township" written in 1928, the author observes that the "over the last ten years the number of house built by Jews composes 8, 1%" (Isics 1928: 94).
49. At present, only in Husyatin (Ternopilska region) does the synagogue building serve the purposes of the local history museum.
50. The Jewish custom to arrange a marriage on a heap of rubbish is also known in Byelorussian Polesie. Among the Byelorussians, a rubbish pile was seen as an impure and contemptible place, as opposed to the place for a proper marriage (Kushkova 1999: 258).
51. According to A. Senyavskiy, the major distinctive feature of the Russian urbanization process was that towns grew out not so much of economical interests of the region, but out of interests of the "expanding Empire" (Senyavskiy 1999: 155).

REFERENCES

Afanasiev (Chuzhbinskyi), A. 1893: *Poyezdka v Yuzhnuyu Rossiyu. Ocherki Dnestra.* Sobr. soch. v 9 t. T. 8. SPb.
Antonovich, V. 1869: *Issledovaniye o gorodakh v Yugo-Zapadnoi Rossii po aktam 1432–1798 godov.* Arkhiv yugo-zapadnoi Rossii Ch. 5 T. 1. Kiev.
Balaban, M. 1910–1911: Pravovoy stroy evreyev v Polshe v sredniie i novyi veka. In: *Yevreyskaya starina* 1910. Ch.II. ¹1; ¹2; ¹3; 1911. Ch.III. ¹1; ¹2.
Baiburin, A. K. 1983: *Zhilishche v obriadakh i prestavleniyakh vostochnykh slavyan.* Leningrad.
Belova, O. & Petrukhin, V. 2002: Demonologicheskie syuzhety v krosskulturnom prostranstve. In: *Mezhdu dvumya mirami: predstavleniia o demonicheskom i potustoronnem v slavyanskoi i yevreyskoi kulturnoi tradicii.* Vyp. 9. Moskva.
Beiser, M. 2002: *Nashe nasledstvo. Sinagogi SNG v proshlom i nastoiashchem.* Moskva – Ierusalim.
Bolshaya Sovetskaya Entsiklopedia. Moskva 1991 Ch. 2.
Isics, I. G. 1928: Sanitarno-bytovoe obsledovanie yevreyskogo mestechka. In: *Voprosy biologii i patologii yevreev* ¹ 3. Vinnitsa.
Yerofeeva, N. N. 1996: K rekonstrukcii arkhetipa istoricheskogo prototipa goroda. In: *Gorod i iskusstvo. Sub"ekty sociokulturnogo dialoga.* Moskva.
Ettinger, Sh. 1993: *Rossiya i yevrei.* Ierusalim.
Yust, Yul 1899: Zapiski Yusta Yulya, datsogo poslannika pri Petre Velikom (1709–1711). In: *Chteniya v Imperatorskom obshchestve istorii i drevnostei rossiiskikh.* Sankt-Peterburg.
Khrenov, N. A. 1996: Kartiny mira i obrazy goroda (psikhologicheskie aspekty obrazovaniya subkultur i ikh vozdeistvie na khudozhestvennuyu kulturu goroda). In: *Gorod i iskusstvo. Sub"ekty sotsiokulturnogo dialoga.* Moskva.
Klier, Dzh. D. 2000: *Rossiya sobiraet svoikh yevreyev (Proishozhdenie yevreyskogo voprosa v Rossii: 1772–1825).* Moskva – Ierusalim.
Kravtsov, S. R. 1999: Galitsiiskie goroda kontsa XVI–XVII vv. (Kompozitsiya i simvolika). In: *Arkhitekturnoe nasledstvo.* Vyp. 43. Moskva
Kompan, Ye. S. & Markina, V. A. 1966: O nekotorykh osobennostiakh sotsialno-ekonomicheskogo razvitiya gorodov Pravoberezhnoi i Levoberezhnoi Ukrainy v XVII–XVIII vv. In: *Goroda feodalnoi Rossii.* Moskva.
Kushkova, A. N. 1999: Sor v slavyanskoi traditsii: na granitse "svoego" i "chuzhogo". In: *Problemy sotsialnogo i gumanitarnogo znania.*
Lukin, V. 2000: Neopalimaya kupina. Yevreiskie obshchiny Podolii: stoletie posle khmelnitchiny. In: *Sto yevreiskikh mestechek Ukrainy. Istoricheskii putevoditel.* Vyp. 2: Podoliya. Sankt-Peterburg.
Melnikov, G. P. 1999: Problemy nemetskoi gorodskoi kolonizatsii kak faktora urbanizatsii Tsentralnoi i Vostochnoi Yevropy. In: *Urbanizatsiya v formirovanii sotsiokulturnogo prostranstva.* Moskva.
Mukha, Ya. 1994: Konflikt, simbioz, izolyatsiya. Etnicheskie otnosheniya v polskom Prikarpat"e. In: *Etnograficheskoe obozrenie* ¹4. Moskva.
Portelli, A. 2003: Osobennosti ustnoi istorii. In: *Khrestomatiya po ustnoi istorii.* Sankt-Peterburg.
Propp, V. Ja. 1986: *Istoricheskie korni volshebnoi skazki.* Moskva.
RYA: *Russko-yevreiskii arkhiv. Dokumenty i materialy dlya istorii yevreyev v Rossii* (sost. Bershadskii S. A.) V 3-h t. Sankt-Peterburg 1882–1903.
Senyavskiy, A. S. 1999: Rossiiskaya urbanizatsiya: nekotorye istoriko-metodologicheskie problemy. In: *Urbanizatsiya v formirovanii sotsiokulturnogo prostranstva.* Moskva.
Sokolova, A. V. 2000a: Etnokulturnaya spetsifika yevreyskogo doma v Podolii. In: *Zhivaya starina* 2/2000. Moskva.
Sokolova, A. V. 2000b: The Podolian Shtetl as Architectural Phenomenon. In: *The Shtetl: Image and Reality. Papers of the Second Mendel Freidman International Conference*

on Yiddish. European Humanities Research Centre of University of Oxford. Oxford, 2000.

Sokolova, A. V. 2002: *Traditsionnaya arkhitekturnaya sreda shtetlov Podolii (XVIII – nachalo XX vv.).* Avtoreferat dissertatsii. Sankt-Peterburg.

Sokha, V. 1991: *Istorichnii naris.* Khmelnytskyi.

Toporov, V. N. 1981: Tekst godora-devy i goroda-bludnitsy v mifopoeticheskom aspekte. In: *Struktura teksta.* Moskva.

Tsyvian, T. V. 1978: Dom v folklornom modeli mira. In: *Semiotika kultury. Trudy po znakovym sistemam.* Tartu.

Utekhin, I. 2001: *Ocherki kommunalnogo byta.* Moskva.

Vadeisha, M. G. 1999: Kolokol i kolokolnyi zvon v traditsionnoi slavyanskoi kulture. In: *Problemy sotsialnogo i gumanitarnogo znaniya.* Vyp. 1. Sankt-Peterburg.

Vladislavlev, I. V. 1925: *Gorod v proizvedeniyakh khudozhestvennoi literatury.* Moskva.

Vishnitser, M. & Shipper, I. 1914: Ekonomicheskii byt. In: *Istoriya yevreyskogo naroda.* T. 11. Moskva.

Weber, M. 1994: *Izbrannoe. Obraz obshchestva.* Moskva.

Zelenin, D. K. 1916: *Opisanie rukopisei uchenogo arkhiva imperatorskogo russkogo geograficheskogo obshchestva.* Vyp. 3. Petrograd.

ABBREVIATIONS

ARGS: Archive of the Russian Geographic society.
b.: born
RJA: Russian-Jewish Archive
RSHA: Russian state historical archive.

Contributors

Oksana Filicheva MA of Ethnology, researcher at the European University in St. Petersburg, Russia

Pekka Hakamies PhD, research fellow at the Karelian Institute, University of Joensuu, Finland

Marina Hakkarainen MA of Ethnology, researcher at the European University in St. Petersburg, Russia

Antti Laine PhD, senior research fellow at the Karelian Institute, University of Joensuu, Finland

Ekaterina Melnikova MA of Ethnology, researcher at the European University in St. Petersburg, Russia

Irina Razumova PhD, chief research worker at the International Center of Science, Culture and Education Development in Euro-Arctic Region, Academy of Science, Kola Research Center, Apatity, Russia

Alla Sokolova Ph. D. in architecture, research fellow at the Jewish Heritage Center "Petersburg Judaica", St. Petersburg, Russia

www.ingramcontent.com/pod-product-compliance
Lightning Source LLC
Chambersburg PA
CBHW080807300426
44114CB00020B/2858